Truth may seem, but cannot be:
Beauty brag, but 'tis not she;
Truth and beauty buried be.

To this urn let those repair
That are either true or fair;
For these dead birds sigh a prayer.

Bacon

CONTENTS.

CONTENTS.

INTRODUCTION.

OF the life of William Hazlitt, no more will be said here than seems needful for considering his work as an Essayist. He was born on the 10th of April 1778, in Mitre Lane, Maidstone. His father was a Unitarian minister, who, after several changes, settled at Wem, in Shropshire. In 1795, amongst other places, young Hazlitt visited Burleigh House, and beheld its pictures, some of which he treasured in his mind to the end of life. In 1796 Coleridge settled at Nether-Stowey, and preached in the Unitarian chapel at Taunton. In January 1798 Coleridge, whilst officiating for Mr. Rowe at Shrewsbury, visited Hazlitt's father at Wem. This proved the great inspiring time of young Hazlitt's intellectual life. He heard Coleridge preach : saw much of him : above all, was invited by the poet to Nether-Stowey in the spring.

During the interval, Hazlitt went to Llangollen Vale, by way of initiating himself into "the mysteries of natural scenery." Coleridge, in December 1796, had published his "Ode to the Departing Year." The poetry, in its character and music, was new to young Hazlitt. Uplifted in spirit by his approaching visit, inspired by the ode, that expedition was fraught with new awakenings. He remembered, long years afterwards, how he sat up half the night at an inn at Bridgwater to read *Paul and Virginia ;* how on his birthday he sat down to a new volume of the *New Hélöise* at a Llangollen inn. Llangollen Vale itself became to him "the cradle of a new existence : in the river that winds through it, my spirit was baptised in the waters of Helicon." Coleridge received him with a welcome. Wordsworth he there met ; heard him *chaunt* some of his poetry ; saw some of his *Lyrical Ballads* in manuscript. Hazlitt spent three weeks at Nether-Stowey. There was a walking excursion to

Linton with Coleridge and a silent admirer of the metaphysician and poet, one John Chester. This was a troublous political time. Wordsworth and Coleridge were watched as suspects by a State spy, and Wordsworth, ultimately, went to Germany with his sister and Coleridge. But young Hazlitt, full of his new poetic experience ; with "the first virgin passion of a soul communing with the glorious universe ;" did not share the high political feelings. He, who became a frenzied politician, who, as such, condemned these same poets for their change of views, was at present in dreamland. Twenty-eight years after these events he wrote :—" I may date my insight into the mysteries of poetry from the commencement of my acquaintance with the authors of the *Lyrical Ballads.*"

We know from one of his essays, that about this time Hazlitt became acquainted with Mr. Joseph Fawcett, who had delivered popular Sunday evening lectures at Old Jewry, but who was then retired to Hedgegrove, in Hertfordshire. He found Fawcett to be a man of keen poetic appreciation, and largely read. "The writings of Sterne, Fielding, Cervantes, Richardson, Rousseau, Godwin, Goethe, etc., were the usual subjects of our discourses." Intended for the ministry, Hazlitt entered the Unitarian College, Hackney, in 1793, but left it in 1795 with the idea given up. His brother John was a miniature-painter. William had a love for painting, which had been stimulated by his visit to Burleigh in 1795. He went to Paris in October 1802, and studied in the Louvre for four months. The remembrance of that visit was always with him.

In 1803 he made a professional tour through the Midland Counties, but not satisfied with the results, he came to London with his thoughts bent on literature. At this time, he formed intimacies with Dr. Stoddart and his sister Sarah, with Charles and Mary Lamb. His friendship with Lamb originated at the house of Godwin, through a flash of Lamb's humour, as told at the conclusion of the second essay.

Hazlitt's first publication was the *Principles of Human Actions* (1805), which he never ceased to esteem as his best work, though a metaphysical choke-pear. Under the stimulus of Coleridge he wrote *Free Thoughts on Public Affairs*, which was published in 1806. Both fell still-born from the press. Pregnant with important consequences was the first sentence of a letter written by Mary Lamb to her friend and correspondent, Miss Stoddart, on the second of July of this year :—
" My dear Sarah, Charles and Hazlitt are going to the Sadler's Wells." This is the beginning of another epoch in Hazlitt's

mental experience—the sowing of the first seed of the theatrical critic.

On Sunday morning, the 1st of May 1808, Hazlitt married Miss Stoddart. There were present at the ceremony Dr. and Mrs. Stoddart, also Charles and Mary Lamb. The newly-wedded couple went to Winterslow, and resided in a cottage which belonged to the bride. Winterslow is a village in Wiltshire, between Andover and Salisbury. It became a favourite resort of Hazlitt's. He found there quiet times for composition. In later years, he took up his quarters at an old inn called Winterslow Hut. The London mails made a busy break in the day; there was Stonehenge to visit; there were in view the "woods that crown the clear lone brow of Norman Court" and "the waving woods of Tuderley." The Lambs visited Mr. and Mrs. Hazlitt in the autumn of the following year. On that occasion they went to Oxford. Hazlitt, in "On Going a Journey," refers to the circumstance :—" I once took a party to Oxford with no mean *éclat.*" The visit was also described by Elia in " Vacation at Oxford." Of this, we speak at a more acceptable time.

Hazlitt, in 1812, fairly settled in London. This year, as Mr. Carew Hazlitt observes, marks " an important era in Hazlitt's life." He soon began to deliver a series of lectures at the Russell Institution, on the " English Philosophers and Metaphysicians." For a short time, he became Parliamentary reporter to the *Morning Chronicle.* Upon giving up this post he retained his connection with the newspaper as the writer of political articles and its theatrical critic. The political contributions were afterwards reprinted in *Political Essays, with Sketches of Public Characters* (1819), and the others in *A View of the English Stage* (1821). He was requested to contribute to the *Edinburgh Review,* and his first contribution appeared in November 1814. By this time, he had become acquainted with Leigh Hunt and his brother John, proprietors of the *Examiner.* Long ere this, Hazlitt was known as a passionate politician, and he remained consistent in his views, his acrimony and his zeal, to the last. Napoleon was his idol. Therefore, the battle of Waterloo, in 1815, struck him severely. Talfourd says, that when he first met Hazlitt after the event, " he was staggering under the blow of Waterloo."

Let us now see Hazlitt, as found in the descriptions of those who were his admirers. He was of middle size, slight, but well formed ; of handsome countenance—eager and pale, and rather worn with thought and pain ; black hair, which curled stiffly over his temples—in later years, plentifully sprinkled with grey ; a sensitive mouth, a sunken, glancing eye.   A man awkward in gait, negligent in dress, painfully bashful in the presence of strangers.   He became a great drinker of fine tea, having given up a stronger stimulant.   Tea with him, as Hunt quoted from Waller, "kept the palace of the soul serene."   He rises at twelve or one o'clock, drinks his tea, and writes his articles till four or five o'clock.   At night he holds an intellectual *levée* at the Southampton, Chancery Lane, where his brilliant talk charms the company, until the grey dawn peeps through the chinks of the shutters.   He haunts the Fives Court, in St. Martin's Street, where he assiduously plays the game, rails at himself, and praises Cavanagh.   In many ways he will

> "Tear his pleasures with rough strife,
> Thorough the iron gates of life."

His temper is suspicious—is genial—he fights with a shadow— he shrinks from general society.   He gives his hand as if it were the fin of a fish.   Hunt noticed it, and reports that some friends wished to place a fish-slice against the hand of such a friend, but no one dared "bell the cat."

Upon his acquaintance with Leigh Hunt and his brother, the *Round Table* essays were commenced in the *Examiner.*   The series were completed in 1817, and republished in two small volumes.   His volume of *Characters of Shakespere's Plays,* dedicated to his friend, Charles Lamb, was published the same year.   The *Characters* sold well.   One edition went off in six weeks ; but the *Quarterly* attacked it, and the sale was stopped.   Almost every event in Hazlitt's life is alluded to in his essays, and he has not forgotten this.   A reckoning with Gifford, the editor of the *Quarterly,* was now imminent.   His attack followed on the heels of other wrongs.   In 1818 were published the lectures delivered by him at the Surrey Institution on the *English Poets.*   Then came his *Letter to William Gifford, Esq.,* followed by lectures on the *English Comic Writers,* and the collection of *Political Essays and Sketches of Public Characters.*   In 1820 the *London Magazine* was commenced, and Hazlitt was amongst the brilliant contributors— enumerated by Talfourd in his *Memorials of Charles Lamb.* The first volume of *Table Talk* (1821) was chiefly composed of essays reprinted from the *London.*

Other events, also, made this a memorable year.   He took apartments at 9 Southampton Buildings, Chancery Lane, London, where he fell in love with one of the daughters of the house. If a ladye-love was called Southampton Buildings, with Hazlitt this might have been "No. 9." He, as well as others of his friends, were rarely without a Dulcinea—the newer the better. From that genial true-heart of wedded life, Charles Cowden Clarke, we learn that, infatuated with Miss Mordaunt, "who was making her appearance at the Haymarket in the first bloom and freshness of her youth and beauty," Hazlitt performed the lunatic, the lover, if not the poet. On another occasion, Clarke, in comparing notes with Leigh Hunt and Vincent Novello, discovered that the whole three were enthralled by a *Viola*, that is by Miss A. M. Tree. Yea, Clarke confesses to Hunt and himself being woefully in love with—(a forgotten name)—a columbine. But then it was different with Hazlitt from his fellows. "No. 9," unfortunately, was in his home : was pretty and engaging. This Hebe brought him Nectar to each meal. Ever the child of passion, he declared his frenzy at all times, in all places. The results were that in two years he was divorced, and the *Liber Amoris ; or, the New Pygmalion*, was published. In this transaction his jesses were not the dear heart-strings of the young lady, Miss Sarah Walker. She whistled him off, and let him down the wind to prey on fortune.

> " Lost, was she, lost ; nor could the sufferer say
> That in the act of preference he had been
> Unjustly dealt with :—but the maid was gone."

In 1820, were published his *Lectures on the Dramatic Literature of the Age of Queen Elizabeth*, followed (1821) by *A View of the English Stage*. In 1821 Lord Byron and Shelley projected a periodical, afterwards named *The Liberal*. Shelley wrote for Leigh Hunt to go to Italy and share the labours and the profits. He went. Hazlitt was made home editor. The *Liberal* appeared in 1822. Four numbers were published. It then ceased to exist, Hazlitt having contributed four articles.

In the few years that remain to be spoken of, we shall name but the chief events. In 1823 he published *Characteristics, in the manner of Rochefoucauld's Maxims*. The book hardly kept the promise of its title; but that is argument for other pages. He married a second time, in 1824, Isabella, widow of Lieutenant-Colonel Bridgwater,—"a lady of some property." With her he visited the Continent. During their wanderings he contributed to the *Morning Chronicle, Notes of a Journey through France and Italy*, which were afterwards collected and published in one volume. His life was a constant paradox. Mrs. Hazlitt did not return to England with him. There is a great deal told of the journey; very little of the companionship. Hazlitt wrote to his wife; she replied that "they had parted for ever" —a brief, but not bright intimacy.

In 1824 appeared his *Sketches of the Principal Picture Galleries in England,* and in 1825, *The Spirit of the Age; or, Contemporary Portraits,* one of the finest volumes of personal and literary criticism, beginning with Jeremy Bentham, ending with Geoffrey Crayon. Hazlitt is searching in his inquisition, sweeping in his judgments, also piquant. Of the first he says, "He writes a language of his own that darkens knowledge. His works have been translated into French—they ought to be translated into English." Of Washington Irving, that his "writings are literary anachronisms. . . . Instead of tracing the changes that have taken place in society since Addison and Fielding wrote, he transcribes their account in a different handwriting, and thus keeps us stationary. . . . A flattering mode of turning fiction into history, or history into fiction. . . . A pardonable error, . . . giving us credit for the virtues of our forefathers." *The Plain Speaker: Opinions on Men, Books, and Things* (1826), was a compilation of essays of similar character to *Table Talk.*

He was now busy with the work on which his heart was set, *The Life of Napoleon Buonaparte.* The first two volumes were published in 1828. That same year he wrote his "Farewell to Essay-Writing." It was not published then, nor was the title true; but, alas, it was too true in its ominous note. Two years afterwards (1830), broken in body and mind, he wrote his essays —"A Free Admission,"—"The Sick Chamber,"—and "Personal Politics," which was his last essay. His *Napoleon Buonaparte* was completed and published the same year. On Saturday, 30th September 1830, he died. Charles Lamb, his old friend, was in his room. Something of peacefulness and light came to him in his latest hours. Was that not gently said, as by a woman, to one who had been talking to him in a soothing undertone, during his illness?—"My sweet friend, go into the next room, and sit there for a time, as quiet as is your nature, for I cannot bear talking at present."

The irritable, discontented temperament was chastened. He saw the past clearly and calmly. His last words were—"Well, I've had a happy life." So confessed that once fiery, stormy spirit, recognising what joys and frequent periods of quiet and restoration had been vouchsafed him, in spite of his passions and his desires.

No writer of merit in this century has been subject to such stupid misrepresentations as William Hazlitt. He has had admirers, he has been a vitalising influence in some minds ; but of the writers of our century, not one has suffered from such reckless distortion and misjudgment. At this moment, the post brings me a sample of those perversions, which affords me a base from which to operate. . . . " The correctness of facts with Hazlitt is nearly in all cases subordinate to the striking construction of a sentence. . . ." This serves my purpose quite as well as though fulminated from an editorial throne. Error and truth, each preserves its native quality, no matter where, no matter by whom it be spoken. That passage is fairly representative of a certain style of criticism, of the mass of misjudgment, in regard to Hazlitt ; it is no exaggeration of the manner in which he has been dealt with by his enemies, by those indifferent to him, and, in their ignorance, by some of his friends. So far as this special charge is concerned, I briefly say that Hazlitt was too passionate a man not to speak the truth sometimes. I do not discern that, as a Truth Speaker as well as a Plain Speaker, he fell beneath his own age, or the present. . . . He was an admirer of Wordsworth's poetry, without degenerating into admiration of his change in politics : he recognised the beauties in the poems of Keats, without discovering the subtle music of Shelley's strains : he was separated from his wife, like a celebrated poet, without possessing the domesticity and self-sacrifice of Lamb : his appreciation of humour was as certain as that of Peter Pindar, without the faculty of turning it into human nature's daily food of smiles and tears, like Tom Hood : he loved a country inn, like Winterslow Hut, without losing his desire for city life, as in the Southampton : he loved the theatre, without giving up his hopes for mankind : he admired the tragic actor, without any diminution of his relish for the comedian : his affection for painters, from Raphael to Rubens and Poussin, was ecstatic, without losing his British taste for Hogarth : his writing displays passion, rapt contemplation, invective, without the serenity, the limpid sweetness, the patient cheerfulness of Leigh Hunt—and a great number of other things, without a great number of other things.

I have already said that the nature of Hazlitt's Essay was after the admiration of Montaigne. " I love a poetic march by leaps and skips : 'tis an art, as Plato says, light, nimble, and a little maddish." He has a Bohemian manner, like his masters. Ever and anon, he breaks away : it is not a mere diversion, but a flight ; frequently he will tell you so. The man's temper being heated, his language obtains therefrom warmth and motion—

> " As full of spirit as the month of May,
>   And gorgeous as the sun at midsummer."

Particularly, he may surprise you by closing his essay, not with the power of logical application, after the orthodox sermon style, but by a complete change of subject. On all occasions you get a great deal more than is in the bond. The true essay with him is like a sweethearts' meeting : good nature and genius are met together : you are never sure what will come next—talk, caresses, or some whisper of lost hearts, dead times : you may get to a flower, or a star—kisses or laughter—or some recollection, to let you know that nothing is

> " So dainty sweet as lovely melancholy."

Something Hazlitt had, which is not so predominant in any other essayist, and which brightens his writings—his intense love of Nature. In this love, he said, was "all the force of individual attachment, combined with its most airy abstraction." Then, as a mind of power, touching more of his fellows at the opening century than anyone except Leigh Hunt, and declaring as to what or with whom he agrees or disagrees—this gives sprightly variety to his pages, and added thereto, is that perfect enrichment of fitly-spoken words in praise of his friends, which, fulfilling the language of the Wise One of old, are "like apples of gold in pictures of silver."

Into his criticisms of painting Hazlitt throws more passionate, personal experience than any other writer. Where Ruskin would, with finest discrimination, analyse a painting —in a style excellent for his generation and all of art— Hazlitt glorifies it in the light of Nature. The colours shine ; the figures breathe and think and glow: being part of his life, he makes the pictures part of yours. When, where, and under what circumstances he has seen a painting is much to him. He is as a pre-Raphaelite ; when he sees a true picture, then you feel he is born anew ; that picture dwells in his spirit for all his years. The pictures that he loved, they live in his pages, there to be beloved by those who love the art.

As a theatrical critic, Hazlitt has his special place. If not possessing the airy graces of Leigh Hunt, he has observation as close, as true a sympathy, and a more resolute judgment. The pleasure of reading what he has written of the stage will increase with the nation's years. . . . At that period England's actors strove to rise and find fame in the best plays. England's theatres, then, produced the best plays. The stock company gave a provincial town each year more of the legitimate drama (as it is called) than the whole kingdom now produces. There was a stimulus to the actor's ambition, when his audience encouraged him to do his best in every character for which he was qualified. Kean having made his hit at Drury Lane as Shylock, the "Merchant of Venice" was not run for a thousand nights. The first of his admirers, in seeing his Shylock a second time, wrote to the *London World*—"We are anxious to see him in Norval and Richard." That was the feeling of the critics and theatre-goers; they longed to witness his personation of other—of all great characters. And the answer was given. Kean opened with Shylock in January, followed with Richard in February, Hamlet in March, Othello and Iago in May. In Hazlitt you have the past times of our theatre renewed in narrative : you have the imperial line of great plays and characters, and those who impersonate them, and therein find the fleeting glory which is the actor's portion. He lets us know the impression produced, the success achieved, by Mrs. Siddons, Kemble, Kean, Miss O'Neill, and the comedians all, with whom he was one in heart for fun and laughter. When fell there upon the stage more lustrous honour than his praise of Mrs. Siddons? And this he would have said of every one worthy of the profession— " She had no need of the robes, of the sweeping train, the ornaments of the stage : in herself, she is as great as any being she ever represented in the ripeness and plenitude of her power ? "

Hazlitt's *Characters of Shakespere's Plays* have been praised by some later Shakesperian critics, also lightly esteemed by others. The difference of circumstances will account for this. Hazlitt judged his characters as a theatre-goer : he interpreted them with the stage before him ; and such plays as he had not seen performed would, in his mind's eye, be reproduced as under similar conditions. The schools of Shakesperian criticism have developed since then, in proportion to the depression of the stage. The consequence of a natural law. The mind seeks for food which it best loves : if not to be found on the stage, it turns to the closet, and makes of it a mansion

" Full of noises,
Sounds, and sweet airs, that give delight and hurt not

alive with gay or tragic incidents, and characters of grace, nobleness, and mirth. The hunger of the soul for the beautiful will be satisfied. Nevertheless, even to the recluse critic, Hazlitt must in much be as correct as he is vigorous and subtle.

His political feelings can be easily explained. When Words-worth, with Beaupuis, during the Revolution days, saw in a French lane a hunger-bitten girl leading a heifer by a cord tied to her arm, to enable it to crop the grass,

> " While the girl, with pallid hands,
> Was busy knitting in a heartless mood
> Of solitude,"

and the soldier, in agitation, cried, "'Tis against *that* we are fighting "—the spirit of Hazlitt was in his words. A dynasty produces that—then down with the dynasty—down with dynasties—the tyranny of monarchy. In time, be came to have no other word in his lexicon of politics than Buonaparte. Buonaparte had risen from the people, he had conquered (Hazlitt did not live to see Wiertz's painting of "Buonaparte in the Shades"); Buonaparte was his sun, his hope— symbol of goodness to all mankind. Buonaparte assumed the purple ; ah ! but on it swarmed the golden bees, and imperialism had become the bountiful giver of honey, and sweetness, and light. If Hazlitt had been a poet, he should have written a "Revolt of Islam." Be that word remem-bered.—I have said thus much of politics, because, ever and anon, in the essays they gleam like the flashing of a shield. Two faces haunted him—Napoleon's and the heroine of the *Liber Amoris.* It was the final and greatest torture in De Quincey's opium experience, the vision of the human face— " the tyranny of the human face," as he called it. His last words of terror were—" My sleep is still tumultuous, and like the gate of Paradise to our first parents, when looking back from afar, it is still (in the tremendous line of Milton)—

> ' With dreadful faces thronged and fiery arms.' "

Hazlitt felt such tyranny in his dream of life. Not with terror, but in the pride of sadness and sorrow, he never concealed it. The two faces shall be seen in his pages, for he boldly spoke, feeling it was better to love them despairing "than have all the world beside."

Hazlitt piqued himself on his metaphysics. We shall not, how-ever, judge him as to that of which he was proudest. We leave them out of our considerations—accept them only as they may steal in to lighten a reflection, or colour a figure ; but in these pages will be found the artist, critic, lover of his special sport, theatre-goer, lover of nature. No one more than myself can be at variance with certain objects of Hazlitt's enthusiasm ; but enthusiasm is so rare : it is such a fire of virtue to inflame the good in man, as well as the evil—that we should pardon him— especially as under its inspiration he has, even in his excesses, so little power with wrong, and such potency with what is best. Here is no " gentle Lamb," no amiable Leigh Hunt, no lethargic Coleridge, no calm, domestic Southey, but a spirit of energy and fearlessness. His self-contradiction has been insisted upon. Evidence of what such complainers allege is here sufficiently plain, in that he admires and hates the same men—Burke, Wordsworth, Coleridge, Scott. On the other hand, it is con- tended that he was consistent in his political views ; and he him- self thinks it virtuous not to allow his political dislikes to blind him to a man's intellectual merit, nor his admiration for a man's genius to excuse his political action. Self-contradiction is in man's nature. If it is exceptionally well illustrated in Hazlitt, then those who laugh at such things can here laugh the more, and those may now laugh that never laughed before—after which, thank the gods that theirs has not been the gift of Hazlitt's outspokenness, nor his genius.—But as to the Essays.

They are not given in sequence of date, but for variety, and with a view to unity; to show the intellectual powers of the man Hazlitt. Altogether, as Essayist, Hazlitt will be found by the reader to be after the heart of the sociable old saint of literature—Montaigne : he will, also, find him a living friend among his book-spirits : of whom, indeed, he can make these words his own, written by Lamb during the one quarrel between them :—"I should belie my own conscience, if I said less than that I think William Hazlitt to be, in his natural and healthy state, one of the finest and wisest spirits breathing."

FRANK CARR.

THE WILLOWS, WALKER-ON-TYNE.

ESSAYS OF WILLIAM HAZLITT.

ON THE PERIODICAL ESSAYISTS.

"The proper study of mankind is man."

I NOW come to speak of that sort of writing which has been so successfully cultivated in this country by our Periodical Essayists, and which consists in applying the talents and resources of the mind to all that mixed mass of human affairs, which, though not included under the head of any regular art, science, or profession, falls under the cognisance of the writer, and "comes home to the business and bosoms of men."

"Quicquid agunt homines nostri farrago libelli," *

is the general motto of this department of literature. It does not treat of minerals or fossils, of the virtues of plants, or the influence of planets; it does not meddle with forms of belief or systems of philosophy, nor launch into the world of spiritual existences; but it makes familiar with the world of men and women, records their actions, assigns their motives, exhibits their whims, characterises their pursuits in all their singular and endless variety, ridicules their absurdities, exposes their inconsistencies, "holds the mirror up to nature, and shows the very age and body of the time, its form and pressure;" takes

---

* "Whatever things men are doing shall germ the motley subject of my page."

minutes of our dress, air, looks, words, thoughts, and actions ; shows us what we are, and what we are not ; plays the whole game of human life over before us, and by making us enlightened spectators of its many-coloured scenes, enables us (if possible) to become tolerably reasonable agents in the one in which we have to perform a part. "The act and practic part of life is thus made the mistress of our theorique." It is the best and most natural course of study. It is in morals and manners what the experimental is in natural philosophy, as opposed to the dogmatical method. It does not deal in sweeping clauses of proscription and anathema, but in nice distinction and liberal constructions. It makes up its general accounts from details, its few theories from many facts. It does not try to prove all black or all white as it wishes, but lays on the intermediate colours (and most of them not unpleasing ones), as it finds them blended with "the web of our life, which is of a mingled yarn, good and ill together." It inquires what human life is and has been, to show what it ought to be. It follows it into courts and camps, into town and country, into rustic sports or learned disputations, into the various shades of prejudice or ignorance, of refinement or barbarism, into its private haunts or public pageants, into its weaknesses and littlenesses, its professions and its practices : before it pretends to distinguish right from wrong, or one thing from another. How, indeed, should it do so otherwise?

> " Quid sit pulchrum, quid turpe, quid utile, quid non,
> Plenius et melius Chrysippo et Crantore dicit."

"It tells what is honourable, what is base, what is expedient, what not, more amply and better than Chrysippus and Crantor."

The writers I speak of are, if not moral philosophers, moral historians, and that's better : or if they are both, they found the one character upon the other ; their premises precede their conclusions ; and we put faith in their testimony, for we know that it is true.

Montaigne was the first person who, in his *Essays*, led the way to this kind of writing among the moderns. The great merit of Montaigne, then, was that he may be said to have been the first who had the courage to say as an author what he felt as a man. And as courage is generally the effect of conscious strength, he was probably led to do so by the richness, truth, and force of his own observations on books and men. He was, in the truest sense, a man of original mind; that is, he had the power of looking at things for himself, or as they really were, instead of blindly trusting to, and fondly repeating what others told him that they were. He got rid of the go-cart of prejudice and affectation, with the learned lumber that follows at their heels, because he could do without them. In taking up his pen he did not set up for a philosopher, wit, orator, or moralist, but he became all these by merely daring to tell us whatever passed through his mind, in its naked simplicity and force, that he thought any-ways worth communicating. He did not, in the abstract character of an author, undertake to say all that could be said upon a subject, but what in his capacity as an inquirer after truth he happened to know about it. He was neither a pedant nor a bigot. He neither supposed that he was bound to know all things, nor that all things were bound to conform to what he had fancied or would have them to be. In treating of men and manners, he spoke of them as he found them, not according to preconceived notions and abstract dogmas ; and he began by teaching us what he himself was. In criticising books he did not compare them with rules and systems, but told us what he saw to like or dislike in them. He did not take his standard of excellence "according to an exact scale" of Aristotle, or fall out with a work that was good for anything, because "not one of the angles at the four corners was a right one." He was, in a word, the first author who was not a book-maker, and who wrote not to make converts of others to established creeds and prejudices, but to satisfy his own mind of the truth of things. In this respect we know not which to be most charmed with, the author or the man. There is an inexpressible frankness and sincerity, as well as power, in what he writes. There is no attempt at imposition or concealment, no juggling tricks or solemn mouthing, no laboured attempts at proving himself always in the right, and everybody else in the wrong ; he says what is uppermost, lays open what floats at the top or the bottom of his mind, and deserves Pope's character of him, where he professes to

"——— pour out all as plain
As downright Shippen, or as old Montaigne."[*]

He does not converse with us like a pedagogue with his pupil, whom he wishes to make as great a blockhead as himself, but like a philosopher and friend who has passed through life with thought and observation, and is willing to enable others to pass through it with pleasure and profit. A writer of this stamp, I confess, appears to me as much superior to a common bookworm, as a library of real books is superior to a mere bookcase, painted and lettered on the outside with the names of celebrated works. As he was the first to attempt this new way of writing, so the same strong natural impulse which prompted the undertaking carried him to the end of his career. The same force and honesty of mind which urged him to throw off the shackles of custom and prejudice would enable him to complete his triumph over them. He has left little for his successors to achieve in the way of just and original speculation on human life. Nearly all the thinking of the two last centuries of that kind which the French denominate *morale observatrice*, is to be found in Montaigne's *Essays:* there is the germ, at least, and generally much more. He sowed the seed and cleared away the rubbish, even where others have reaped the fruit, or cultivated and decorated the soil to a greater degree of nicety and perfection. There is no one to whom the old Latin adage is more applicable than to Montaigne, "*Pereant isti qui ante nos nostra dixerunt*" (Confound the fellows who have said our good things before us). There has been no new impulse

* Why Pope should say in reference to him, "Or *more wise* Charron," is not easy to determine.

given to thought since his time. Among the specimens of criticisms on authors which he has left us, are those on Virgil, Ovid, and Boccaccio, in the account of books which he thinks worth reading, or (which is the same thing) which he finds he can read in his old age, and which may be reckoned among the few criticisms which are worth reading at any age.

Montaigne's *Essays* were translated into English by Charles Cotton, who was one of the wits and poets of the age of Charles II.; and Lord Halifax, one of the noble critics of that day, declared it to be "the book in the world he was the best pleased with." This mode of familiar essay-writing, free from the trammels of the schools, and the airs of professed authorship, was successfully imitated, about the same time, by Cowley and Sir William Temple, in their miscellaneous *Essays*, which are very agreeable and learned talking upon paper. Lord Shaftesbury, on the contrary, who aimed at the same easy, *degagé* mode of communicating his thoughts to the world, has quite spoiled his matter, which is sometimes valuable, by his manner, in which he carries a certain flaunting, flowery, figurative, flirting style of amicable condescension to the reader, to an excess more tantalising than the most starched and ridiculous formality of the age of James I. There is nothing so tormenting as the affectation of ease and freedom from affectation.

The ice being thus thawed, and the barrier that kept authors at a distance from common-sense and feeling broken through, the transition was not difficult from Montaigne and his imitators to our Periodical Essayists. These last applied the same unrestrained expression of their thoughts to the more immediate and passing scenes of life, to temporary and local matters; and in order to discharge the invidious office of *Censor Morum* more freely, and with less responsibility, assumed some fictitious and humorous disguise, which, however, in a great degree corresponded to their own peculiar habits and character. By thus concealing their own name and person under the title of the *Tatler*, *Spectator*, etc., they were enabled to inform us more fully of what was passing in the world, while the dramatic contrast and ironical point of view to which the whole is subjected, added a greater liveliness and *piquancy* to the descriptions. The philosopher and wit here commences newsmonger, makes himself master of " the perfect spy o' th' time," and from his various walks and turns through life, brings home little curious specimens of the humours, opinions, and manners of his contemporaries, as the botanist brings home different plants and weeds, or the mineralogist different shells and fossils, to illustrate their several theories, and be useful to mankind.

The first of these papers that was attempted in this country was set up by Steele in the beginning of the last century ; and of all our Periodical Essayists, the *Tatler* (for that was the name he assumed) has always appeared to me the most amusing and agreeable. Montaigne, whom I have proposed to consider as the father of this kind of personal authorship among the moderns, in which the reader is admitted behind the curtain, and sits down with the writer in his gown and slippers, was a most magnanimous and undisguised egotist ; but Isaac Bickerstaff, Esq., was the more disinterested gossip of the two. The French author is contented to describe the peculiarities of his own mind and constitution, which he does with a copious and unsparing hand. The English journalist good-naturedly lets you into the secret both of his own affairs and those of others. A young lady, on the other side Temple Bar, cannot be seen at her glass for half a day together, but Mr. Bickerstaff takes due notice of it ; and he has the first intelligence of the symptoms of the *belle* passion appearing in any young gentleman at the West-end of the town. The departures and arrivals of widows with handsome jointures, either to bury their grief in the country, or to procure a second husband in town, are punctually recorded in his pages. He is well acquainted with the celebrated beauties of the preceding age at the court of Charles II. ; and the old gentleman (as he feigns himself) often grows romantic in recounting "the disastrous strokes which his youth suffered" from the glances of their bright eyes, and their unaccountable caprices. In particular, he dwells with a secret satisfaction on the recollection of one of his mistresses, who left him for a richer rival, and whose constant reproach to her husband, on occasion of any quarrel between them, was, " I, that might have married the famous Mr. Bickerstaff, to be treated in this manner ! " The club at the Trumpet consists of a set of persons almost as well worth knowing as himself. The cavalcade of the justice of the peace, the knight of the shire, the country squire, and the young gentleman, his nephew, who came to wait on him at his chambers, in such form and ceremony, seem not to have settled the order of their precedence to this hour ; and I should hope that the upholsterer and his companions, who used to sun themselves in the Green Park, and who broke their rest and fortunes to maintain the balance of power in Europe, stand as fair a chance for immortality as some modern politicians. Mr. Bickerstaff himself is a gentleman and a scholar, a humorist, and a man of the world ; with a great deal of nice easy *naïveté* about him. If he walks out and is caught in a shower of rain, he makes amends for this unlucky accident by a criticism on the shower in Virgil, and concludes with a burlesque copy of verses on a city shower. He entertains us, when he dates from his own apartments, with a quotation from Plutarch, or a moral reflection : from the Grecian coffee-house, with politics ; and from Will's or the Temple, with the poets and players, the beaux and men of wit and pleasure about town. In reading the pages of the *Tatler*, we seem as if suddenly carried back to the age of Queen Anne, of toupees and full-bottomed periwigs. The whole appearance of our dress and manners undergoes a delightful metamorphosis. The beaux and the belles are of a quite different species from what they are at present ; we distinguish the dappers, the smarts, and the pretty fellows, as they pass by Mr. Lilly's shop-windows in the Strand ; we are introduced to Betterton and Mrs. Oldfield behind the scenes ; are made familiar with the persons and performances of Will Estcourt or Tom Durfey ; we listen to a dispute at a tavern on the merits of the Duke of Marlborough or Marshal Turenne ; or are present at the first rehearsal of a play by Vanbrugh, or the reading of a new poem by Mr. Pope. The privilege of thus virtually transporting ourselves to past times is even greater than that of visiting distant places in reality. London, a hundred years ago, would be much better worth seeing than Paris at the present moment.

It will be said, that all this is to be found, in the same or a greater degree, in the *Spectator*. For myself, I do not think so ; or at least, there is in the last work a much greater proportion of commonplace matter. I have, on this account, always preferred the *Tatler* to the *Spectator*. Whether it is owing to my having been earlier or better acquainted with the one than the other, my pleasure in reading these two admirable works is not in proportion to their comparative reputation. The *Tatler* contains only half the number of volumes, and, I will venture to say, nearly an equal quantity of sterling wit and sense. "The first sprightly runnings" are there : it has more of the original spirit, more of the freshness and stamp of nature. The indications of character and strokes of humour are more true and frequent ; the reflections that suggest themselves arise more from the occasion, and are less spun out into regular dissertations. They are more like the remarks which occur in sensible conversation, and less like a lecture. Something is left to the understanding of the reader. Steele seems to have gone into his closet chiefly to set down what he observed out of doors. Addison seems to have spent most of his time in his study, and to have spun out and wire-drawn the hints, which he borrowed from Steele, or took from nature, to the utmost. I am far from wishing to depreciate Addison's talents, but I am anxious to do justice to Steele, who was, I think, upon the whole, a less artificial and more original writer. The humorous descriptions of Steele resemble loose sketches, or fragments of a comedy ; those of Addison are rather comments or ingenious paraphrases on the genuine text. The characters of the club, not only in the *Tatler*, but in the *Spectator*, were drawn by Steele. That of Sir Roger de Coverley is among the number. Addison has, however, gained himself immortal honour by his manner of filling up this last character. Who is there that can forget, or be insensible to, the inimitable nameless graces and

varied traits of nature and of old English character in it : to his
unpretending virtues and amiable weaknesses : to his modesty,
generosity, hospitality, and eccentric whims : to the respect of
his neighbours, and the affection of his domestics : to his
wayward, hopeless, secret passion for his fair enemy, the widow,
in which there is more of real romance and true delicacy than in
a thousand tales of knight-errantry (we perceive the hectic flush
of his cheek, the faltering of his tongue in speaking of her
bewitching airs and "the whiteness of her hand") : to the
havoc he makes among the game in his neighbourhood : to his
speech from the bench, to show the *Spectator* what is thought of
him in the country : to his unwillingness to be put up as a
sign-post, and his having his own likeness turned into the
Saracen's head : to his gentle reproof of the baggage of a gipsy
that tells him "he has a widow in his line of life :" to his doubts
as to the existence of witchcraft, and protection of reputed
witches : to his account of the family pictures, and his choice of
a chaplain : to his falling asleep at church, and his reproof of
John Williams, as soon as he recovered from his nap, for
talking in sermon-time. The characters of Will Wimble and
Will Honeycomb are not a whit behind their friend, Sir Roger,
in delicacy and felicity. The delightful simplicity and good-
humoured officiousness in the one are set off by the graceful
affectation and courtly pretension in the other. How long
since I first became acquainted with these two characters
in the *Spectator!* What old-fashioned friends they seem,
and yet I am not tired of them like so many other friends,
nor they of me! How airy these abstractions of the poet's
pen stream over the dawn of our acquaintance with human
life! how they glance their fairest colours on the prospect
before us! how pure they remain in it to the last, like the
rainbow in the evening-cloud, which the rude hand of time and
experience can neither soil nor dissipate! What a pity that we
cannot find the reality, and yet if we did, the dream would be
over. I once thought I knew a Will Wimble, and a Will
Honeycomb, but they turned out but indifferently ; the originals
in the *Spectator* still read, word for word, the same that they

always did. We have only to turn to the page, and find them where we left them! Many of the most exquisite pieces in the *Tatler*, it is to be observed, are Addison's, as the "Court of Honour" and the "Personification of Musical Instruments," with almost all those papers that form regular sets or series. I do not know whether the picture of the family of an old college acquaintance, in the *Tatler*, where the children run to let Mr. Bickerstaff in at the door, and where the one that loses the race that way, turns back to tell the father that he is come : with the nice gradation of incredulity in the little boy who is got into *Guy of Warwick* and the *Seven Champions*, and who shakes his head at the improbability of Æsop's *Fables*, is Steele's or Addison's, though I believe it belongs to the former. The account of the two sisters, one of whom held up her head higher than ordinary, from having on a pair of flowered garters, and that of the married lady who complained to the *Tatler* of the neglect of her husband, with her answers to some *home* questions that were put to her, are unquestionably Steele's. If the *Tatler* is not inferior to the *Spectator* as a record of manners and character, it is superior to it in the interest of many of the stories. Several of the incidents related there by Steele have never been surpassed in the heart-rending pathos of private distress. I might refer to those of the lover and his mistress, when the theatre, in which they were, caught fire ; of the bridegroom, who by accident kills his bride on the day of their marriage ; the story of Mr. Eustace and his wife ; and the fine dream about his own mistress when a youth. What has given its superior reputation to the *Spectator*, is the greater gravity of its pretensions, its moral dissertations and critical reasonings, by which I confess myself less edified than by other things, which are thought more lightly of. Systems and opinions change, but nature is always true. It is the moral and didactic tone of the *Spectator* which makes us apt to think of Addison (according to Mandeville's sarcasm) as "a parson in a tie-wig." Many of his moral Essays are, however, exquisitely beautiful and quite happy. Such are the reflections on cheerfulness, those in Westminster Abbey, on the Royal Exchange, and particularly some very affecting ones on the death of a young lady in the fourth volume. These, it must be allowed, are the perfection of elegant sermonising. His critical Essays are not so good. I prefer Steele's occasional selection of beautiful poetical passages, without any affectation of analysing their beauties, to Addison's finer-spun theories. The best criticism in the *Spectator*, that on the "Cartoons of Raphael," of which Mr. Fuseli has availed himself with great spirit in his *Lectures*, is by Steele.* I owed this acknowledgment to a writer who has so often put me in good humour with myself, and everything about me, when few things else could, and when the tomes of casuistry and ecclesiastical history, with which the little duodecimo volumes of the *Tatler* were overwhelmed and surrounded, in the only library to which I had access when a boy, had tried their tranquillising effects upon me in vain. I had not long ago in my hands, by favour of a friend, an original copy of the quarto edition of the *Tatler*, with a list of the subscribers. It is curious to see some names there which we should hardly think of (that of Sir Isaac Newton is among them), and also to observe the degree of interest excited by those of the different persons, which is not determined according to the rules of the Heralds' College. One literary name lasts as long as a whole race of heroes and their descendants! The *Guardian*, which followed the *Spectator*, was, as may be supposed, inferior to it.

The dramatic and conversational turn which forms the distinguishing feature and greatest charm of the *Spectator* and *Tatler*, is quite lost in the *Rambler* by Dr. Johnson. There is no reflected light thrown on human life from an assumed character, nor any direct one from a display of the author's own. The *Tatler* and *Spectator* are, as it were, made up of notes and memorandums of the events and incidents of the day, with finished studies after nature, and characters fresh from the life,

---

* The antithetical style and verbal paradoxes which Burke was so fond of, in which the epithet is a seeming contradiction to the substantive, such as "proud submission and dignified obedience," are, I think, first to be found in the *Tatler*.

which the writer moralises upon, and turns to account as they come before him : the *Rambler* is a collection of moral Essays, or scholastic theses, written on set subjects, and of which the individual characters and incidents are merely artificial illustrations, brought in to give a pretended relief to the dryness of didactic discussion. The *Rambler* is a splendid and imposing commonplace book of general topics, and rhetorical declamation on the conduct and business of human life. In this sense, there is hardly a reflection that had been suggested on such subjects which is not to be found in this celebrated work, and there is, perhaps, hardly a reflection to be found in it which had not been already suggested and developed by some other author, or in the common course of conversation. The mass of intellectual wealth here heaped together is immense ; but it is rather the result of gradual accumulation, the produce of the general intellect labouring in the mine of knowledge and reflection, than dug out of the quarry, and dragged into the light by the industry and sagacity of a single mind. I am not here saying that Dr. Johnson was a man without originality, compared with the ordinary run of men's minds ; but he was not a man of original thought or genius, in the sense in which Montaigne or Lord Bacon was. He opened no new vein of precious ore, nor did he light upon any single pebbles of uncommon size and unrivalled lustre. We seldom meet with anything to "give us pause ; " he does not set us thinking for the first time. His reflections present themselves like reminiscences ; do not disturb the ordinary march of our thoughts ; arrest our attention by the stateliness of their appearance and the costliness of their garb, but pass on and mingle with the throng of our impressions. After closing the volumes of the *Rambler*, there is nothing that we remember as a new truth gained to the mind, nothing indelibly stamped upon the memory ; nor is there any passage that we wish to turn to as embodying any known principle or observation with such force and beauty that justice can only be done to the idea in the author's own words. Such, for instance, are many of the passages to be found in Burke, which shine by their own light, belong to no class, have neither equal nor counterpart, and of which we say that no one but the author could have written them ! There is neither the same boldness of design, nor mastery of execution in Johnson. In the one, the spark of genius seems to have met with its congenial matter : the shaft is sped ; the forked lightning dresses up the face of nature in ghastly smiles, and the loud thunder rolls far away from the ruin that is made. Dr. Johnson's style, on the contrary, resembles rather the rumbling of mimic thunder at one of our theatres ; and the light he throws upon a subject is like the dazzling effect of phosphorus, or an *ignis fatuus* of words. There is a wide difference, however, between perfect originality and perfect commonplace : neither ideas nor expressions are trite or vulgar because they are not quite new. They are valuable, and ought to be repeated, if they have not become quite common ; and Johnson's style both of reasoning and imagery holds the middle rank between startling novelty and vapid commonplace. Johnson has as much originality of thinking as Addison ; but then he wants his familiarity of illustration, knowledge of character, and delightful humour. What most distinguishes Dr. Johnson from other writers is the pomp and uniformity of his style. All his periods are cast in the same mould, are of the same size and shape, and consequently have little fitness to the variety of things he professes to treat of. His subjects are familiar, but the author is always upon stilts. He has neither ease nor simplicity, and his efforts at playfulness, in part, remind one of the lines in Milton :—

> " —— The elephant
> To make them sport wreath'd his proboscis lithe."

. . . .

. . . .

The fault of Dr. Johnson's style is, that it reduces all things to the same artificial and unmeaning level. It destroys all shades of difference, the association between words and things. It is a perpetual paradox and innovation. He condescends to the familiar till we are ashamed of our interest in it : he expands the little till it looks big. " If he were to write a fable of little fishes," as Goldsmith said of him, "he would make them speak like great whales." We can no more distinguish the most familiar objects in his description of them, than we can a well-known face under a huge painted mask. The structure of his sentences, which was his own invention, and which has been generally imitated since his time, is a species of rhyming in prose, where one clause answers to another in measure and quantity, like the tagging of syllables at the end of a verse ; the close of the period follows as mechanically as the oscillation of a pendulum, the sense is balanced with the sound ; each sentence, revolving round its centre of gravity, is contained with itself like a couplet, and each paragraph forms itself into a stanza. Dr. Johnson is also a complete balance-master in the topics of morality. He never encourages hope, but he counteracts it by fear ; he never elicits a truth, but he suggests some objection in answer to it. He seizes and alternately quits the clue of reason, lest it should involve him in the labyrinths of endless error : he wants confidence in himself and his fellows.

   .   .   .   .   .   .

The most triumphant record of the talents and character of Johnson is to be found in Boswell's Life of him. The man was superior to the author. When he threw aside his pen, which he regarded as an incumbrance, he became not only learned and thoughtful, but acute, witty, humorous, natural, honest ; hearty and determined, "the king of good fellows and wale of old men." There are as many smart repartees, profound remarks, and keen invectives to be found in Boswell's "inventory of all he said," as are recorded of any celebrated man. The life and dramatic play of his conversation forms a contrast to his written works. His natural powers and undisguised opinions were called out in convivial intercourse. In public, he practised with the foils on : in private, he unsheathed the sword of controversy, and it was "the Ebro's temper." The eagerness of opposition roused him from his natural sluggishness and acquired timidity ; he returned blow for blow ; and whether the trial were of argument or wit, none of his rivals could boast much of the encounter. Burke seems to have been the only person who had a chance with him ; and it is the unpardonable sin of Boswell's work, that he has purposely omitted their combats of strength and skill. Goldsmith asked, " Does he wind into a subject like a serpent, as Burke does?" And when exhausted with sickness, he himself said, " If that fellow Burke were here now, he would kill me." It is to be observed, that Johnson's colloquial style was as blunt, direct, and downright, as his style of studied composition was involved and circuitous. As when Topham Beauclerc and Langton knocked him up at his chambers, at three in the morning, and he came to the door with the poker in his hand, but seeing them, exclaimed, " What, is it you, my lads? then I'll have a frisk with you!" And he afterwards reproaches Langton, who was a literary milksop, for leaving them to go to an engagement " with some *un-idead* girls." What words to come from the mouth of the great moralist and lexicographer ! His good deeds were as many as his good sayings. His domestic habits, his tenderness to servants, and readiness to oblige his friends ; the quantity of strong tea that he drank to keep down sad thoughts ; his many labours reluctantly begun and irresolutely laid aside ; his honest acknowledgment of his own, and indulgence to the weaknesses of others ; his throwing himself back in the post-chaise with Boswell, and saying, " Now I think I am a good-humoured fellow," though nobody thought him so, and yet he was ; his quitting the society of Garrick and his actresses, and his reason for it ; his dining with Wilkes, and his kindness to Goldsmith ; his sitting with the young ladies on his knee at the Mitre, to give them good advice, in which situation, if not explained, he might be taken for Falstaff ; and last and noblest, his carrying the unfortunate victim of disease and dissipation on his back up through Fleet Street (an act which realises the parable of the good Samaritan)—all these, and innumerable others, endear him to the reader, and must be remembered to his lasting honour. He had faults, but they lie buried with him.

He had his prejudices and his intolerant feelings; but he suffered enough in the conflict of his own mind with them. For if no man can be happy in the free exercise of his reason, no wise man can be happy without it. His were not time-serving, heartless, hypocritical prejudices; but deep, inwoven, not to be rooted out but with life and hope, which he found from old habit necessary to his own peace of mind, and thought so to the peace of mankind. I do not hate, but love him for them. They were between himself and his conscience; and should be left to that higher tribunal, "where they in trembling hope repose, the bosom of his Father and his God." In a word, he has left behind him few wiser or better men.

The herd of his imitators showed what he was by their disproportionate effects. The Periodical Essayists that succeeded the *Rambler* are, and deserve to be, little read at present. The *Adventurer*, by Hawksworth, is completely trite and vapid, aping all the faults of Johnson's style, without anything to atone for them. The sentences are often absolutely unmeaning; and one half of each might regularly be left blank. The *World*, and *Connoisseur*, which followed, are a little better; and in the last of these there is one good idea, that of a man in indifferent health, who judges of every one's title to respect from their possession of this blessing, and bows to a sturdy beggar with sound limbs and a florid complexion, while he turns his back upon a lord who is a valetudinarian.

Goldsmith's *Citizen of the World*, like all his works, bears the stamp of the author's mind. It does not "go about to cozen reputation without the stamp of merit." He is more observing, more original, more natural and picturesque than Johnson. His work is written on the model of the *Persian Letters*; and contrives to give an abstracted and somewhat perplexing view of things, by opposing foreign prepossessions to our own, and thus stripping objects of their customary disguises. Whether truth is elicited in this collision of contrary absurdities, I do not know; but I confess the process is too ambiguous and full of intricacy to be very amusing to my plain understanding. For light summer reading. It is like walking in a garden full of traps and pitfalls. It necessarily gives rise to paradoxes, and there are some very bold ones in the Essays, which would subject an author less established to no very agreeable sort of *censura literaria.* Thus the Chinese philosopher exclaims very unadvisedly, "The bonzes and priests of all religions keep up superstition and imposture : all reformations begin with the laity." Goldsmith, however, was staunch in his practical creed, and might bolt speculative extravagances with impunity. There is a striking difference in this respect between him and Addison, who, if he attacked authority, took care to have common sense on his side, and never hazarded anything offensive to the feelings of others, or on the strength of his own discretional opinion. There is another inconvenience in this assumption of an exotic character and tone of sentiment, that it produces an inconsistency between the knowledge which the individual has time to acquire, and which the author is bound to communicate. Thus the Chinese has not been in England three days before he is acquainted with the characters of the three countries which compose this kingdom, and describes them to his friend at Canton, by extracts from the newspapers of each metropolis. The nationality of Scotchmen is thus ridiculed :—"*Edinburgh.* We are positive when we say that Sanders Macgregor, lately executed for horse-stealing, is not a native of Scotland, but born at Carrickfergus." Now this is very good ; but how should our Chinese philosopher find it out by instinct ? Beau Tibbs, a prominent character in this little work, is the best comic sketch since the time of Addison ; unrivalled in his finery, his vanity, and his poverty.

MY FIRST ACQUAINTANCE WITH POETS.

My father was a Dissenting minister at Wem, in Shropshire, and in the year 1798 (the figures that compose the date are to me like the "dreaded name of Demogorgon") Mr. Coleridge came to Shrewsbury to succeed Mr. Rowe in the spiritual charge of a Unitarian congregation there.   He did not come till late on the Saturday afternoon before he was to preach, and Mr. Rowe, who himself went down to the coach in a state of anxiety and expectation to look for the arrival of his successor, could find no one at all answering the description but a round-faced man in a short black coat (like a shooting-jacket) which hardly seemed to have been made for him, but who seemed to be talking at a great rate to his fellow-passengers.   Mr. Rowe had scarce returned to give an account of his disappointment when the round-faced man in black entered, and dissipated all doubts on the subject by beginning to talk.   He did not cease while he stayed, nor has he since, that I know of.   He held the good town of Shrewsbury in delightful suspense for three weeks that he remained there, "fluttering the *proud Salopians* like an eagle in a dove-cote ;" and the Welsh mountains that skirt the horizon with their tempestuous confusion agree to have heard no such mystic sounds since the days of

" High-born Hoel's harp or soft Llewellyn's lay."

As we passed along between Wem and Shrewsbury, and I eyed their blue tops seen through the wintry branches, or the red rustling leaves of the sturdy oak-trees by the road-side, a sound was in my ears as of a Syren's song ; I was stunned, startled with it, as from deep sleep; but I had no notion then that I should ever be able to express my admiration to others in motley imagery or quaint allusion, till the light of his genius shone into my soul, like the sun's rays glittering in the puddles of the road. I was at that time dumb, inarticulate, helpless, like a worm by the way-side, crushed, bleeding, lifeless; but now, bursting the deadly bands that "bound them,

"With Styx nine times round them,"

my ideas float on winged words, and as they expand their plumes, catch the golden light of other years. My soul has indeed remained in its original bondage, dark, obscure, with longings infinite and unsatisfied; my heart, shut up in the prison-house of this rude clay, has never found, nor will it ever find, a heart to speak to; but that my understanding also did not remain dumb and brutish, or at length found a language to express itself, I owe to Coleridge. But this is not to my purpose.

My father lived ten miles from Shrewsbury, and was in the habit of exchanging visits with Mr. Rowe, and with Mr. Jenkins, of Whitchurch (nine miles further on), according to the custom of Dissenting ministers in each other's neighbourhood. A line of communication is thus established, by which the flame of civil and religious liberty is kept alive, and nourishes its smouldering fire unquenchable, like the fires in the *Agamemnon* of Æschylus, placed at different stations, that waited for ten long years to announce with their blazing pyramids the destruction of Troy. Coleridge had agreed to come over and see my father, according to the courtesy of the country, as Mr. Rowe's probable successor; but, in the meantime, I had gone to hear him preach the Sunday after his arrival. A poet and a philosopher getting up into a Unitarian pulpit to preach the Gospel was a romance in these degenerate days, a sort of revival of the primitive spirit of Christianity which was not to be resisted.

It was in January of 1798 that I rose one morning before daylight, to walk ten miles in the mud to hear this celebrated person preach.   Never, the longest day I have to live, shall I have such another walk as this cold, raw, comfortless one, in the winter of the year 1798. *Il y a des impressions qui ni le tems ni les circonstances peuvent effacer. Dusse-je vivre des siècles entiers, le doux tems de ma jeunesse ne peut renaître pour moi, ni s'effacer jamais dans ma mémoire.*   When I got there the organ was playing the 100th Psalm, and when it was done Mr. Coleridge rose and gave out his text, "And he went up into the mountain to pray, HIMSELF, ALONE."   As he gave out this text his voice "rose like a steam of rich distilled perfumes," and when he came to the two last words, which he pronounced loud, deep, and distinct, it seemed to me, who was then young, as if the sounds had echoed from the bottom of the human heart, and as if that prayer might have floated in solemn silence through the universe.   The idea of St. John came into my mind, "of one crying in the wilderness, who had his loins girt about, and whose food was locusts and wild honcy."   The preacher then launched into his subject like an eagle dallying with the wind.   The sermon was upon peace and war ; upon church and state—not their alliance but their separation—on the spirit of the world and the spirit of Christianity, not as the same, but as opposed to one another.   He talked of those who had "inscribed the cross of Christ on banners dripping with human gore."   He made a poetical and pastoral excursion—and to show the fatal effects of war, drew a striking contrast between the simple shepherd-boy, driving his team afield, or sitting under the hawthorn, piping to his flock, "as though he should never be old," and the same poor country lad, crimped, kidnapped, brought into town, made drunk at an alehouse, turned into a wretched drummer-boy, with his hair sticking on end with powder and pomatum, a long cue at his back, and tricked out in the loathsome finery of the profession of blood :

"Such were the notes our once-loved poet sung.'

And for myself, I could not have been more delighted if I had heard the music of the spheres.   Poetry and Philosophy had

met together. Truth and Genius had embraced, under the eye
and with the sanction of Religion. This was even beyond my
hopes. I returned home well satisfied. The sun that was still
labouring pale and wan through the sky, obscured by thick
mists, seemed an emblem of the *good cause;* and the cold, dank
drops of dew that hung half melted on the beard of the thistle
had something genial and refreshing in them ; for there was a
spirit of hope and youth in all nature that turned everything
into good. The face of nature had not then the brand of JUS
DIVINUM on it :

"Like to that sanguine flower, inscrib'd with woe."

On the Tuesday following the half-inspired speaker came. I
was called down into the room where he was, and went half-
hoping, half-afraid. He received me very graciously, and I
listened for a long time without uttering a word. I did not
suffer in his opinion by my silence. "For those two hours," he
afterwards was pleased to say, "he was conversing with
William Hazlitt's forehead !" His appearance was different
from what I had anticipated from seeing him before. At a
distance, and in the dim light of the chapel, there was to me a
strange wildness in his aspect, a dusky obscurity, and I thought
him pitted with the small-pox. His complexion was at that
time clear, and even bright—

"As are the children of yon azure sheen."

His forehead was broad and high, light as if built of ivory, with
large projecting eyebrows, and his eyes rolling beneath them,
like a sea with darkened lustre. "A certain tender bloom his
face o'erspread," a purple tinge as we see it in the pale thoughtful complexions of the Spanish portrait-painters, Murillo and
Valasquez. His mouth was gross, voluptuous, open, eloquent ;
his chin good-humoured and round ; but his nose, the rudder
of the face, the index of the will, was small, feeble, nothing—
like what he has done. It might seem that the genius of his
face as from a height surveyed and projected him (with
sufficient capacity and huge aspiration) into the world unknown

of thought and imagination, with nothing to support or guide his veering purpose, as if Columbus had launched his adventurous course for the New World in a scallop, without oars or compass. So, at least, I comment on it after the event. Coleridge, in his person, was rather above the common size, inclining to the corpulent, or like Lord Hamlet, "somewhat fat and pursy." His hair (now, alas! grey) was then black and glossy as the raven's, and fell in smooth masses over his forehead. This long pendulous hair is peculiar to enthusiasts, to those whose minds tend heavenward, and is traditionally inseparable (though of a different colour) from the pictures of Christ. It ought to belong, as a character, to all who preach *Christ crucified*, and Coleridge was at that time one of those!

It was curious to observe the contrast between him and my father, who was a veteran in the cause, and then declining into the vale of years. He had been 'a poor Irish lad, carefully brought up by his parents, and sent to the University of Glasgow (where he studied under Adam Smith) to prepare him for his future destination. It was his mother's proudest wish to see her son a Dissenting Minister. So, if we look back to past generations (as far as eye can reach), we see the same hopes, fears, wishes, followed by the same disappointments, throbbing in the human heart ; and so we may see them (if we look forward) rising up for ever, and disappearing, like vapourish bubbles, in the human breast! After being tossed about from congregation to congregation in the heats of the Unitarian controversy, and squabbles about the American war, he had been relegated to an obscure village, where he was to spend the last thirty years of his life, far from the only converse that he loved, the talk about disputed texts of Scripture, and the cause of civil and religious liberty. Here he passed his days, repining, but resigned, in the study of the Bible, and the perusal of the Commentators—huge folios, not easily got through, one of which would outlast a winter! Why did he pore on these from morn to night (with the exception of a walk in the fields or a turn in the garden to gather broccoli-plants or kidney beans of his own rearing, with no small degree of pride and pleasure)? Here were "no figures nor no fantasies"—neither poetry nor philosophy—nothing to dazzle, nothing to excite modern curiosity; but to his lack-lustre eyes there appeared within the pages of the ponderous, unwieldly, neglected tomes, the sacred name of JEHOVAH in Hebrew capitals: pressed down by the weight of the style, worn to the last fading thinness of the understanding, there were glimpses, glimmering notions of the patriarchal wanderings, with palm-trees hovering in the horizon, and processions of camels at the distance of three thousand years; there was Moses with the Burning Bush, the number of the Twelve Tribes, types, shadows, glosses on the law and the prophets; there were discussions (dull enough) on the age of Methuselah, a mighty speculation ! there were outlines, rude guesses at the shape of Noah's Ark and of the riches of Solomon's Temple; questions as to the date of the creation, predictions of the end of all things; the great lapses of time, the strange mutations of the globe were unfolded with the voluminous leaf, as it turned over; and though the soul might slumber with an hieroglyphic veil of inscrutable mysteries drawn over it, yet it was in a slumber ill-exchanged for all the sharpened realities of sense, wit, fancy, or reason. My father's life was comparatively a dream; but it was a dream of infinity and eternity, of death, the resurrection, and a judgment to come !

No two individuals were ever more unlike than were the host and his guest. A poet was to my father a sort of nondescript; yet whatever added grace to the Unitarian cause was to him welcome. He could hardly have been more surprised or pleased if our visitor had worn wings. Indeed, his thoughts had wings: and as the silken sounds rustled round our little wainscoted parlour, my father threw back his spectacles over his forehead, his white hairs mixing with its sanguine hue; and a smile of delight beamed across his rugged, cordial face, to think that Truth had found a new ally in Fancy ! Besides, Coleridge seemed to take considerable notice of me, and that of itself was enough. He talked very familiarly, but agreeably, and glanced over a variety of subjects. At dinner-

time he grew more animated, and dilated in a very edifying
manner on Mary Wolstonecraft and Mackintosh. The last,
he said, he considered (on my father's speaking of his *Vindiciæ
Gallicæ* as a capital performance) as a clever, scholastic man—
a master of the topics—or, as the ready warehouseman of
letters, who knew exactly where to lay his hand on what he
wanted, though the goods were not his own. He thought
him no match for Burke, either in style or matter. Burke
was a metaphysician, Mackintosh a mere logician. Burke
was an orator (almost a poet) who reasoned in figures, because
he had an eye for nature : Mackintosh, on the other hand,
was a rhetorician, who had only an eye to commonplaces.
On this I ventured to say that I had always entertained a
great opinion of Burke, and that (as far as I could find) the
speaking of him with contempt might be made the test of a
vulgar, democratical mind. This was the first observation I
ever made to Coleridge, and he said it was a very just and
striking one. I remember the leg of Welsh mutton and the
turnips on the table that day had the finest flavour imaginable.
Coleridge added that Mackintosh and Tom Wedgwood (of
whom, however, he spoke highly) had expressed a very indifferent opinion of his friend Mr. Wordsworth, on which he
remarked to them—"He strides on so far before you that he
dwindles in the distance!" Godwin had once boasted to him
of having carried on an argument with Mackintosh for three
hours with dubious success ; Coleridge told him—"If there
had been a man of genius in the room he would have settled
the question in five minutes." He asked me if I had ever seen
Mary Wolstonecraft, and I said, I had once for a few moments,
and that she seemed to me to turn off Godwin's objections
to something she advanced with quite a playful, easy air.
He replied, that "this was only one instance of the ascend-
ency which people of imagination exercised over those of
mere intellect." He did not rate Godwin very high* (this

---

* He complained in particular of the presumption of his attempting to establish the future immortality of man, "without" (as he

was caprice or prejudice, real or affected), but he had a great idea of Mrs. Wolstonecraft's powers of conversation; none at all of her talent for bookmaking. We talked a little about Holcroft. He had been asked if he was not much struck *with* him, and he said, he thought himself in more danger of being struck *by* him. I complained that he would not let me get on at all, for he required a definition of every the commonest word, exclaiming, "What do you mean by a *sensation*, sir? What do you mean by an *idea?*" This, Coleridge said, was barricadoing the road to truth; it was setting up a turnpike-gate at every step we took. I forget a great number of things, many more than I remember; but the day passed off pleasantly, and the next morning Mr. Coleridge was to return to Shrewsbury. When I came down to break-fast I found that he had just received a letter from his friend, T. Wedgwood, making him an offer of £150 a-year if he chose to waive his present pursuit and devote himself entirely to the study of poetry and philosophy. Coleridge seemed to make up his mind to close with this proposal in the act of tying on one of his shoes. It threw an additional damp on his departure. It took the wayward enthusiast quite from us to cast him into Deva's winding vales, or by the shores of old romance. Instead of living at ten miles' distance, of being the pastor of a Dissent-ing congregation at Shrewsbury, he was henceforth to inhabit the Hill of Parnassus, to be a Shepherd on the Delectable Mountains. Alas! I knew not the way thither, and felt very little gratitude for Mr. Wedgwood's bounty. I was presently relieved from this dilemma; for Mr. Coleridge, asking for a pen and ink, and going to a table to write something on a bit of card, advanced towards me with undulating step, and giving me the precious document, said that that was his address, Mr. Coleridge, Nether-Stowey, Somersetshire; and that he should be glad to see me there in a few weeks' time, and, if I chose,

said) "knowing what Death was or what Life was"—and the tone in which he pronounced these two words seemed to convey a complete image of both.

would come half-way to meet me. I was not less surprised
than the shepherd-boy (this simile is to be found in " Cas-
sandra "), when he sees a thunderbolt fall close at his feet. I
stammered out my acknowledgments and acceptance of this
offer (I thought Mr. Wedgwood's annuity a trifle to it) as well
as I could ; and this mighty business being settled, the poet
preacher took leave, and I accompanied him six miles on the
road. It was a fine morning in the middle of winter, and he
talked the whole way. The scholar in Chaucer is described as
going

> " ——Sounding on his way."

So Coleridge went on his. In digressing, in dilating, in passing from subject to subject, he appeared to me to float in air, to
slide on ice. He told me in confidence (going along) that he
should have preached two sermons before he accepted the
situation at Shrewsbury, one on Infant Baptism, the other on
the Lord's Supper, showing that he could not administer
either, which would have effectually disqualified him for the
object in view. I observed that he continually crossed me on
the way by shifting from one side of the footpath to the other.
This struck me as an odd movement ; but I did not at that
time connect it with any instability of purpose or involuntary
change of principle, as I have done since. He seemed
unable to keep on in a straight line. He spoke slightingly
of Hume (whose *Essay on Miracles* he said was stolen from
an objection started in one of South's sermons—*Credat Judæus
Appella !*) I was not very much pleased at this account of
Hume, for I had just been reading, with infinite relish, that
completest of all metaphysical *choke-pears*, his *Treatise on
Human Nature*, to which the *Essays*, in point of scholastic
subtilty and close reasoning, are mere elegant trifling, light
summer reading. Coleridge even denied the excellence of
Hume's general style, which I think betrayed a want of taste or
candour. He, however, made me amends by the manner in
which he spoke of Berkeley. He dwelt particularly on his *Essay
on Vision* as a masterpiece of analytical reasoning. So it

undoubtedly is. He was exceedingly angry with Dr. Johnson for striking the stone with his foot, in allusion to this author's *Theory of Matter and Spirit*, and saying, "Thus I confute him, Sir." Coleridge drew a parallel (I don't know how he brought about the connection) between Bishop Berkeley and Tom Paine. He said the one was an instance of a subtle, the other of an acute mind, than which no two things could be more distinct. The one was a shop-boy's quality, the other the characteristic of a philosopher. He considered Bishop Butler as a true philosopher, a profound and conscientious thinker, a genuine reader of nature and his own mind. He did not speak of his *Analogy*, but of his *Sermons at the Rolls' Chapel*, of which I had never heard. Coleridge somehow always contrived to prefer the *unknown* to the *known*. In this instance he was right. The *Analogy* is a tissue of sophistry, of wire-drawn, theological special-pleading ; the *Sermons* (with the preface to them) are in a fine vein of deep, matured reflection, a candid appeal to our observation of human nature, without pedantry and without bias. I told Coleridge I had written a few remarks, and was sometimes foolish enough to believe that I had made a discovery on the same subject (the *Natural disinterestedness of the Human Mind*)—and I tried to explain my view of it to Coleridge, who listened with great willingness, but I did not succeed in making myself understood. I sat down to the task shortly afterwards for the twentieth time, got new pens and paper, determined to make clear work of it, wrote a few meagre sentences in the skeleton style of a mathematical demonstration, stopped half-way down the second page ; and, after trying in vain to pump up any words, images, notions, apprehensions, facts, or observations, from that gulf of abstraction in which I had plunged myself for four or five years preceding, gave up the attempt as labour in vain, and shed tears of helpless despondency on the blank, unfinished paper. I can write fast enough now. Am I better than I was then ? Oh no ! One truth discovered, one pang of regret at not being able to express it, is better than all the fluency and flippancy in the world. Would that I could go back to what I then was !

Why can we not revive past times as we can revisit old places? If I had the quaint Muse of Sir Philip Sidney to assist me, I would write a Sonnet to the Road between Wem and Shrewsbury, and immortalise every step of it by some fond enigmatical conceit. I would swear that the very milestones had ears, and that Harmer Hill stooped, with all its pines, to listen to a poet, as he passed! I remember but one other topic of discourse in this walk. He mentioned Paley, praised the naturalness and clearness of his style, but condemned his sentiments, thought him a mere time-serving casuist, and said that "the fact of his work on Moral and Political Philosophy being made a text-book in our Universities was a disgrace to the national character." We parted at the six-mile stone; and I returned homeward, pensive, but much pleased. I had met with unexpected notice from a person whom I believed to have been prejudiced against me. "Kind and affable to me had been his condescension, and should be honoured ever with suitable regard." He was the first poet I had known, and he certainly answered to that inspired name. I had heard a great deal of his powers of conversation and was not disappointed. In fact, I never met with anything at all like them, either before or since. I could easily credit the accounts which were circulated of his holding forth to a large party of ladies and gentlemen, an evening or two before, on the Berkeleian Theory, when he made the whole material universe look like a transparency of fine words; and another story (which I believe he has somewhere told himself) of his being asked to a party at Birmingham, of his smoking tobacco and going to sleep after dinner on a sofa, where the company found him, to their no small surprise, which was increased to wonder when he started up of a sudden, and rubbing his eyes, looked about him, and launched into a three-hours' description of the third heaven, of which he had had a dream, very different from Mr. Southey's "Vision of Judgment," and also from that other "Vision of Judgment," which Mr. Murray, the Secretary of the Bridge Street Junta, took into his especial keeping.

On my way back I had a sound in my ears—it was the voice

of Fancy; I had a light before me—it was the face of Poetry.
The one still lingers there, the other has not quitted my side!
Coleridge, in truth, met me half-way on the ground of philosophy,
or I should not have been won over to his imaginative creed.
I had an uneasy, pleasurable sensation all the time, till I was to
visit him. During those months the chill breath of winter gave
me a welcoming; the vernal air was balm and inspiration to
me. The golden sunsets, the silver star of evening, lighted me
on my way to new hopes and prospects. *I was to visit Coleridge
in the spring.* This circumstance was never absent from my
thoughts, and mingled with all my feelings. I wrote to him at
the time proposed, and received an answer postponing my
intended visit for a week or two, but very cordially urging me to
complete my promise then. This delay did not damp, but
rather increased my ardour. In the meantime, I went to
Llangollen Vale, by way of initiating myself in the mysteries
of natural scenery; and I must say I was enchanted with it.
I had been reading Coleridge's description of England in
his fine "Ode on the Departing Year," and I applied it, *con
amore,* to the objects before me. That valley was to me (in
a manner) the cradle of a new existence: in the river that
winds through it, my spirit was baptised in the waters of
Helicon!

I returned home, and soon after set out on my journey with
unworn heart, and untired feet. My way lay through Worcester
and Gloucester, and by Upton, where I thought of Tom Jones
and the adventure of the muff. I remember getting completely
wet through one day, and stopping at an inn (I think it was at
Tewkesbury) where I sat up all night to read *Paul and Virginia.* Sweet were the showers in early youth that drenched
my body, and sweet the drops of pity that fell upon the books I
read! I recollect a remark of Coleridge's upon this very book
that nothing could show the gross indelicacy of French manners
and the entire corruption of their imagination more strongly
than the behaviour of the heroine in the last fatal scene, who
turns away from a person on board the sinking vessel, that
offers to save her life, because he has thrown off his clothes to

assist him in swimming. Was this a time to think of such a circumstance? I once hinted to Wordsworth, as we were sailing in his boat on Grasmere lake, that I thought he had borrowed the idea of his *Poems on the Naming of Places* from the local inscriptions of the same kind in *Paul and Virginia.* He did not own the obligation, and stated some distinction without a difference in defence of his claim to originality. Any, the slightest variation, would be sufficient for this purpose in his mind ; for whatever *he* added or altered would inevitably be worth all that anyone else had done, and contain the marrow of the sentiment, I was still two days before the time fixed for my arrival, for I had taken care to set out early enough. I stopped these two days at Bridgewater ; and when I was tired of sauntering on the banks of its muddy river, returned to the inn and read *Camilla.* So have I loitered my life away, reading books, looking at pictures, going to plays, hearing, thinking, writing on what pleased me best. I have wanted only one thing to make me happy ; but wanting that have wanted everything !

I arrived, and was well received. The country about Nether-Stowey is beautiful, green and hilly, and near the sea-shore. I saw it but the other day, after an interval of twenty years, from a hill near Taunton. How was the map of my life spread out before me, as the map of the country lay at my feet ! In the afternoon, Coleridge took me over to All-Foxden, a romantic old family mansion of the St. Aubins, where Wordsworth lived. It was then in the possession of a friend of the poet's, who gave him the free use of it. Somehow, that period (the time just after the French Revolution) was not a time when *nothing was given for nothing.* The mind opened and a softness might be perceived coming over the hearts of individuals, beneath "the scales that fence" our self-interest. Wordsworth himself was from home, but his sister kept house, and set before us a frugal repast ; and we had free access to her brother's poems, the *Lyrical Ballads,* which were still in manuscript, or in the form of *Sybilline Leaves.* I dipped into a few of these with great satisfaction, and with the faith of a novice. I slept that night in an old room with blue hangings, and covered with the round-faced family portraits of the age of George I. and II., and from the wooded declivity of the adjoining park that overlooked my window, at the dawn of day, could

"—— hear the loud stag speak."

In the outset of life (and particularly at this time I felt it so) our imagination has a body to it. We are in a state between sleeping and waking, and have indistinct but glorious glimpses of strange shapes, and there is always something to come better than what we see. As in our dreams the fulness of the blood gives warmth and reality to the coinage of the brain, so in youth our ideas are clothed, and fed, and pampered with our good spirits ; we breathe thick with thoughtless happiness, the weight of future years presses on the strong pulses of the heart, and we repose with undisturbed faith in truth and good. As we advance, we exhaust our fund of enjoyment and of hope. We are no longer wrapped in *lamb's-wool*, lulled in Elysium. As we taste the pleasures of life, their spirit evaporates, the sense palls ; and nothing is left but the phantoms, the lifeless shadows of what *has been !*

That morning, as soon as breakfast was over, we strolled out into the park, and seating ourselves on the trunk of an old ash-tree that stretched along the ground, Coleridge read aloud, with a sonorous and musical voice, the ballad of "Betty Foy." I was not critically or sceptically inclined. I saw touches of truth and nature, and took the rest for granted. But in the "Thorn," and the "Mad Mother," and the "Complaint of a Poor Indian Woman," I felt that deeper power and pathos which have been since acknowledged,

"In spite of pride, in erring reason's spite,"

as the characteristics of this author ; and the sense of a new style and a new spirit in poetry came over me. It had to me something of the effect that arises from the turning up of the fresh soil, or of the first welcome breath of Spring :

" While yet the trembling year is unconfirmed."

Coleridge and myself walked back to Stowey that evening, and his voice sounded high

" Of Providence, foreknowledge, will, and fate,
    Fix'd fate, free-will, foreknowledge absolute."

as we passed through echoing grove, by fairy stream or water-fall, gleaming in the summer moonlight ! He lamented that Wordsworth was not prone enough to believe in the traditional superstitions of the place, and that there was a something cor-poreal, a *matter-of-fact-ness*, a clinging to the palpable, or often to the petty, in his poetry, in consequence. His genius was not a spirit that descended to him through the air; it sprung out of the ground like a flower, or unfolded itself from a green spray, on which the goldfinch sang. He said, however (if I remember right), that this objection must be confined to his descriptive pieces, that his philosophic poetry had a grand and comprehen-sive spirit in it, so that his soul seemed to inhabit the universe like a palace, and to discover truth by intuition, rather than by deduction. The next day Wordsworth arrived from Bristol at Coleridge's cottage. I think I see him now. He answered in some degree to his friend's description of him, but was more gaunt and Don Quixote-like. He was quaintly dressed (accord-ing to the *costume* of that unconstrained period) in a brown fustian jacket and striped pantaloons. There was something of a roll, a lounge in his gait, not unlike his own "Peter Bell." There was a severe, worn pressure of thought about his temples, a fire in his eye (as if he saw something in objects more than the outward appearance), an intense, high, narrow forehead, a Roman nose, cheeks furrowed by strong purpose and feeling, and a convulsive inclination to laughter about the mouth, a good deal at variance with the solemn, stately expression of the rest of his face. Chantrey's bust wants the marking traits; but he was teased into making it regular and heavy: Haydon's head of him, introduced into the "Entrance of Christ into Jerusalem," is the most like his drooping weight of thought and expression. He sat down and talked very naturally and freely, with a mixture of clear, gushing accents in his voice, a deep guttural intonation, and a strong tincture of the northern *burr*, like the crust on wine. He instantly began to make havoc of the half of a Cheshire cheese on the table, and said, triumphantly, that " his marriage with experience had not been so productive as Mr. Southey's in teaching him a knowledge of the good things of this life."   He had been to see the " Castle Spectre," by Monk Lewis, while at Bristol, and described it very well.   He said " it fitted the taste of the audience like a glove." This *ad captandum* merit was however by no means a recommendation of it, according to the severe principles of the new school, which reject rather than court popular effect.   Wordsworth, looking out of the low, latticed window, said, "How beautifully the sun sets on that yellow bank !"   I thought within myself, " With what eyes these poets see nature ! " and ever after, when I saw the sunset stream upon the objects facing it, conceived I had made a discovery, or thanked Mr. Wordsworth for having made one for me !   We went over to All-Foxden again the day following, and Wordsworth read us the story of " Peter Bell " in the open air ; and the comment upon it by his face and voice was very different from that of some later critics !   Whatever might be thought of the poem, " his face was as a book where men might read strange matters," and he announced the fate of his hero in prophetic tones.   There is a *chaunt* in the recitation both of Coleridge and Wordsworth, which acts as a spell upon the hearer, and disarms the judgment.   Perhaps they have deceived themselves by making habitual use of this ambiguous accompaniment.   Coleridge's manner is more full, animated, and varied ; Wordsworth's more equable, sustained, and internal. The one might be termed more *dramatic*, the other more *lyrical*.   Coleridge has told me that he himself liked to compose in walking over uneven ground, or breaking through the straggling branches of a copse-wood ; whereas Wordsworth always wrote (if he could) walking up and down a straight gravel walk, or in some spot where the continuity of his verse met with no collateral interruption. · Returning that same evening, I got into a metaphysical argument with Wordsworth, while Coleridge was explaining the different notes of the nightingale to his sister, in which we neither of us succeeded in making ourselves perfectly clear and intelligible. Thus I passed three weeks at Nether Stowey and in the neighbourhood, generally devoting the afternoons to a delightful chat in an arbour made of bark by the poet's friend Tom Poole, sitting under two fine elm-trees, and listening to the bees humming round us, while we quaffed our *flip*. It was agreed, among other things, that we should make a jaunt down the Bristol Channel, as far as Linton. We set off together on foot, Coleridge, John Chester, and I. This Chester was a native of Nether Stowey, one of those who were attracted to Coleridge's discourse as flies are to honey, or bees in swarming-time to the sound of a brass pan. He "followed in the chase like a dog who hunts, not like one that made up the cry." He had on a brown cloth coat, boots, and corduroy breeches, was low in stature, bow-legged, had a drag in his walk like a drover, which he assisted by a hazel switch, and kept on a sort of trot by the side of Coleridge, like a running footman by a state coach, that he might not lose a syllable or sound that fell from Coleridge's lips. He told me his private opinion, that Coleridge was a wonderful man. He scarcely opened his lips, much less offered an opinion the whole way : yet of the three, had I to choose during that journey, I would be John Chester. He afterwards followed Coleridge into Germany, where the Kantean philosophers were puzzled how to bring him under any of their categories. When he sat down at table with his idol, John's felicity was complete ; Sir Walter Scott's, or Mr. Blackwood's, when they sat down at the same table with the King, was not more so. We passed Dunster on our right, a small town between the brow of a hill and the sea. I remember eyeing it wistfully as it lay below us : contrasted with the woody scene around, it looked as clear, as pure, as *embrowned* and ideal as any landscape I have seen since, of Gaspar Poussin's or Domenichino's. We had a long day's march (our feet kept time to the echoes of Coleridge's tongue) through Minehead and by the Blue Anchor, and on to Linton, which we did

not reach till near midnight, and where we had some difficulty
in making a lodgment. We, however, knocked the people of
the house up at last, and we were repaid for our apprehensions
and fatigue by some excellent rashers of fried bacon and eggs.
The view in coming along had been splendid. We walked
for miles and miles on dark brown heaths overlooking the
Channel, with the Welsh hills beyond, and at times descended
into little sheltered valleys close by the sea-side, with a
smuggler's face scowling by us, and then had to ascend conical
hills with a path winding up through a coppice to a barren
top, like a monk's shaven crown, from one of which I pointed
out to Coleridge's notice the bare masts of a vessel on the very
edge of the horizon, and within the red-orbed disk of the
setting sun, like his own spectre-ship in the "Ancient Mariner."
At Linton the character of the sea-coast becomes more
marked and rugged. There is a place called the *Valley of
Rocks* (I suspect this was only the poetical name for it), bedded
among precipices overhanging the sea, with rocky caverns
beneath, into which the waves dash, and where the sea-gull
for ever wheels its screaming flight. On the tops of these
are huge stones thrown transverse, as if an earthquake had
tossed them there, and behind these is a fretwork of perpen-
dicular rocks, something like the *Giant's Causeway*. A
thunderstorm came on while we were at the inn, and Coleridge
was running out bareheaded to enjoy the commotion of the
elements in the *Valley of Rocks*, but, as if in spite, the clouds
only muttered a few angry sounds, and let fall a few refreshing drops. Coleridge told me that he and Wordsworth were
to have made this place the scene of a prose-tale, which
was to have been in the manner of, but far superior to,
the "Death of Abel," but they had relinquished the design.
In the morning of the second day we breakfasted luxuri-
ously in an old-fashioned parlour on tea, toast, eggs, and
honey, in the very sight of the bee-hives from which it had
been taken, and a garden full of thyme and wild flowers that
had produced it. On this occasion Coleridge spoke of Virgil's
Georgics, but not well. I do not think he had much feeling for

the classical or elegant.* It was in this room that we found a little worn-out copy of the *Seasons,* lying in a window-seat, on which Coleridge exclaimed, " *That* is true fame ! " He said Thomson was a great poet, rather than a good one ; his style was as meretricious as his thoughts were natural. He spoke of Cowper as the best modern poet. He said the *Lyrical Ballads* were an experiment about to be tried by him and Wordsworth, to see how far the public taste would endure poetry written in a more natural and simple style than had hitherto been attempted ; totally discarding the artifices of poetical diction, and making use only of such words as had probably been common in the most ordinary language since the days of Henry II. Some comparison was introduced between Shakespeare and Milton. He said "he hardly knew which to prefer. Shakespeare appeared to him a mere stripling in the art ; he was as tall and as strong, with infinitely more activity, than Milton, but he never appeared to have come to man's estate ; or if he had, he would not have been a man, but a monster." He spoke with contempt of Gray, and with intolerance of Pope. He did not like the versification of the latter. He observed that "the ears of these couplet-writers might be charged with having short memories, that could not retain the harmony of whole passages." He thought little of Junius as a writer ; he had a dislike of Dr. Johnson ; and a much higher opinion of Burke as an orator and politician, than of Fox or Pitt. He, however, thought him very inferior in richness of style and imagery to some of our elder prose-writers, particularly Jeremy Taylor. He liked Richardson, but not Fielding ; nor could I get him to enter into the merits of *Caleb Williams.* In short, he was profound and discriminating with respect to those authors

* He had no idea of pictures, of Claude or Raphael, and at this time I had as little as he. He sometimes gives a striking account at present of the Cartoons at Pisa by Buffamalco and others ; of one in particular, where Death is seen in the air brandishing his scythe, and the great and mighty of the earth shudder at his approach, while the beggars and the wretched kneel to him as their deliverer. He would, of course, understand so broad and fine a moral as this at any time.

whom he liked, and where he gave his judgment fair-play; capricious, perverse, and prejudiced in his antipathies and distastes. We loitered on the "ribbed sea-sands," in such talk as this, a whole morning, and, I recollect, met with a curious sea-weed, of which John Chester told us the country name! A fisherman gave Coleridge an account of a boy that had been drowned the day before, and that they had tried to save him at the risk of their own lives. He said "he did not know how it was that they ventured, but, Sir, we have a *nature* towards one another." This expression, Coleridge remarked to me, was a fine illustration of that theory of disinterestedness which I (in common with Butler) had adopted. I broached to him an argument of mine to prove that *likeness* was not mere association of ideas. I said that the mark in the sand put one in mind of a man's foot, not because it was part of a former impression of a man's foot (for it was quite new), but because it was like the shape of a man's foot. He assented to the justness of this distinction (which I have explained at length elsewhere, for the benefit of the curious) and John Chester listened; not from any interest in the subject, but because he was astonished that I should be able to suggest anything to Coleridge that he did not already know. We returned on the third morning, and Coleridge remarked the silent cottage-smoke curling up the valleys where, a few evenings before, we had seen the lights gleaming through the dark.

In a day or two after we arrived at Stowey, we set out, I on my return home, and he for Germany. It was a Sunday morning, and he was to preach that day for Dr. Toulmin of Taunton. I asked him if he had prepared anything for the occasion? He said he had not even thought of the text, but should as soon as we parted. I did not go to hear him—this was a fault—but we met in the evening at Bridgewater. The next day we had a long day's walk to Bristol, and sat down, I recollect, by a well-side on the road, to cool ourselves and satisfy our thirst, when Coleridge repeated to me some descriptive lines of his tragedy of "Remorse"; which I must say became his mouth and that occasion better than they, some years after, did Mr. Elliston's and the Drury Lane boards—

> " Oh memory ! shield me from the world's poor strife,
> And give those scenes thine everlasting life."

I saw no more of him for a year or two, during which period he had been wandering in the Hartz Forest, in Germany ; and his return was cometary, meteorous, unlike his setting out. It was not till some time after that I knew his friends, Lamb and Southey. The last always appears to me (as I first saw him) with a commonplace book under his arm, and the first with a *bon-mot* in his mouth. It was at Godwin's that I met him with Holcroft and Coleridge, where they were disputing fiercely which was the best—*Man as he was, or man as he is to be.* " Give me," says Lamb, "man as he is *not* to be." This saying was the beginning of a friendship between us, which I believe still continues. Enough of this for the present.

> " But there is matter for another rhyme,
> And I to this may add a second tale."

ON THE PLEASURE OF PAINTING.

"THERE is a pleasure in painting which none but painters know." In writing, you have to contend with the world ; in painting, you have only to carry on a friendly strife with Nature. You sit down to your task, and are happy. From the moment that you take up the pencil, and look Nature in the face, you are at peace with your own heart. No angry passions rise to disturb the silent progress of the work, to shake the hand, or dim the brow : no irritable humours are set afloat : you have no absurd opinions to combat, no point to strain, no adversary to crush, no fool to annoy—you are actuated by fear or favour to no man. There is "no juggling here," no sophistry, no intrigue, no tampering with the evidence, no attempt to make black white, or white black : but you resign yourself into the hands of a greater power, that of Nature, with the simplicity of a child, and the devotion of an enthusiast— "study with joy her manner, and with rapture taste her style." The mind is calm, and full at the same time. The hand and eye are equally employed. In tracing the commonest object, a plant or the stump of a tree. you learn something every moment. You perceive unexpected differences, and discover likenesses where you looked for no such thing. You try to set down what you see—find out your error, and correct it. You need not play tricks, or purposely mistake : with all your pains, you are still far short of the mark. Patience grows out of the endless pursuit, and turns it into a luxury. A streak in a flower, a wrinkle in a leaf, a tinge in a cloud, a

stain in an old wall or ruin grey, are seized with avidity as
the *spolia opima* of this sort of mental warfare, and furnish
out labour for another half-day. The hours pass away
untold, without chagrin, and without weariness ; nor would
you ever wish to pass them otherwise. Innocence is joined
with industry, pleasure with business ; and the mind is
satisfied, though it is not engaged in thinking or in doing any
mischief. *

I have not much pleasure in writing these Essays, or
in reading them afterwards ; though I own I now and then
meet with a phrase that I like, or a thought that strikes me as

---

* There is a passage in *Werter* which contains a very pleasing
illustration of this doctrine, and is as follows :—

"About a league from the town is a place called Walheim. It is
very agreeably situated on the side of a hill : from one of the paths
which leads out of the village you have a view of the whole country ;
and there is a good old woman who sells wine, coffee, and tea there :
but better than all this are two lime-trees before the church, which
spread their branches over a little green, surrounded by barns and
cottages. I have seen few places more retired and peaceful. I send
for a chair and table from the old woman's, and there I drink my
coffee and read Homer. It was by accident that I discovered this
place one fine afternoon : all was perfect stillness ; everybody was in
the fields except a little boy about four years old, who was sitting on
the ground, and holding between his knees a child of about six
months ; he pressed it to his bosom with his little arms, which made
a sort of great chair for it ; and notwithstanding the vivacity which
sparkled in his eyes, he sat perfectly still. Quite delighted with the
scene, I sat down on a plough opposite, and had great pleasure
in drawing this little picture of brotherly tenderness. I added a
bit of the hedge, the barn-door, and some broken cart-wheels, without
any order, just as they happened to lie ; and in about an hour I
found I had made a drawing of great expression and very correct
design, without having put in anything of my own. This confirmed
me in the resolution I had made before, only to copy Nature for the
future. Nature is inexhaustible, and alone forms the greatest masters.
Say what you will of rules, they alter the true features, and the
natural expression."

a true one. But after I begin them, I am only anxious to get to the end of them, which I am not sure I shall do, for I seldom see my way a page or even a sentence beforehand ; and when I have as by a miracle escaped, I trouble myself little more about them. I sometimes have to write them twice over : then it is necessary to read the *proof*, to prevent mistakes by the printer ; so that by the time they appear in a tangible shape, and one can con them over with a conscious, side-long glance to the public approbation, they have lost their gloss and relish, and become "more tedious than a twice-told tale." For a person to read his own works over with any great delight, he ought first to forget that he ever wrote them. Familiarity naturally breeds contempt. It is, in fact, like poring fondly over a piece of blank paper : from repetition, the words convey no distinct meaning to the mind—are mere idle sounds, except that our vanity claims an interest and property in them. I have more satisfaction in my own thoughts than in dictating them to others : words are necessary to explain the impression of certain things upon me to the reader, but they rather weaken and draw a veil over than strengthen it to myself. However I might say with the poet, "My mind to me a kingdom is," yet I have little ambition "to set a throne or chair of state in the understandings of other men." The ideas we cherish most exist best in a kind of shadowy abstraction,

" Pure in the last recesses of the mind,"

and derive neither force nor interest from being exposed to public view. They are old, familiar acquaintance, and any change in them, arising from the adventitious ornaments of style or dress, is little to their advantage. After I have once written on a subject, it goes out of my mind : my feelings about it have been melted down into words, and *them* I forget. I have, as it were, discharged my memory of its old habitual reckoning, and rubbed out the score of real sentiment. For the future, it exists only for the sake of others.—But I cannot say, from my own experience, that the same process takes place in transferring our ideas to canvas : they gain more than they lose in the mechanical transformation. One is never tired of painting, because you have to set down not what you knew already, but what you have just discovered. In the former case, you translate feelings into words ; in the latter, names into things. There is a continual creation out of nothing going on. With every stroke of the brush a new field of inquiry is laid open ; new difficulties arise, and new triumphs are prepared over them. By comparing the imitation with the original, you see what you have done, and how much you have still to do. The test of the senses is severer than that of fancy, and an overmatch even for the delusions of our self-love. One part of a picture shames another, and you determine to paint up to yourself, if you cannot come up to nature. Every object becomes lustrous from the light thrown back upon it by the mirror of art ; and by the aid of the pencil we may be said to touch and handle the objects of sight. The air-drawn visions that hover on the verge of existence have a bodily presence given them on the canvas : the form of beauty is changed into a substance : the dream and the glory of the universe is made "palpable to feeling as to sight."—And see ! a rainbow starts from the canvas, with all its humid train of glory, as if it were drawn from its cloudy arch in heaven. The spangled landscape glitters with drops of dew after the shower. The "fleecy fools" show their coats in the gleams of the setting sun. The shepherds pipe their farewell notes in the fresh evening air. And is this bright vision made from a dead dull blank, like a bubble reflecting the mighty fabric of the universe? Who would think this miracle of Rubens's pencil possible to be performed? Who, having seen it, would not spend his life to do the like ? See how the rich fallows, the bare stubble-field, the scanty harvest-home, drag in Rembrandt's landscapes ! How often have I looked at them and nature, and tried to do the same, till the very "light thickened," and there was an earthiness in the feeling of the air ! There is no end of the refinements of art and nature in this respect. One may look at the misty glimmering horizon till the eye dazzles and the imagination is lost, in hopes to transfer the whole interminable expanse at one blow upon the canvas. Wilson said, he used to try to paint the effect of the motes dancing in the setting sun. At another time, a friend coming into his painting-room when he was sitting on the ground in a melancholy posture, observed that his picture looked like a landscape after a shower : he started up with the greatest delight, and said, "That is the effect I intended to produce, but thought I had failed." Wilson was neglected ; and, by degrees, neglected his art to apply himself to brandy. His hand became unsteady, so that it was only by repeated attempts that he could reach the place, or produce the effect he aimed at ; and when he had done a little to a picture, he would say to any acquaintance who chanced to drop in, "I have painted enough for one day : come, let us go somewhere." It was not so Claude left his pictures, or his studies on the banks of the Tiber, to go in search of other enjoyments, or ceased to gaze upon the glittering sunny vales and distant hills ; and while his eye drank in the clear sparkling hues and lovely forms of nature, his hand stamped them on the lucid canvas to last there for ever ! One of the most delightful parts of my life was one fine summer, when I used to walk out of an evening to catch the last light of the sun, gemming the green slopes or russet lawns, and gilding tower or tree, while the blue sky gradually turning to purple and gold, or skirted with dusky grey, hung its broad marble pavement over all, as we see it in the great master of Italian landscape. But to come to more particular explanation of the subject :—

The first head I ever tried to paint was an old woman with the upper part of the face shaded by her bonnet, and I certainly laboured [at] it with great perseverance. It took me number- less sittings to do it. I have it by me still, and sometimes look at it with surprise, to think how much pains were thrown away to little purpose—yet not altogether in vain if it taught me to see good in everything, and to know that there is nothing vulgar in nature seen with the eye of science or of true art. Refinement creates beauty everywhere : it is the grossness of the spectator that discovers nothing but grossness in the object. Be this as it may, I spared no pains to do my best. If art was long, I thought that life was so too at that moment. I got in the general effect the first day; and pleased and surprised enough I was at my success. The rest was a work of time—of weeks and months (if need were), of patient toil and careful finishing. I had seen an old head by Rembrandt at Burleigh House, and if I could produce a head at all like Rembrandt in a year, in my lifetime, it would be glory and felicity and wealth and fame enough for me! The head I had seen at Burleigh was an exact and wonderful fac-simile of nature, and I resolved to make mine (as nearly as I could) an exact fac-simile of nature. I did not then, nor do I now believe, with Sir Joshua, that the perfection of art consists in giving general appearances without individual details, but in giving general appearances with individual details. Otherwise, I had done my work the first day. But I saw something more in nature than general effect, and I thought it worth my while to give it in the picture. There was a gorgeous effect of light and shade: but there was a delicacy as well as depth in the *chiaro scuro* which I was bound to follow into all its dim and scarce perceptible variety of tone and shadow. Then I had to make the transition from a strong light to as dark a shade, preserving the masses, but gradually softening off the intermediate parts. It was so in nature; the difficulty was to make it so in the copy. I tried, and failed again and again; I strove harder, and succeeded as I thought. The wrinkles in Rembrandt were not hard lines, but broken and irregular. I saw the same appearance in nature, and strained every nerve to give it. If I could hit off this edgy appearance, and insert the reflected light in the furrows of old age in half a morning, I did not think I had lost a day. Beneath the shrivelled, yellow parchment look of the skin there was here and there a streak of the blood-colour tinging the face; this I made a point of conveying, and did not cease to compare what I saw with what I did (with jealous lynx-eyed watchfulness) till I succeeded to the best of my ability and judgment. How many revisions were there! How many attempts to catch an expression which I had seen the day before! How often did we try to get the old position, and wait for the return of the same light! There was a puckering up of the lips, a cautious introversion of the eye under the shadow of the bonnet, indicative of the feebleness and suspicion of old age, which at last we managed, after many trials and some quarrels, to a tolerable nicety. The picture was never finished, and I might have gone on with it to the present hour.* I used to set it on the ground when my day's work was done, and saw revealed to me with swimming eyes the birth of new hopes, and of a new world of objects. The painter thus learns to look at nature with different eyes. He before saw her "as in a glass darkly, but now face to face." He understands the texture and meaning of the visible universe, and "sees into the life of things," not by the help of mechanical instruments, but of the improved exercise of his faculties, and an intimate sympathy with nature. The meanest thing is not lost upon him, for he looks at it with an eye to itself, not merely to his own vanity or interest, or the opinion of the world. Even where there is neither beauty nor use—if that ever were—still there is truth, and a sufficient source of gratification in the indulgence of curiosity and activity of mind. The humblest painter is a true scholar ; and the best of scholars—the scholar of nature. For myself, and for the real comfort and satisfaction of the thing, I had rather had been Jan Steen, or Gerard Dow, than the greatest casuist or philologer that ever lived. The painter does not view things in clouds or "mist, the common gloss of theologians," but applies the same standard of truth and dis-interested spirit of inquiry that influence his daily practice to other subjects. He perceives form, he distinguishes character. He reads men and books with an intuitive eye. He is a critic as well as a connoisseur. The conclusions he draws are clear and convincing, because they are taken from the things them-selves. He is not a fanatic, a dupe, or a slave ; for the habit of seeing for himself also disposes him to judge for himself. The

---

* It is at present covered with a thick slough of oil and varnish (the perishable vehicle of the English school), like an envelope of gold-beaters' skin, so as to be hardly visible.

most sensible men I know (taken as a class) are painters ; that is, they are the most lively observers of what passes in the world about them, and the closest observers of what passes in their own minds. From their profession they in general mix more with the world than authors ; and if they have not the same fund of acquired knowledge, are obliged to rely more on individual sagacity. I might mention the names of Opie, Fuseli, Northcote, as persons distinguished for striking description and acquaintance with the subtle traits of character.* Painters in ordinary society, or in obscure situations where their value is not known, and they are treated with neglect and indifference, have sometimes a forward self-sufficiency of manner ; but this is not so much their fault as that of others. Perhaps their want of regular education may also be in fault in such cases. Richardson, who is very tenacious of the respect in which the profession ought to be held, tells a story of Michael Angelo, that after a quarrel between him and Pope Julius II., "upon account of a slight the artist conceived the pontiff had put upon him, Michael Angelo was introduced by a bishop, who, thinking to serve the artist by it, made it an argument that the Pope should be reconciled to him, because men of his profession were commonly ignorant, and of no consequence otherwise ; his holiness, enraged at the bishop, struck him with his staff, and told him, it was he that was the blockhead, and affronted the man himself would not offend. The prelate was driven out of the chamber, and Michael Angelo had the Pope's benediction, accompanied with presents. This bishop had fallen into the vulgar error, and was rebuked accordingly."

Besides the exercise of the mind, painting exercises the body.

* Men in business, who are answerable with their fortunes for the consequences of their opinions, and are therefore accustomed to ascertain pretty accurately the grounds on which they act, before they commit themselves on the event, are often men of remarkably quick and sound judgments. Artists in like manner must know tolerably well what they are about, before they can bring the result of their observations to the test of ocular demonstration.

It is a mechanical as well as a liberal art. To do anything, to dig a hole in the ground, to plant a cabbage, to hit a mark, to move a shuttle, to work a pattern—in a word, to attempt to produce any effect, and to *succeed*—has something in it that gratifies the love of power, and carries off the restless activity of the mind of man. Indolence is a delightful but distressing state ; we must be doing something to be happy. Action is no less necessary than thought to the instinctive tendencies of the human frame ; and painting combines them both incessantly.* The hand furnishes a practical test of the correctness of the eye ; and the eye thus admonished, imposes fresh tasks of skill and industry upon the hand. Every stroke tells, as the verifying of a new truth ; and every new observation, the instant it is made, passes into an act and emanation of the will. Every step is nearer what we wish, and yet there is always more to do. In spite of the facility, the fluttering grace, the evanescent hues, that play round the pencil of Rubens and Vandyke, however I may admire, I do not envy them this power so much as I do the slow, patient, laborious execution of Correggio, Leonardo da Vinci, and Andrea del Sarto, where every touch appears conscious of its charge, emulous of truth, and where the painful artist has so distinctly wrought,

" That you might almost say his picture thought ! "

In the one case, the colours seem breathed on the canvas as if by magic, the work and the wonder of a moment ; in the other, they seem inlaid in the body of the work, and as if it took the artist years of unremitting labour, and of delightful never-ending progress to perfection.† Who would wish ever to come to the close of such works—not to dwell on them, to

---

* The famous Schiller used to say, that he found the great happiness of life, after all, to consist in the discharge of some mechanical duty.

† The rich *impasting* of Titian and Giorgione combines something of the advantages of both these styles, the felicity of the one with the carefulness of the other, and is perhaps to be preferred to either.

return to them, to be wedded to them to the last? Rubens, with his florid, rapid style, complained that when he had just learned his art, he should be forced to die. Leonardo, in the slow advances of his, had lived long enough!

Painting is not, like writing, what is properly understood by a sedentary employment. It requires not indeed a strong, but a continued and steady exertion of muscular power. The precision and delicacy of the manual operation, makes up for the want of vehemence—as to balance himself for any time in the same position the rope-dancer must strain every nerve. Painting for a whole morning gives one as excellent an appetite for one's dinner as old Abraham Tucker acquired for his by riding over Banstead Downs. It is related of Sir Joshua Reynolds, that "he took no other exercise than what he used in his painting-room"—the writer means, in walking backwards and forwards to look at his picture; but the act of painting itself, of laying on the colours in the proper place, and proper quantity, was a much harder exercise than this alternate receding from and returning to the picture. This last would be rather a relaxation and relief than an effort. It is not to be wondered at, that an artist like Sir Joshua, who delighted so much in the sensual and practical part of his art, should have found himself at a considerable loss when the decay of his sight precluded him, for the last year or two of his life, from the following up of his profession—"the source," according to his own remark, "of thirty years' uninterrupted enjoyment and prosperity to him." It is only those who never think at all, or else who have accustomed themselves to brood incessantly on abstract ideas, that never feel *ennui*.

To give one instance more, and then I will have done with this rambling discourse. One of my first attempts was a picture of my father, who was then in a green old age, with strong-marked features, and scarred with the small-pox. I drew it out with a broad light crossing the face, looking down, with spectacles on, reading. The book was Shaftesbury's *Characteristics*, in a fine old binding, with Gribelin's etchings. My father would as lieve it had been any other book: but for him to read was to be content, was "riches fineless." The sketch promised well ; and I set to work to finish it, determined to spare no time nor pains. My father was willing to sit as long as I pleased ; for there is a natural desire in the mind of man to sit for one's picture, to be the object of continued attention, to have one's likeness multiplied ; and besides his satisfaction in the picture, he had some pride in the artist, though he would rather I should have written a sermon than painted like Rembrandt or like Raphael. Those winter days, with the gleams of sunshine coming through the chapel windows, and cheered by the notes of the robin-redbreast in our garden (that "ever in the haunch of winter sings")—as my afternoon's work drew to a close—were among the happiest of my life. When I gave the effect I intended to any part of the picture for which I had prepared my colours ; when I imitated the roughness of the skin by a lucky stroke of the pencil ; when I hit the clear pearly tone of a vein ; when I gave the ruddy complexion of health, the blood circulating under the broad shadows of one side of the face, I thought my fortune made ; or rather it was already more than made, in my fancying that I might one day be able to say with Correggio, "*I also am a painter!*" It was an idle thought, a boy's conceit ; but it did not make me less happy at the time. I used regularly to set my work in the chair to look at it through the long evenings ; and many a time did I return to take leave of it before I could go to bed at night. I remember sending it with a throbbing heart to the Exhibition, and seeing it hung up there by the side of one of the Honourable Mr. Skeffington (now Sir George). There was nothing in common between them, but that they were the portraits of two very good-natured men. I think, but am not sure, that I finished this portrait (or another afterwards) on the same day that the news of the battle of Austerlitz came ; I walked out in the afternoon, and, as I returned, saw the evening star set over a poor man's cottage with other thoughts and feelings than I shall ever have again. Oh for the revolution of the great Platonic year, that those times might come over again! I could sleep out the three hundred and

576

sixty-five thousand intervening years very contentedly !—The picture is left : the table, the chair, the window where I learned to construe Livy, the chapel where my father preached, remain where they were ; but he himself is gone to rest, full of years, of faith, of hope, and charity !

ON ACTORS AND ACTING.

PLAYERS are "the abstracts and brief chronicles of the times," the motley representatives of human nature. They are the only honest hypocrites. Their life is a voluntary dream, a studied madness. The height of their ambition is to be *beside themselves*. To-day kings, to-morrow beggars, it is only when they are themselves that they are nothing. Made up of mimic laughter and tears, passing from the extremes of joy or woe at the prompter's call, they wear the livery of other men's fortunes; their very thoughts are not their own. They are, as it were, train-bearers in the pageant of life, and hold a glass up to humanity, frailer than itself. We see ourselves at second-hand in them ; they show us all that we are, all that we wish to be, and all that we dread to be. The stage is an epitome, a bettered likeness, of the world, with the dull part left out ; and indeed, with this omission, it is nearly big enough to hold·all the rest. What brings the resemblance nearer is, that, as *they* imitate us, we, in our turn, imitate them. How many fine gentlemen do we owe to the stage! How many romantic lovers are mere Romeos in masquerade! How many soft bosoms have heaved with Juliet's sighs! They teach us when to laugh and when to weep, when to love and when to hate, upon principle and with a good grace. Wherever there is a playhouse the world will go on not amiss. The stage not only refines the manners, but it is the best teacher of morals, for it is the truest and most intelligible picture of life. It stamps the image of virtue on the mind by first softening the rude materials of which it is composed by a sense of pleasure. It regulates the passions by giving a loose to the imagination. It points out the selfish and depraved to our detestation, the amiable and generous to our admiration ; and if it clothes the more seductive vices with the borrowed graces of wit and fancy, even those graces operate as a diversion to the coarser poison of experience and bad example, and often prevent or carry off the infection by inoculating the mind with a certain taste and elegance. To show how little we agree with the common declamations against the immoral tendency of the stage on this score, we will hazard a conjecture that the acting of the "Beggar's Opera" a certain number of nights every year since it was first brought out has done more towards putting down the practice of highway robbery than all the gibbets that ever were erected. A person after seeing this piece is too deeply imbued with a sense of humanity, is in too good humour with himself and the rest of the world, to set about cutting throats or rifling pockets. Whatever makes a jest of vice leaves it too much a matter of indifference for any one in his senses to rush desperately on his ruin for its sake. We suspect that just the contrary effect must be produced by the representation of "George Barnwell," which is too much in the style of the ordinary's sermon to meet with any better success. The mind, in such cases, instead of being deterred by the alarming consequences held out to it, revolts against the denunciation of them as an insult offered to its freewill, and, in a spirit of defiance, returns a practical answer to them by daring the worst that can happen. The most striking lesson ever read to levity and licentiousness is in the last act of "The Inconstant," where young Mirabel is preserved by the fidelty of his mistress, Orinda, in the disguise of a page, from the hands of assassins, into whose power he has been allured by the temptations of vice and beauty. There never was a rake who did not become in imagination a reformed man during the representation of the last trying scenes of this admirable comedy.

If the stage is useful as a school of instruction, it is no less so as a scource of amusement. It is the source of the greatest enjoyment at the time, and a never-failing fund of agreeable reflection afterwards. The merits of a new play or of a new actor are always among the first topics of polite conversation. One way in which public exhibitions contribute to refine and humanise mankind is by supplying them with ideas and subjects of conversation and interest in common. The progress of civilisation is in proportion to the number of commonplaces current in society. For instance, if we meet with a stranger at an inn or in a stage-coach, who knows nothing but his own affairs, his shop, his customers, his farm, his pigs, his poultry, we can carry on no conversation with him on these local and personal matters ; the only way is to let him have all the talk to himself. But if he has fortunately ever seen Mr. Liston act, this is an immediate topic of mutual conversation, and we agree together the rest of the evening in discussing the merits of that inimitable actor, with the same satisfaction as in talking over the affairs of the most intimate friend.

If the stage thus introduces us familiarly to our contemporaries, it also brings us acquainted with former times. It is an interesting revival of past ages, manners, opinions, dresses, persons, and actions—whether it carries us back to the wars of York and Lancaster, or half-way back to the heroic times of Greece and Rome, in some translation from the French, or quite back to the age of Charles II. in the scenes of Congreve and of Etherege (the gay Sir George !)—happy age, when kings and nobles led purely ornamental lives ; when the utmost stretch of a morning's study went no further than the choice of a sword-knot or the adjustment of a side-curl ; when the soul spoke out in all the pleasing eloquence of dress ; and beaux and belles, enamoured of themselves in one another's follies, fluttered like gilded butterflies in giddy mazes through the walks of St. James's Park !

A good company of comedians, a theatre royal judiciously managed, is your true Heralds' College—the only Antiquarian Society that is worth a rush. It is for this reason that there is such an air of romance about players, and that it is·pleasanter to see them, even in their own persons, than any of the three learned professions. We feel more respect for John Kemble in a plain coat than for the Lord Chancellor on the woolsack. He is surrounded, to our eyes, with a greater number of imposing recollections ; he is a more reverend piece of formality—a more complicated tissue of costume. We do not know whether to look upon this accomplished actor as Pierre, or King John, or Coriolanus, or Cato, or Leontes, or the Stranger. But we see in him a stately hieroglyphic of humanity, a living monument of departed greatness, a sombre comment on the rise and fall of kings. We look after him till he is out of sight as we listen to a story of one of Ossian's heroes, to "a tale of other times !"

One of the most affecting things we know is to see a favourite actor take leave of the stage. We were present not long ago when Mr. Bannister quitted it. We do not wonder that his feelings were overpowered on the occasion : ours were nearly so too. We remembered him, in the first heyday of our youthful spirits, in " The Prize," in which he played so delight-fully with that fine old croaker Suett, and Madame Storace—in the farce of " My Grandmother," in the " Son-in-Law," in Autolycus, and in Scrub, in which our satisfaction was at its height. At that time King, and Parsons, and Dodd, and Quick, and Edwin, were in the full vigour of their reputation, who are now all gone. We still feel the vivid delight with which we used to see their names in the playbills as we went along to the theatre. Bannister was one of the last of these that remained ; and we parted with him as we should with one of our oldest and best friends. The most pleasant feature in the profession of a player, and which indeed is peculiar to it, is, that we not only admire the talents of those who adorn it, but we contract a personal intimacy with them. There is no class of society whom so many persons regard with affection as actors. We greet them on the stage ; we like to meet them in the streets ; they almost always recall to us pleasant associations ; and we feel our gratitude excited without the uneasiness of a sense of obligation. The very gaiety and popularity, however, which surround the life of a favourite performer make the retiring from it a very serious business. It glances a mortifying reflection on the shortness of human life and the vanity of human pleasures. Something reminds us that "all the world's a stage, and all the men and women merely players."

It has been considered as the misfortune of first-rate talents for the stage that they leave no record behind them except that of vague rumour, and that the genius of a great actor perishes with him, "leaving the world no copy." This is a misfortune, or at least an unpleasant circumstance, to actors; but it is, perhaps, an advantage to the stage. It leaves an opening to originality. The stage is always beginning anew; the candidates for theatrical reputation are always setting out afresh, unencumbered by the affectation of the faults or the excellences of their predecessors. In this respect we should imagine that the average quantity of dramatic talent remains more nearly the same than that in any other walk of art. In no other instance do the complaints of the degeneracy of the moderns seem so unfounded as in this; and Colley Cibber's account of the regular decline of the stage, from the time of Shakespeare to that of Charles II., and from the time of Charles II. to the beginning of George II., appears quite ridiculous. The stage is a place where genius is sure to come upon its legs, in a generation or two at furthest. In the other arts (as painting and poetry) it has been contended that what has been well done already, by giving rise to endless vapid imitations, is an obstacle to what might be done well hereafter; that the models or *chefs-d'œuvre* of art, where they are accumulated, choke up the path to excellence; and that the works of genius, where they can be rendered permanent and handed down from age to age, not only prevent, but render superfluous, future productions of the same kind. We have not, neither do we want, two Shakespeares, two Miltons, two Raphaels, any more than we require two suns in the same sphere. Even Miss O'Neill stands a little in the way of our recollections of Mrs. Siddons. But Mr. Kean is an excellent substitute for the memory of Garrick, whom we never saw. When an author dies it is no matter, for his works remain. When a great actor dies there

is a void produced in society, a gap which requires to be filled
up. Who does not go to see Kean? Who, if Garrick were
alive, would go to see him? At least one or the other must
have quitted the stage. We have seen what a ferment has
been excited among our living artists by the exhibition of the
works of the old masters at the British Gallery. What would the
actors say to it if, by any spell or power of necromancy, all the
celebrated actors for the last hundred years could be made to
appear again on the boards of Covent Garden and Drury Lane,
for the last time, in all their most brilliant parts? What a rich
treat to the town, what a feast for the critics, to go and see
Betterton, and Booth, and Wilks, and Sandford, and Nokes,
and Leigh, and Penkethman, and Bullock, and Estcourt, and
Dogget, and Mrs. Barry, and Mrs. Montfort, and Mrs. Oldfield,
and Mrs. Bracegirdle, and Mrs. Cibber, and Cibber himself, the
prince of coxcombs, and Macklin, and Quin, and Rich, and
Mrs. Clive, and Mrs. Pritchard, and Mrs. Abington, and
Weston, and Shutter, and Garrick, and all the rest of those
who "gladdened life, and whose deaths eclipsed the gaiety of
nations !" We should certainly be there. We should buy a
ticket for the season. We should enjoy *our hundred days*
again. We should not lose a single night. We would not,
for a great deal, be absent from Betterton's Hamlet or his
Brutus, or from Booth's Cato, as it was first acted to the
contending applause of Whigs and Tories. We should be
in the first row when Mrs. Barry (who was kept by
Lord Rochester, and with whom Otway was in love) played
Monimia or Belvidera ; and we suppose we should go to
see Mrs. Bracegirdle (with whom all the world was in
love) in all her parts. We should then know exactly whether
Penkethman's manner of picking a chicken and Bullock's mode
of devouring asparagus answered to the ingenious account of
them in the *Tatler* ; and whether Dogget was equal to Dowton
—whether Mrs. Montfort or Mrs. Abington was the finest
lady—whether Wilks or Cibber was the best Sir Harry Wildair
—whether Macklin was really "the Jew that Shakespeare
drew," and whether Garrick was, upon the whole, so great an

actor as the world have made him out. Many people have a
strong desire to pry into the secrets of futurity: for our own
part, we should be satisfied if we had the power to recall the
dead, and live the past over again as often as we pleased.
Players, after all, have little reason to complain of their hard-
earned, short-lived popularity. One thunder of applause from
pit, boxes, and gallery is equal to a whole immortality of
posthumous fame ; and when we hear an actor, whose modesty
is equal to his merit, declare that he would like to see a dog
wag his tail in approbation, what must he feel when he sees the
whole house in a roar ! Besides, Fame, as if their reputation
had been entrusted to her alone, has been particularly careful
of the renown of her theatrical favourites ; she forgets one by
one, and year by year, those who have been great lawyers, great
statesmen, and great warriors in their day, but the name of
Garrick still survives with the works of Reynolds and of
Johnson.

Actors have been accused, as a profession, of being extravagant and dissipated. While they are said to be so, as a piece
of common cant, they are likely to continue so. But there is a
sentence in Shakespeare which should be stuck as a label in
the mouths of our beadles and whippers-in of morality : "The
web of our life is of a mingled yarn, good and ill together : our
virtues would be proud if our faults whipped them not ; and
our vices would despair if they were not cherished by our
virtues." With respect to the extravagance of actors, as a
traditional character, it is not to be wondered at. They
live from hand to mouth : they plunge from want into luxury ;
they have no means of making money *breed*, and all professions
that do not live by turning money into money, or have not
a certainty of accumulating it in the end by parsimony, spend
it. Uncertain of the future, they make sure of the present
moment. This is not unwise. Chilled with poverty, steeped in
contempt, they sometimes pass into the sunshine of fortune,
and are lifted to the very pinnacle of public favour ; yet even
there cannot calculate on the continuance of success, but are,
"like the giddy sailor on the mast, ready with every blast to

topple down into the fatal bowels of the deep." Besides, if the young enthusiast who is smitten with the stage, and with the public as a mistress, were naturally a close *hunks,* he would become or remain a city clerk, instead of turning player. Again, with respect to the habit of convivial indulgence, an actor, to be a good one, must have a great spirit of enjoyment in himself, strong impulses, strong passions, and a strong sense of pleasure ; for it is his business to imitate the passions, and to communicate pleasure to others. A man of genius is not a machine. The neglected actor may be excused if he drinks oblivion of his disappointments ; the successful one, if he quaffs the applause of the world, and enjoys the friendship of those who are the friends of the favourites of fortune, in draughts of nectar. There is no path so steep as that of fame : no labour so hard as the pursuit of excellence. The intellectual excite- ment inseparable from those professions which call forth all our sensibility to pleasure and pain requires some correspond- ing physical excitement to support our failure, and not a little to allay the ferment of the spirits attendant on success. If there is any tendency to dissipation beyond this in the pro- fession of a player, it is owing to the prejudices entertained against them—to that spirit of bigotry which, in a neigbouring country, would deny actors Christian burial after their death, and to that cant of criticism which, in our own, slurs over their characters, while living, with a half-witted jest.

A London engagement is generally considered by actors as the *ne plus ultra* of their ambition, as "a consummation devoutly to be wished," as the great prize in the lottery of their professional life. But this appears to us, who are not in the secret, to be rather the prose termination of their adventurous career ; it is the provincial commencement that is the poetical and truly enviable part of it. After that, they have com- paratively little to hope or fear. "The wine of life is drunk, and but the lees remain." In London they become gentlemen, and the King's servants ; but it is the romantic mixture of the hero and the vagabond that constitutes the essence of the player's life. It is the transition from their real to their assumed characters, from the contempt of the world to the applause of the multitude, that gives its zest to the latter, and raises them as much above common humanity at night, as in the daytime they are depressed below it. "Hurried from fierce extremes, by contrast made more fierce,"—it is rags and a flock-bed which give their splendour to a plume of feathers and a throne. We should suppose, that if the most admired actor on the London stage were brought to confession on this point, he would acknowledge that all the applause he had received from "brilliant and overflowing audiences" was nothing to the light-headed intoxication of unlooked-for success in a barn. In town, actors are criticised : in country-places, they are wondered at, or hooted at ; it is of little consequence which, so that the interval is not too long between. For ourselves, we own that the description of the strolling player in *Gil Blas*, soaking his dry crusts in the well by the roadside, presents to us a perfect picture of human felicity.

ON MR. KEAN'S IAGO.

WE certainly think Mr. Kean's performance of the part of Iago one of the most extraordinary exhibitions on the stage. There is no one within our remembrance who has so completely foiled the critics as this celebrated actor. One sagacious person imagines that he must perform a part in a certain manner; another virtuoso chalks out a different path for him; and when the time comes, he does the whole off in a way that neither of them had the least conception of, and which both of them are therefore very ready to condemn as entirely wrong. It was ever the trick of genius to be thus. We confess that Mr. Kean has thrown us out more than once. For instance, we are very much inclined to adopt the opinion of a contemporary critic, that his Richard is not gay enough, and that his Iago is not grave enough. This he may perhaps conceive to be the mere caprice of idle criticism; but we will try to give our reasons, and shall leave them to Mr. Kean's better judgment. It is to be remembered, then, that Richard was a princely villain, borne along in a sort of triumphal car of royal state, buoyed up with the hopes and privileges of his birth, reposing even on the sanctity of religion, trampling on his devoted victims without remorse, and who looked out and laughed from the high watch-tower of his confidence and his expectations on the desolation and misery he had caused around him. He held on his way, unquestioned, "hedged in with the divinity of kings," amenable to no tribunal, and abusing his power *in contempt of mankind.* But as for Iago, we conceive differently of him. He had not the same natural advantages. He was a mere adventurer in mischief—a painstaking, plodding knave, without patent or pedigree, who was obliged to work his uphill way by wit, not by will, and to be the founder of his own fortune. He was, if we may be allowed a vulgar allusion, a sort of prototype of modern Jacobinism, who thought that talents ought to decide the place—a man of " morbid sensibility " (in the fashionable phrase), full of distrust, of hatred, of anxious and corroding thoughts, and who, though he might assume a temporary superiority over others by superior adroitness, and pride himself in his skill, could not be supposed to assume it as a matter of course, as if he had been entitled to it from his birth. We do not here mean to enter into the characters of the two men, but something must be allowed to the difference of their situations. There might be the same insensibility in both as to the end ·in view, but there could not well be the same security as to the success of the means. Iago had to pass through a different ordeal : he had no appliances and means to boot—no royal road to the completion of his tragedy. His pretensions were not backed by authority ; they were baptised at the font ; they were not holy-water-proof. He had the whole to answer for in his own person, and could not shift the responsibility to the heads of others. Mr. Kean's Richard was therefore, we think, deficient in something of that regal jollity and reeling triumph of success which the part would bear ; but this we can easily account for, because it is the traditional commonplace idea of the character, that he is to " play the dog—to bite and snarl." The extreme unconcern and laboured levity of his Iago, on the contrary, is a refinement and original device of the actor's own mind, and therefore deserves consideration. The character of Iago, in fact, belongs to a class of characters common to Shakespeare, and at the same time peculiar to him—namely, that of great intellectual activity, accompanied with a total want of moral principle, and therefore displaying itself at the constant expense of others, making use of reason as a pander to will, employing its ingenuity and its resources to palliate its own crimes and aggravate the faults of others, and seeking to confound the practical distinctions of right and wrong by referring them to some overstrained standard of speculative refinement. Some persons, more nice than wise, have thought the whole of the character of Iago unnatural. Shakespeare, who was quite as good a philosopher as he was a poet, thought otherwise. He knew that the love of power, which is another name for the love of mischief, was natural to man. He would know this as well or better than if it had been demonstrated to him by a logical diagram, merely from seeing children paddle in the dirt, or kill flies for sport. We might ask those who think the character of Iago not natural, why they go to see it performed, but from the interest it excites, the sharper edge which it sets on their curiosity and imagination? Why do we go to see tragedies in general, why do we always read the accounts in the newspapers of dreadful fires and shocking murders, but for the same reason? Why do so many persons frequent executions and trials, or why do the lower classes almost universally take delight in barbarous sports and cruelty to animals, but because there is a natural tendency in the mind to strong excitement, a desire to have its faculties roused and stimulated to the utmost? Whenever this principle is not under the restraint of humanity or the sense of moral obligation, there are no excesses to which it will not of itself give rise, without the assistance of any other motive, either of passion or self-interest. Iago is only an extreme instance of the kind—that is, of diseased intellectual activity, with an almost perfect indifference to moral good or evil, or rather with a preference for the latter, because it falls more in with his favourite propensity, gives greater zest to his thoughts, and scope to his actions. Be it observed, too (for the sake of those who are for squaring all human actions by the maxims of Rochefoucault), that he is quite or nearly as indifferent to his own fate as to that of others; that he runs all risks for a trifling and doubtful advantage; and is himself the dupe and victim of his ruling passion—an incorrigible love of mischief, an insatiable craving after action of the most difficult and dangerous kind. Our "ancient" is a philosopher, who fancies that a lie that kills has more point in it than an alliteration or an antithesis; who thinks a fatal experiment on the peace of a family a better thing than watching the palpitations in the heart of a flea in an air-pump ; who plots the ruin of his friends as an exercise for his understanding, and stabs men in the dark to prevent ennui. Now this, though it be sport, yet it is dreadful sport. There is no room for trifling and indifference, nor scarcely for the appearance of it ; the very object of his whole plot is to keep his faculties stretched on the rack, in a state of watch and ward, in a sort of breathless suspense, without a moment's interval of repose. He has a desperate stake to play for, like a man who fences with poisoned weapons, and has business enough on his hands to call for the whole stock of his sober circumspection, his dark duplicity, and insidious gravity. He resembles a man who sits down to play at chess for the sake of the difficulty and complication of the game, and who immediately becomes absorbed in it. His amusements, if they are amusements, are severe and saturnine—even his wit blisters. His gaiety arises from the success of his treachery ; his ease from the sense of the torture he has inflicted on others. Even, if other circumstances permitted it, the part he has to play with Othello requires that he should assume the most serious concern, and something of the plausibility of a confessor. "His cue is villainous melancholy, with a sigh like Tom o' Bedlam." He is repeatedly called "honest Iago," which looks as if there were something suspicious in his appearance, which admitted a different construction. The tone which he adopts in the scenes with Roderigo, Desdemona, and Cassio is only a relaxation from the more arduous business of the play. Yet there is in all his conversation an inveterate misanthropy, a licentious keenness of perception, which is always sagacious of evil, and snuffs up the tainted scent of its quarry with rancorous delight. An exuberance of spleen is the essence of the character. The view which we have here taken of the subject (if at all correct) will not therefore justify the extreme alteration which Mr. Kean has introduced into the part. Actors in general have been struck only with the wickedness of the character, and have exhibited an assassin going to the place of execution. Mr. Kean has

abstracted the wit of the character, makes Iago appear throughout an excellent good fellow and lively bottle-companion. But
though we do not wish him to be represented as a monster or
fiend, we see no reason why he should instantly be converted
into a pattern of comic gaiety and good-humour. The light
which illumines the character should rather resemble the flashes
of lightning in the murky sky, which make the darkness more
terrible. Mr. Kean's Iago is, we suspect, too much in the sun.
His manner of acting the part would have suited better with the
character of Edmund in " King Lear," who, though in other
respects much the same, has a spice of gallantry in his constitution, and has the favour and countenance of the ladies, which
always gives a man the smug appearance of a bridegroom.

MRS. SIDDONS.

MRS. SIDDONS was in the meridian of her reputation when I first became acquainted with the stage. She was an established veteran, when I was an unfledged novice ; and, perhaps, played those scenes without emotion, which filled me, and so many others, with delight and awe. So far I had the advantage of her, and of myself too. I did not then analyse her excellences as I should now, or divide her merits into physical and intellectual advantages, or see that her majestic form rose up against misfortune in equal sublimity, an antagonist power to it ; but the total impression (unquestioned, unrefined upon) overwhelmed and drowned me in a flood of tears. I was stunned and torpid after seeing her in any of her great parts. I was uneasy, and hardly myself ; but I felt (more than ever) that human life was something very far from being indifferent, and I seemed to have got a key to unlock the springs of joy and sorrow in the human heart. This was no mean possession, and I availed myself of it with no sparing hand. The pleasure I anticipated at that time in witnessing her dullest performance, was certainly greater than I should have now in seeing her in the most brilliant. The very sight of her name in the play-bills in " Tamarlane" or " Alexander the Great" threw a light upon the day, and drew after it a long trail of Eastern glory, a joy and felicity unutterable, that has since vanished in the mists of criticism and idle distinctions. I was in a trance, and my dreams were of mighty empires fallen, of vast burning zones, of waning time, of Persian thrones and them that sat on them, of sovereign beauty, and of victors vanquished by love. Death and Life played their pageant before me. The gates were

unbarred, the folding-doors of fancy were thrown open, and
I saw all that mankind had been, or that I myself could
conceive, pass in review before me.

The homage she has received is greater than that which is
paid to queens. The enthusiasm she excited had something
idolatrous about it ; she was regarded less with admiration
than with wonder, as if a being of a superior order had dropped
from another sphere to awe the world with the majesty of her
appearance. She raised tragedy to the skies, or brought it
down from thence. It was something above nature. We can
conceive of nothing grander. She embodied to our imagination the fables of mythology, of the heroic and deified mortals
of elder time. She was not less than a goddess, or than a
prophetess inspired by the gods. Power was seated on her
brow, passion emanated from her breast as from a shrine. She
was tragedy personified. She was the stateliest ornament of
the public mind. She was not only the idol of the people, she
not only hushed the tumultuous shouts of the pit in breathless
expectation, and quenched the blaze of surrounding beauty in
silent tears, but to the retired and lonely student, through long
years of solitude, her face has shone as if an eye had appeared
from heaven ; her name has been as if a voice had opened the
chambers of the human heart, or as if a trumpet had awakened
the sleeping and the dead. To have seen Mrs. Siddons was an
event in every one's life ; and does she think we have forgot
her ?

Who shall give us Mrs. Siddons again, but in a waking
dream, a beatific vision of past years, crowned with other hopes
and other feelings, whose pomp is almost faded, and their glory
and their power gone? Who shall in our time (or can ever
to the eye of fancy) fill the stage like her, with the dignity
of their persons and the emanations of their minds? Or who
shall sit majestic on the throne of tragedy—a Goddess, a
prophetess, and a Muse—from which the lightning of her eye
flashed o'er the mind, startling its inmost thoughts, and the

thunder of her voice circled through the labouring breast, rousing deep and scarce-known feelings from their slumber? Who shall stalk over the stage of horrors, its presiding genius, or "play the hostess" at the banqueting scene of murder? Who shall walk in sleepless ecstasy of soul, and haunt the mind's eye ever after with the dread pageantry of suffering and of guilt? Who shall make tragedy once more stand with its feet upon the earth, and with its head raised above the skies, weeping tears and blood? That loss is not to be repaired. While the stage lasts, there will never be another Mrs. Siddons. Tragedy seemed to set with her; and the rest are but blazing comets, or fiery exhalations.

.   .   .   .   .

Mrs. Siddons seldom if ever goes (into the boxes), and yet she is almost the only thing left worth seeing there. She need not stay away on account of any theory that I can form. She is out of the pale of all theories, and annihilates all rules. Wherever she sits there is grace and grandeur, there is tragedy personified. Her seat is the undivided throne of the Tragic Muse. She had no need of the robes, the sweeping train, the ornaments of the stage ; in herself she is as great as any being she ever represented in the ripeness and plenitude of her power

ON A LANDSCAPE OF NICOLAS POUSSIN.

" And blind Orion hungry for the morn."

ORION, the subject of this landscape, was the classical Nimrod; and is called by Homer, "a hunter of shadows, himself a shade." He was the son of Neptune; and having lost an eye in some affray between the Gods and men, was told that if he would go to meet the rising sun he would recover his sight. He is represented setting out on his journey, with men on his shoulders to guide him, a bow in his hand, and Diana in the clouds greeting him. He stalks along, a giant upon earth, and reels and falters in his gait, as if just awakened out of sleep, or uncertain of his way; you see his blindness, though his back is turned. Mists rise around him, and veil the sides of the green forests; earth is dank and fresh with dews, the "grey dawn and the Pleiades before him dance," and in the distance are seen the blue hills and sullen ocean. Nothing was ever more finely conceived or done. It breathes the spirit of the morning; its moisture, its repose, its obscurity, waiting the miracle of light to kindle it into smiles; the whole is, like the principal figure in it, "a forerunner of the dawn." The same atmosphere tinges and imbues every object, the same dull light "shadowy sets off" the face of nature: one feeling of vastness, of strangeness, and of primeval forms pervades the painter's canvas, and we are thrown back upon the first integrity of things. This great and learned man might be said to see nature through the glass of time; he alone has a right to be considered as the painter of classical antiquity. Sir Joshua has done him justice in this respect. He could give to the scenery of his heroic fables that unimpaired look of original nature, full, solid, large, luxuriant, teeming with life and power; or deck it with all the pomp of art, with temples and towers, and mythologic groves. His pictures "denote a foregone conclusion." He applies nature to his purposes, works out her images according to the standard of his thoughts, embodies high fictions; and the first conception being given, all the rest seems to grow out of, and be assimilated to it, by the unfailing process of a studious imagination. Like his own "Orion," he overlooks the surrounding scene, appears to "take up the isles as a very little thing, and to lay the earth in a balance." With a laborious and mighty grasp, he put nature into the mould of the ideal and antique; and was among painters (more than any one else) what Milton was among poets. There is in both something of the same pedantry, the same stiffness, the same elevation, the same grandeur, the same mixture of art and nature, the same richness of borrowed materials, the same unity of character. Neither the poet nor the painter lowered the subjects they treated, but filled up the outline in the fancy, and added strength and reality to it; and thus not only satisfied, but surpassed the expectations of the spectator and the reader. This is held for the triumph and the perfection of works of art. To give us nature, such as we see it, is well and deserving of praise; to give us nature, such as we have never seen, but have often wished to see it, is better, and deserving of higher praise. He who can show the world in its first naked glory, with the hues of fancy spread over it, or in its high and palmy state, with the gravity of history stamped on the proud monuments of vanished empire—who, by his "so potent art," can recall time past, transport us to distant places, and join the regions of imagination (a new conquest) to those of reality—who shows us not only what nature is, but what she has been, and is capable of—he who does this, and does it with simplicity, with truth, and grandeur, is lord of nature and her powers, and his mind is universal, and his art the master-art !

There is nothing in this "more than natural," if criticism could be persuaded to think so. The historic painter does not neglect or contravene nature, but follows her more closely up into her fantastic heights, or hidden recesses. He demonstrates what she would be in conceivable circumstances, and under implied conditions. He "gives to airy nothing a local habitation," not "a name." At his touch, words start up into images, thoughts become things. He clothes a dream, a phantom with form and colour and the wholesome attributes of reality. *His* art is a second nature; not a different one. There are those, indeed, who think that not to copy nature is the rule for attaining perfection. Because they cannot paint the objects which they have seen, they fancy themselves qualified to paint the ideas which they have not seen. But it is possible to fail in this latter and more difficult style of imitation, as well as in the former humbler one. The detection, it is true, is not so easy, because the objects are not so nigh at hand to compare, and therefore there is more room both for false pretension and for self-deceit. They take an epic motto or subject, and conclude that the spirit is implied as a thing of course. They paint inferior portraits, maudlin lifeless faces, without ordinary expression, or one look, feature, or particle of nature in them, and think that this is to rise to the truth of history. They vulgarise and degrade whatever is interesting or sacred to the mind, and suppose that they thus add to the dignity of their profession. They represent a face that seems as if no thought or feeling of any kind had ever passed through it, and would have you believe that this is the very sublime of expression, such as it would appear in heroes, or demi-gods of old, when rapture or agony was raised to its height. They show you a landscape that looks as if the sun never shone upon it, and tell you that it is not modern—that so earth looked when Titan first kissed it with his rays. This is not the true *ideal.* It is not to fill the moulds of the imagination, but to deface and injure them ; it is not to come up to, but to fall short of the poorest conception in the public mind. Such pictures should not be hung in the same room with that of "Orion."*

Poussin was, of all painters, the most poetical. He was the painter of ideas. No one ever told a story half so well, nor so well knew what was capable of being told by the pencil. He seized on, and struck off with grace and precision, just that point of view which would be likely to catch the reader's fancy. There is a significance, a consciousness in whatever he does (sometimes a vice, but oftener a virtue) beyond any other painter. His Giants sitting on the tops of craggy mountains, as huge themselves, and playing idly on their Pan's pipes, seem to have been seated there these three thousand years, and to know the beginning and the end of their own story. An infant

* Everything tends to show the manner in which a great artist is formed. If any person could claim an exemption from the careful imitation of individual objects, it was Nicolas Poussin. He studied the antique, but he also studied nature. "I have often admired," says Vignuel de Marville, who knew him at a late period of his life, "the love he had for his art. Old as he was, I frequently saw him among the ruins of ancient Rome, out in the Campagna, or along the banks of the Tyber, sketching a scene that had pleased him; and I often met him with his handkerchief full of stones, moss, or flowers, which he carried home, that he might copy them exactly from nature. One day I asked him how he had attained to such a degree of perfection as to have gained so high a rank among the great painters of Italy? He answered, I HAVE NEGLECTED NOTHING."—*See his Life lately published.* It appears from this account that he had not fallen into a recent error, that Nature puts the man of genius out. As a contrast to the foregoing description, I might mention that I remember an old gentleman once asking Mr. West, in the British Gallery, if he had ever been at Athens? To which the President made answer, No; nor did he feel any great desire to go; for that he thought he had as good an idea of the place from the Catalogue as he could get by living there for any number of years. What would he have said if anyone had told him he could get as good an idea of the subject of one of his great works from reading the Catalogue of it as from seeing the picture itself! Yet the answer was characteristic of the genius of the painter.

Bacchus or Jupiter is big with his future destiny. Even inanimate and dumb things speak a language of their own. His snakes, the messengers of fate, are inspired with human intellect. His trees grow and expand their leaves in the air, glad of the rain, proud of the sun, awake to the winds of heaven. In his " Plague of Athens," the very buildings seem stiff with horror. His picture of " The Deluge " is, perhaps, the finest historical landscape in the world. You see a waste of waters, wide, interminable : the sun is labouring, wan and weary, up the sky ; the clouds, dull and leaden, lie like a load upon the eye, and heaven and earth seem commingling into one confused mass ! His human figures are sometimes "o'er-informed" with this kind of feeling. Their actions have too much gesticulation, and the set expression of the features borders too much on the mechanical and caricatured style. In this respect they form a contrast to Raphael's, whose figures never appear to be sitting for their pictures, or to be conscious of a spectator, or to have come from the painter's hand. In Nicolas Poussin, on the contrary, everything seems to have a distinct understanding with the artist ; "the very stones prate of their whereabout ;" each object has its part and place assigned, and is in a sort of compact with the rest of the picture. It is this conscious keeping, and, as it were, *internal* design, that gives their peculiar character to the works of this artist. There was a picture of "Aurora" in the British Gallery a year or two ago. It was a suffusion of golden light. The Goddess wore her saffron-coloured robes, and appeared just risen from the gloomy bed of old Tithonus. Her very steeds, milk-white, were tinged with the yellow dawn. It was a personification of the morning. Poussin succeeded better in classic than in sacred subjects. The latter are comparatively heavy, forced, full of violent contrasts of colour, of red, blue, and black, and without the true prophetic inspiration of the characters. But in his Pagan allegories and fables he was quite at home. The native gravity and native levity of the Frenchman were combined with Italian scenery and an antique gusto, and gave even to his colouring an air of learned indifference. He wants, in one respect, grace, form, expression; but he has everywhere sense and meaning, perfect costume and propriety. His personages always belong to the class and time represented, and are strictly versed in the business in hand. His grotesque compositions in particular, his Nymphs and Fauns, are superior (at least, as far as style is concerned) even to those of Rubens'. They are taken more immediately out of fabulous history. Rubens' Satyrs and Bacchantes have a more jovial and voluptuous aspect, are more drunk with pleasure, more full of animal spirits and riotous impulses; they laugh and bound along—

" Leaping like wanton kids in pleasant spring ; "

but those of Poussin have more of the intellectual part of the character, and seem vicious on reflection, and of set purpose. Rubens' are noble specimens of a class; Poussin's are allegorical abstractions of the same class, with bodies less pampered, but with minds more secretly depraved. The Bacchanalian groups of the Flemish painter were, however, his masterpieces in composition. Witness those prodigies of colour, character, and expression at Blenheim. In the more chaste and refined delineation of classic fable, Poussin was without a rival. Rubens, who was a match for him in the wild and picturesque, could not pretend to vie with the elegance and purity of thought in his picture of Apollo giving a poet a cup of water to drink, nor with the gracefulness of design in the figure of a nymph squeezing the juice of a bunch of grapes from her fingers (a rosy wine-press) which falls into the mouth of a chubby infant below. But, above all, who shall celebrate, in terms of fit praise, his picture of the shepherds in the Vale of Tempe going out in a fine morning of the spring, and coming to a tomb with this inscription :—ET EGO IN ARCADIA VIXI ! The eager curiosity of some, the expression of others who start back with fear and surprise, the clear breeze playing with the branches of the shadowing trees, "the valleys low, where the mild zephyrs use." the distant. uninterrupted. sunny prospects speak (and for ever will speak on) of ages past to ages yet to come !*.

Pictures are a set of chosen images, a stream of pleasant thoughts passing through the mind. It is a luxury to have the walls of our rooms hung round with them, and no less so to have such a gallery in the mind, to con over the relics of ancient art bound up " within the book and volume of the brain, unmixed (if it were possible) with baser matter ! " A life passed among pictures, in the study and the love of art, is a happy noiseless dream : or rather, it is to dream and to be awake at the same time ; for it has all " the sober certainty of waking bliss," with the romantic voluptuousness of a visionary and abstracted being. They are the bright consummate essences of things, and " he who knows of these delights to taste and interpose them oft, is not unwise !" The "Orion," which I have here taken occasion to descant upon, is one of a collection of excellent pictures, as this collection is itself one of a series from the old masters, which have for some years back embrowned the walls of the British Gallery and enriched the public eye. What hues (those of nature mellowed by time) breathe around, as we enter ! What forms are there woven into the memory ! What looks, which only the answering looks of the spectator can express ! What intellectual stores have been yearly poured forth from the shrine of ancient art ! The works are various, but the names the same— heaps of Rembrandts frowning from the darkened walls, Rubens' glad gorgeous groups, Titians more rich and rare, Claudes always exquisite, sometimes beyond compare, Guido's endless cloying sweetness, the learning of Poussin and the Caracci, and Raphael's princely magnificence crowning all. We read certain letters and syllables in the catalogue, and at the well-known magic sound, a miracle of skill and beauty starts to

* Poussin has repeated this subject more than once, and appears to have revelled in its witcheries. I have before alluded to it, and may again. It is hard that we should not be allowed to dwell as often as we please on what delights us, when things that are disagreeable recur so often against our will.

view. One might think that one year's prodigal display of such perfection would exhaust the labours of one man's life; but the next year, and the next to that, we find another harvest reaped and gathered in to the great garner of art by the same immortal hands—

"Old GENIUS the porter of them was ;
He letteth in, he letteth out to wend."—

Their works seem endless as their reputation—to be many as they are complete—to multiply with the desire of the mind to see more and more of them ; as if there were a living power in the breath of Fame, and in the very names of the great heirs of glory "there were propagation too !" It is something to have a collection of this sort to count upon once a year ; to have one last, lingering look yet to come. Pictures are scattered like stray gifts through the world; and while they remain, earth has yet a little gilding left, not quite rubbed off, dishonoured, and defaced. There are plenty of standard works still to be found in this country, in the collections at Blenheim, at Burleigh, and in those belonging to Mr. Angerstein, Lord Grosvenor, the Marquis of Stafford, and others, to keep up this treat to the lovers of art for many years ; and it is the more desirable to reserve a privileged sanctuary of this sort, where the eye may dote, and the heart take its fill of such pictures as Poussin's "Orion," since the Louvre is stripped of its triumphant spoils, and since he, who collected it, and wore it as a rich jewel in his Iron Crown, the hunter of greatness and of glory, is himself a shade !

ON HOGARTH'S "MARRIAGE A LA MODE."

THE superiority of the pictures of Hogarth to the common prints is confined chiefly to the "Marriage à la mode." We shall attempt to illustrate a few of their most striking excellences, more particularly with reference to the expression of character. Their merits are indeed so prominent, and have been so often discussed, that it may be thought difficult to point out any new beauties ; but they contain so much truth of nature, they present the objects to the eye under so many aspects and bearings, admit of so many constructions, and are so pregnant with meaning, that the subject is in a manner inexhaustible.

Boccaccio, the most refined and sentimental of all the novel-writers, has been stigmatised as a mere inventor of licentious tales, because readers in general have only seized on those things in his works which were suited to their own taste, and have reflected their own grossness back upon the writer. So it has happened that the majority of critics having been most struck with the strong and decided expression in Hogarth, the extreme delicacy and subtle gradations of character in his pictures have almost entirely escaped them. In the first picture of the "Marriage à la mode" the three figures of the young nobleman, his intended bride, and her inamorato the lawyer, show how much Hogarth excelled in the power of giving soft and effeminate expression. They have, however, been less noticed than the other figures, which tell a plainer story and convey a more palpable moral. Nothing can be more finely managed than the differences of character in these delicate personages. The beau sits smiling at the looking-glass, with a reflected simper of self-admiration and a languishing inclination of the head, while the rest of his body is perked up on his high heels with a certain air of tiptoe elevation. He is the Narcissus of the reign of George II., whose powdered peruke, ruffles, gold lace, and patches divide his self-love unequally with his own person—the true Sir Plume of his day :

> " Of amber-lidded snuff-box justly vain,
> And the nice conduct of a clouded cane."

There is the same felicity in the figure and attitude of the bride courted by the lawyer. There is the utmost flexibility and yielding softness in her whole person, a listless languor and tremulous suspense in the expression of her face. It is the precise look and air which Pope has given to his favourite, Belinda, just at the moment of the "Rape of the Lock." The heightened glow, the forward intelligence, and loosened soul of love in the same face, in the assignation scene before the masquerade, form a fine and instructive contrast to the delicacy, timidity, and coy reluctance expressed in the first. The lawyer in both pictures is much the same—perhaps too much so ; though even this unmoved, unaltered appearance may be designed as characteristic. In both cases he has "a person and a smooth dispose, framed to make woman false." He is full of that easy good-humour and easy good opinion of himself with which the sex are delighted. There is not a sharp angle in his face to obstruct his success or give a hint of doubt or difficulty. His whole aspect is round and rosy, lively and unmeaning, happy without the least expense of thought, careless and inviting, and conveys a perfect idea of the uninterrupted glide and pleasing murmur of the soft periods that flow from his tongue.

The expression of the bride in the morning scene is the most highly seasoned, and at the same time the most vulgar in the series. The figure, face, and attitude of the husband are inimitable. Hogarth has with great skill contrasted the pale countenance of the husband with the yellow-whitish colour of the marble chimney-piece behind him in such a manner as to preserve the fleshy tone of the former. The airy splendour of the view of the inner room in this picture is probably not exceeded by any of the productions of the Flemish School.

The young girl in the third picture, who is represented as the victim of fashionable profligacy, is unquestionably one of the artist's *chefs-d'œuvre*. The exquisite delicacy of the painting is only surpassed by the felicity and subtlety of the conception. Nothing can be more striking than the contrast between the extreme softness of her person and the hardened indifference of her character. The vacant stillness, the docility to vice, the premature suppression of youthful sensibility, the doll-like mechanism of the whole figure, which seems to have no other feeling but a sickly sense of pain—show the deepest insight into human nature, and into the effects of those refinements in depravity by which it has been good-naturedly asserted that "vice loses half its evil by losing all its grossness." The story of this picture is in some parts very obscure and enigmatical. It is certain that the nobleman is not looking straight forward to the quack, whom he seems to have been threatening with his cane, but that his eyes are turned up with an ironical leer of triumph to the procuress. The commanding attitude and size of this woman—the swelling circumference of her dress, spread out like a turkey-cock's feathers—the fierce, ungovernable, inveterate malignity of her countenance, which hardly needs the comment of the clasp-knife to explain her purpose—are all admirable in themselves, and still more so they are opposed to the mute insensibility, the as elegant negligence of the dress, and the childish figure of the girl who is supposed to be her *protégée*. As for the quack, there can be no doubt entertained about him. His face seems as if it were composed of salve, and his features exhibit all the chaos and confusion of the most gross, ignorant, and impudent empiricism.

The gradations of ridiculous affectation in the music scene are finely imagined and preserved. The preposterous, overstrained admiration of the lady of quality ; the sentimental, insipid, patient delight of the man with his hair in papers and sipping his tea ; the pert, smirking, conceited, half-distorted approbation of the figure next to him ; the transition to the total insensibility of the round face in profile, and then to the wonder of the negro boy at the rapture of his mistress, form a perfect whole. The sanguine complexion and flame-coloured hair of the female virtuoso throw an additional light on the character. This is lost in the print. The continuing the red colour of the hair into the back of the chair has been pointed out as one of those instances of alliteration in colouring of which these pictures are everywhere full. The gross, bloated appearance of the Italian singer is well relieved by the hard features of the instrumental performer behind him, which might be carved of wood. The negro boy holding the chocolate, both in expression, colour, and execution, is a masterpiece. The gay, lively derision of the other negro boy, playing with the Actæon, is an ingenious contrast to the profound amazement of the first. Some account has already been given of the two lovers in this picture. It is curious to observe the infinite activity of mind which the artist displays on every occasion. An instance occurs in the present picture. He has so contrived the papers in the hair of the bride as to make them look almost like a wreath of half-blown flowers, while those which he has placed on the head of the musical amateur very much resemble a *cheval de frise* of horns, which adorn and fortify the lack-lustre expression and mild resignation of the face beneath.

The night scene is inferior to the rest of the series. The attitude of the husband, who is just killed, is one in which it would be impossible for him to stand or even to fall. It resembles the loose pasteboard figures they make for children. The characters in the last picture, in which the wife dies, are all masterly. We would particularly refer to the captious, petulant self-sufficiency of the apothecary, whose face and figure are constructed on exact physiognomical principles, and to the fine example of passive obedience and non-resistance in the servant, whom he is taking to task, and whose coat of green-and-yellow livery is as long and melancholy as his face. The disconsolate look, the haggard eyes, the open mouth, the comb sticking in the hair, the broken, gapped teeth, which, as it were, hitch in an answer—everything about him denotes the utmost perplexity and dismay. The harmony and gradations of colour in this picture are uniformly preserved with the greatest nicety, and are well worthy the attention of the artist.

It has been observed that Hogarth's pictures are exceedingly unlike any other representations of the same kind of subjects— that they form a class, and have a character peculiar to them-selves. It may be worth while to consider in what this general distinction consists.

In the first place, they are, in the strictest sense, *historical* pictures; and if what Fielding says be true, that his novel of *Tom Jones* ought to be regarded as an epic prose poem, because it contained a regular development of fable, manners, character, and passion, the compositions of Hogarth will, in like manner, be found to have a higher claim to the title of epic pictures than many which have of late arrogated that denom-ination to themselves. When we say that Hogarth treated his subjects historically, we mean that his works represent the manners and humours of mankind in action, and their characters by varied expression. Everything in his pictures has life and motion in it. Not only does the business of the scene never stand still, but every feature and muscle is put into full play ; the exact feeling of the moment is brought out and carried to its utmost height, and then instantly seized and stamped on the canvas for ever. The expression is always taken *en passant*, in a state of progress or change, and, as it were, at the salient point. Besides the excellence of each individual face, the reflection of the expression from face to face, the contrast and struggle of particular motives and feelings in the different actors in the scene—as of anger, contempt, laughter, compassion—are conveyed in the happiest and most lively manner. His figures

are not like the background on which they are painted ; even
the pictures on the wall have a peculiar look of their own.
Again, with the rapidity, variety, and scope of history, Hogarth's
heads have all the reality and correctness of portraits. He
gives the extremes of character and expression, but he gives
them with perfect truth and accuracy. This is, in fact, what
distinguishes his compositions from all others of the same kind,
that they are equally remote from caricature, and from mere
still life. It of course happens in subjects from common life,
that the painter can procure real models, and he can get them
to sit as long as he pleases. Hence, in general, those attitudes
and expressions have been chosen which could be assumed the
longest, and in imitating which the artist, by taking pains and
time, might produce almost as complete fac-similes as he could
of a flower or a flower-pot, of a damask curtain or a china vase.
The copy was as perfect and as uninteresting in the one case
as in the other. On the contrary, subjects of drollery and
ridicule, affording frequent examples of strange deformity and
peculiarity of features, these have been eagerly seized by
another class of artists, who, without subjecting themselves to
the laborious drudgery of the Dutch School and their imitators,
have produced our popular caricatures, by rudely copying or
exaggerating the casual irregularities of the human countenance. Hogarth has equally avoided the faults of both these
styles—the insipid tameness of the one, and the gross vulgarity
of the other—so as to give to the productions of his pencil equal
solidity and effect. For his faces go to the very verge of
caricature, and yet never (we believe in any single instance) go
beyond it : they take the very widest latitude, and yet we
always see the links which bind them to nature : they bear all
the marks and carry all the conviction of reality with them, as
if we had seen the actual faces for the first time, from the
precision, consistency, and good sense with which the whole
and every part is made out. They exhibit the most uncommon
features with the most uncommon expressions, but which are
yet as familiar and intelligible as possible, because with all
the boldness they have all the truth of nature. Hogarth has

left behind him as many of these memorable faces, in their memorable moments, as perhaps most of us remember in the course of our lives, and has thus doubled the quantity of our observation.

We have attempted to point out the fund of observation, physical and moral, contained in one set of Hogarth's pictures, the "Marriage à la mode." The rest would furnish as many topics to descant upon, were the patience of the reader as inexhaustible as the painter's invention. But as this is not the case, we shall content ourselves with barely referring to some of those figures in the other pictures which appear the most striking, and which we see not only while we are looking at them, but which we have before us at all other times. For instance, who having seen can easily forget that exquisite frost-piece of religion and morality, and antiquated prude in the morning scene? or that striking commentary on the *good old times*, the little wretched appendage of a footboy, who crawls half famished and half frozen behind her? The Frenchman and woman in the "Noon" are the perfection of flighty affectation and studied grimace; the amiable *fraternisation* of the two old women saluting each other is not enough to be admired; and in the little master, in the same national group, we see the early promise and personification of that eternal principle of wondrous self-complacency, proof against all circumstances, and which makes the French the only people who are vain even of being cuckolded and being conquered. Or shall we prefer to this the outrageous distress and unmitigated terrors of the boy, who has dropped his dish of meat, and who seems red all over with shame and vexation, and bursting with the noise he makes? Or what can be better than the good housewifery of the girl underneath, who is devouring the lucky fragments?—or than the plump, ripe, florid, luscious look of the servant-wench, embraced by a greasy rascal of an Othello, with her pie-dish tottering like her virtue, and with the most precious parts of its contents running over? Just—no, not quite—as good is the joke of the woman overhead, who, having quarrelled with her husband, is throwing their Sunday's dinner

out of the window, to complete this chapter of accidents of baked
dishes.   The husband in the evening scene is certainly as meek
as any recorded in history; but we cannot say that we admire
this picture, or the night scene after it.   But then, in the "Taste
in High Life," there is that inimitable pair, differing only in sex,
congratulating and delighting one another by "all the mutually
reflected charities" of folly and affectation—with the young
lady coloured like a rose, dandling her little, black, pug-faced,
white-teethed, chuckling favourite, and with the portrait of
Monsieur Des Noyers in the background, dancing in a grand
ballet, surrounded by butterflies.   And again, in "The Election
Dinner," is the immortal cobbler, surrounded by his peers, who,
"frequent and full"—

"In *loud* recess and *brawling* conclave sit"—

the Jew in the second picture, a very Jew in grain—innumerable
fine sketches of heads in the "Polling for Votes," of which the
nobleman overlooking the caricaturist is the best; and then the
irresistible, tumultuous display of broad humour in the "Chairing
the Member," which is, perhaps, of all Hogarth's pictures, the
most full of laughable incidents and situations—the yellow, rusty-
faced thresher, with his swinging flail, breaking the head of one
of the chairmen, and his redoubted antagonist, the sailor, with
his oak-stick, and stumping wooden leg, a supplemental cudgel
—the persevering ecstasy of the hobbling blind fiddler, who, in
the fray, appears to have been trod upon by the artificial
excrescence of the honest tar—Monsieur the monkey, with
piteous aspect, speculating the impending disaster of the
triumphant candidate, and his brother, Bruin, appropriating the
paunch—the precipitous flight of the pigs, souse over head into
the water, the fine lady fainting, with vermilion lips, and the two
chimney-sweepers, satirical young rogues!   We had almost
forgot "The Politician," who is burning a hole through his hat
with a candle in reading the newspaper; and the chickens, in
the "March to Finchley," wandering in search of their lost
dam, which is found in the pocket of the sergeant.   Of the
pictures in the "Rake's Progress" we shall not here say anything,

because we think them, on the whole, inferior to the prints, and because they have already been criticised by a writer, to whom we could add nothing, in a paper which ought to be read by every lover of Hogarth and of English genius.*

---

* See an " Essay on the Genius of Hogarth," by C. Lamb, published in a periodical work called the *Reflector*.

ON GOING A JOURNEY.

ONE of the pleasantest things in the world is going a journey; but I like to go by myself. I can enjoy society in a room; but out of doors, nature is company enough for me. I am then never less alone than when alone.

> " The fields his study, nature was his book."

I cannot see the wit of walking and talking at the same time. When I am in the country, I wish to vegetate like the country. I am not for criticising hedge-rows and black cattle. I go out of town in order to forget the town and all that is in it. There are those who for this purpose go to watering-places, and carry the metropolis with them. I like more elbow-room, and fewer incumbrances. I like solitude, when I give myself up to it, for the sake of solitude; nor do I ask for

> "——a friend in my retreat,
> Whom I may whisper, solitude is sweet."

The soul of a journey is liberty, perfect liberty, to think, feel, do, just as one pleases. We go a journey chiefly to be free of all impediments and of all inconveniences; to leave ourselves behind much more to get rid of others. It is because I want a little breathing-space to muse on indifferent matters, where Contemplation

> " May plume her feathers and let grow her wings,
> That in the various bustle of resort
> Were all too ruffled, and sometimes impair'd."

that I absent myself from the town for a while, without feeling at a loss the moment I am left by myself. Instead of a friend in a post-chaise or in a Tilbury, to exchange good things with and vary the same stale topics over again, for once let me have a truce with impertinence. Give me the clear blue sky over my head, and the green turf beneath my feet, a winding road before me, and a three hours' march to dinner—and then to thinking! It is hard if I cannot start some game on these lone heaths. I laugh, I run, I leap, I sing for joy. From the point of yonder rolling cloud, I plunge into my past being, and revel there, as the sun-burnt Indian plunges headlong into the wave that wafts him to his native shore. Then long-forgotten things, like "sunken wrack and sumless treasuries," burst upon my eager sight, and I begin to feel, think, and be myself again. Instead of an awkward silence, broken by attempts at wit or dull commonplaces, mine is that undisturbed silence of the heart which alone is perfect eloquence. No one likes puns, alliterations, antitheses, argument, and analysis better than I do; but I sometimes had rather be without them. "Leave, oh, leave me to my repose!" I have just now other business in hand, which would seem idle to you, but is with me "very stuff o' the conscience." Is not this wild rose sweet without a comment? Does not this daisy leap to my heart set in its coat of emerald? Yet if I were to explain to you the circumstance that has so endeared it to me, you would only smile. Had I not better then keep it to myself, and let it serve me to brood over, from here to yonder craggy point, and from thence onward to the far-distant horizon? I should be but bad company all that way, and therefore prefer being alone. I have heard it said that you may, when the moody fit comes on, walk or ride on by yourself, and indulge your reveries. But this looks like a breach of manners, a neglect of others, and you are thinking all the time that you ought to rejoin your party. "Out upon such half-faced fellowship," say I. I like to be either entirely to myself, or entirely at the disposal of others; to talk or be silent, to walk or sit still, to be sociable or solitary. I was pleased with an observation of Mr. Cobbett's, that "he thought it a bad

French custom to drink our wine with our meals, and that an Englishman ought to do only one thing at a time." So I cannot talk and think, or indulge in melancholy musing and lively conversation by fits and starts. "Let me have a companion of my way," says Sterne, "were it but to remark how the shadows lengthen as the sun declines." It is beautifully said ; but in my opinion, this continual comparing of notes interferes with the involuntary impression of things upon the mind, and hurts the sentiment. If you only hint what you feel in a kind of dumb show, it is insipid : if you have to explain it, .t is making a toil of a pleasure. You cannot read the book of nature without being perpetually put to the trouble of translating it for the benefit of others. I am for this synthetical method on a journey in preference to the analytical. I am content to lay in a stock of ideas then, and to examine and anatomise them afterwards. I want to see my vague notions float like the down of the thistle before the breeze, and not to have them entangled in the briars and thorns of controversy. For once, I like to have it all my own way ; and this is impossible unless you are alone, or in such company as I do not covet. I have no objection to argue a point with any one for twenty miles of measured road, but not for pleasure. If you remark the scent of a bean-field crossing the road, perhaps your fellow-traveller has no smell. If you point to a distant object, perhaps he is short-sighted, and has to take out his glass to look at it. There is a feeling in the air, a tone in the colour of a cloud which hits your fancy, but the effect of which you are unable to account for. There is then no sympathy, but an uneasy craving after it, and a dissatisfaction which pursues you on the way, and in the end probably produces ill-humour. Now, I never quarrel with myself, and take all my own conclusions for granted till I find it necessary to defend them against objections. It is not merely that you may not be of accord on the objects and circumstances that present themselves before you—these may recall a number of objects, and lead to associations too delicate and refined to be possibly communicated to others. Yet these I love to cherish. and sometimes still fondly clutch them, when I can escape from the throng to do so. To give way to our feelings before company seems extravagance or affectation; and, on the other hand, to have to unravel this mystery of our being at every turn, and to make others take an equal interest in it (otherwise the end is not answered), is a task to which few are competent. We must "give it an understanding, but no tongue." My old friend Coleridge, however, could do both. He could go on in the most delightful explanatory way over hill and dale a summer's day, and convert a landscape into a didactic poem or a Pindaric ode. "He talked far above singing." If I could so clothe my ideas in sounding and flowing words, I might perhaps wish to have some one with me to admire the swelling theme; or I could be more content, were it possible for me still to hear his echoing voice in the woods of All-Foxden. They had "that fine madness in them which our first poets had;" and if they could have been caught by some rare instrument, would have breathed such strains as the following:—

"——Here be woods as green
As any, air likewise as fresh and sweet
As when smooth Zephyrus plays on the fleet
Face of the curled streams, with flow'rs as many
As the young spring gives, and as choice as any;
Here be all new delights, cool streams and wells;
Arbours o'ergrown with woodbines, caves and dells:
Choose where thou wilt, whilst I sit by and sing.
Or gather rushes, to make many a ring
For thy long fingers; tell thee tales of love;
How the pale Phœbe, hunting in a grove,
First saw the boy Endymion, from whose eyes
She took eternal fire that never dies;
How she conveyed him softly in a sleep,
His temples bound with poppy, to the steep
Head of old Latmos, where she stoops each night,
Gilding the mountain with her brother's light,
To kiss her sweetest." *

* Fletcher's "Faithful Shepherdess.

Had I words and images at command like these, I would attempt to wake the thoughts that lie slumbering on golden ridges in the evening clouds : but at the sight of nature my fancy, poor as it is, droops and closes up its leaves, like flowers at sunset. I can make nothing out on the spot—I must have time to collect myself.

In general, a good thing spoils out-of-door prospects : it should be reserved for Table-talk. Lamb is for this reason, I take it, the worst company in the world out of doors ; because he is the best within. I grant there is one subject on which it is pleasant to talk on a journey ; and that is, what one shall have for supper when we get to our inn at night. The open air improves this sort of conversation or friendly altercation, by setting a keener edge on appetite. Every mile of the road heightens the flavour of the viands we expect at the end of it. How fine it is to enter some old town, walled and turreted, just at approach of nightfall, or to come to some straggling village, with the lights streaming through the surrounding gloom ; and then, after inquiring for the best entertainment that the place affords, to "take one's ease at one's inn !" These eventful moments in our lives' history are too precious, too full of solid, heartfelt happiness to be frittered and dribbled away in imperfect sympathy. I would have them all to myself, and drain them to the last drop : they will do to talk of or to write about afterwards. What a delicate speculation it is, after drinking whole goblets of tea,

" The cups that cheer, but not inebriate,"

and letting the fumes ascend into the brain, to sit considering what we shall have for supper—eggs and a rasher, a rabbit smothered in onions, or an excellent veal cutlet ! Sancho in such a situation once fixed on cow-heel ; and his choice, though he could not help it, is not to be disparaged. Then, in the intervals of pictured scenery and Shandean contemplation, to catch the preparation and the stir in the kitchen. *Procul, O procul este profani!* ("Avaunt! avaunt! ye unhallowed.") These hours are sacred to silence and to musing, to be treasured up in the memory, and to feed the source of smiling thoughts here-after. I would not waste them in idle talk ; or if I must have the integrity of fancy broken in upon, I would rather it were by a stranger than a friend. A stranger takes his hue and character from the time and place ; he is a part of the furniture and costume of an inn. If he is a Quaker, or from the West Riding of Yorkshire, so much the better. I do not even try to sympathise with him, and he breaks no squares. I associate nothing with my travelling companion but present objects and passing events. In his ignorance of me and my affairs, I in a manner forgot myself. But a friend reminds one of other things, rips up old grievances, and destroys the abstraction of the scene. He comes in ungraciously between us and our imaginary character. Something is dropped in the course of conversation that gives a hint of your profession and pursuits ; or from having someone with you that knows the less sublime portions of your history, it seems that other people do. You are no longer a citizen of the world ; but your "unhoused free condition is put into circumspection and confine." The *incognito* of an inn is one of its striking privileges—"lord of one's self, uncumbered with a name." Oh ! it is great to shake off the trammels of the world and of public opinion—to lose our importunate, tormenting, ever-lasting personal identity in the elements of nature, and become the creature of the moment, clear of all ties—to hold to the universe only by a dish of sweetbreads, and to owe nothing but the score of the evening—and no longer seeking for applause and meeting with contempt, to be known by no other title than *the Gentleman in the parlour !* One may take one's choice of all characters in this romantic state of uncertainty as to one's real pretensions, and become indefinitely respect-able and negatively right-worshipful. We baffle prejudice and disappoint conjecture ; and from being so to others, begin to be objects of curiosity and wonder even to ourselves. We are no more those hackneyed commonplaces that we appear in the world ; an inn restores us to the level of nature, and quits scores with society ! I have certainly spent some enviable hours at inns—sometimes when I have been left entirely to myself, and have tried to solve some metaphysical problem, as once at Witham Common, where I found out the proof that likeness is not a case of the association of ideas—at other times, when there have been pictures in the room, as at St. Neot's (I think it was), where I first met with Gribelin's engravings of the Cartoons, into which I entered at once, and at a little inn on the borders of Wales, where there happened to be hanging some of Westall's drawings, which I compared triumphantly (for a theory that I had, not for the admired artist) with the figure of a girl who had ferried me over the Severn, standing up in a boat between me and the twilight—at other times I might mention luxuriating in books, with a peculiar interest in this way, as I remember sitting up half the night to read *Paul and Virginia*, which I picked up at an inn at Bridgewater, after being drenched in the rain all day ; and at the same place I got through two volumes of Madame D'Arblay's *Camilla.* It was on the 10th of April 1798 that I sat down to a volume of the *New Eloise*, at the inn at Llangollen, over a bottle of sherry and a cold chicken. The letter I chose was that in which St. Preux describes his feelings as he first caught a glimpse from the heights of the Jura of the Pays de Vaud, which I had brought with me as a *bon bouche* to crown the evening with. It was my birthday, and I had for the first time come from a place in the neighbourhood to visit this delightful spot. The road to Llangollen turns off between Chirk and Wrexham ; and on passing a certain point, you come all at once upon the valley, which opens like an amphitheatre, broad, barren hills rising in majestic state on either side, with "green upland swells that echo to the bleat of flocks" below, and the river Dee babbling over its stony bed in the midst of them. The valley at this time "glittered green with sunny showers," and a budding ash-tree dipped its tender branches in the chiding stream. How proud, how glad I was to walk along the high road that overlooks the delicious prospect, repeating the lines which I have just quoted from Mr.

Coleridge's poems ! But besides the prospect which opened beneath my feet, another also opened to my inward sight, a heavenly vision, on which were written, in letters large as Hope could make them, these four words, LIBERTY, GENIUS, LOVE, VIRTUE ; which have since faded into the light of common day, or mock my idle gaze.

"The beautiful is vanished, and returns not."

Still I would return some time or other to this enchanted spot ; but I would return to it alone. What other self could I find to share that influx of thoughts, of regret, and delight, the fragments of which I could hardly conjure up to myself, so much have they been broken and defaced. I could stand on some tall rock, and overlook the precipice of years that separates me from what I then was. I was at that time going shortly to visit the poet whom I have above named. Where is he now ? Not only I myself have changed ; the world, which was then new to me, has become old and incorrigible. Yet will I turn to thee in thought, O sylvan Dee, in joy, in youth and gladness as thou then wert ; and thou shalt always be to me the river of Paradise, where I will drink of the waters of life freely !

There is hardly anything that shows the short-sightedness or capriciousness of the imagination more than travelling does. With change of place we change our ideas ; nay, our opinions and feelings. We can by an effort indeed transport ourselves to old and long-forgotten scenes, and then the picture of the mind revives again ; but we forget those that we have just left. It seems that we can think but of one place at a time. The canvas of the fancy is but of a certain extent, and if we paint one set of objects upon it, they immediately efface every other. We cannot enlarge our conceptions, we only shift our point of view. The landscape bares its bosom to the enraptured eye, we take our fill of it, and seem as if we could form no other image of beauty or grandeur. We pass on, and think no more of it ; the horizon that shuts it from our sight also blots it from our memory like a dream. In travelling through a wild, barren country, I can form no idea of a woody and cultivated one. It appears to me that all the world must be barren, like what I see of it. In the country we forget the town, and in town we despise the country. " Beyond Hyde Park," says Sir Fopling Flutter "all is a desert." All that part of the map that we do not see before us is blank. The world in our conceit of it is not much bigger than a nutshell. It is not one prospect expanded into another, county joined to county, kingdom to kingdom, land to seas, making an image voluminous and vast ;—the mind can form no larger idea of space than the eye can take in at a single glance. The rest is a name written in a map, a calculation of arithmetic. For instance, what is the true signification of that immense mass of territory and population, known by the name of China to us? An inch of pasteboard on a wooden globe, of no more account than a China orange! Things near us are seen of the size of life : things at a distance are diminished to the size of the understanding. We measure the universe by ourselves, and even comprehend the texture of our own being only piecemeal. In this way, however, we remember an infinity of things and places. The mind is like a mechanical instrument that plays a great variety of tunes, but it must play them in succession. One idea recalls another, but it at the same time excludes all others. In trying to renew old recollections, we cannot as it were unfold the whole web of our existence ; we must pick out the single threads. So in coming to a place where we have formerly lived, and with which we have intimate associations, every one must have found that the feeling grows more vivid the nearer we approach the spot, from the mere anticipation of the actual impression : we remember circumstances, feelings, persons, faces, names that we had not thought of for years ; but for the time all the rest of the world is forgotten !—To return to the question I have quitted above :—

I have no objection to go to see ruins, aqueducts, pictures, in company with a friend or a party, but rather the contrary, for the former reason reversed. They are intelligible matters, and will bear talking about. The sentiment here is not tacit.

but communicable and overt. Salisbury Plain is barren of criticism, but Stonehenge will bear a discussion antiquarian, picturesque, and philosophical. In setting out on a party of pleasure, the first consideration always is where we shall go to : in taking a solitary ramble, the question is what we shall meet with by the way. "The mind is its own place ; " nor are we anxious to arrive at the end of our journey. I can myself do the honours indifferently well to works of art and curiosity. I once took a party to Oxford with no mean *éclat*—showed them that seat of the Muses at a distance,

" With glistering spires and pinnacles adorn'd "—

descanted on the learned air that breathes from the grassy quadrangles and stone walls of halls and cottages—was at home in the Bodleian ; and at Blenheim quite superseded the powdered Cicerone that attended us, and that pointed in vain with his wand to commonplace beauties in matchless pictures. As another exception to the above reasoning, I should not feel confident in venturing on a journey in a foreign country without a companion. I should want at intervals to hear the sound of my own language. There is an involuntary antipathy in the mind of an Englishman to foreign manners and notions that requires the assistance of social sympathy to carry it off. As the distance from home increases, this relief, which was at first a luxury, becomes a passion and an appetite. A person would almost feel stifled to find himself in the deserts of Arabia without friends and countrymen : there must be allowed to be something in the view of Athens or old Rome that claims the utterance of speech ; and I own that the Pyramids are too mighty for any single contemplation. In such situations, so opposite to all one's ordinary train of ideas, one seems a species by one's-self, a limb torn off from society, unless one can meet with instant fellowship and support. Yet I did not feel this want or craving very pressing once, when I first set my foot on the laughing shores of France. Calais was peopled with novelty and delight. The confused, busy murmur of the place was like oil and wine poured into my ears ; nor did the Mariners' Hymn,

which was sung from the top of an old crazy vessel in the
harbour, as the sun went down, send an alien sound into my
soul. I only breathed the air of general humanity. I walked over
"the vine-covered hills and gay regions of France," erect and
satisfied ; for the image of man was not cast down and chained
to the foot of arbitrary thrones : I was at no loss for language,
for that of all the great schools of painting was open to me.
The whole is vanished like a shade. Pictures, heroes, glory,
freedom, all are fled : nothing remains but the Bourbons and the
French people !—There is undoubtedly a sensation in travelling
into foreign parts that is to be had nowhere else : but it is more
pleasing at the time than lasting. It is too remote from our
habitual associations to be a common topic of discourse or
reference, and, like a dream or another state of existence, does
not piece into our daily modes of life. It is an animated but a
momentary hallucination. It demands an effort to exchange our
actual for our ideal identity ; and to feel the pulse of our old
transports revive very keenly, we must "jump" all our present
comforts and connections. Our romantic and itinerant character is not to be domesticated. Dr. Johnson remarked how
little foreign travel added to the facilities of conversation in
those who had been abroad. In fact, the time we have spent
there is both delightful, and, in one sense, instructive ; but it
appears to be cut out of our substantial, downright existence,
and never to join kindly on to it. We are not the same, but
another, and perhaps more enviable individual, all the time we
are out of our own country. We are lost to ourselves, as well
as our friends. So the poet somewhat quaintly sings,

"Out of my country and myself I go."

Those who wish to forget painful thoughts, do well to absent
themselves for a while from the ties and objects that recall
them : but we can be said only to fulfil our destiny in the place
that gave us birth. I should on this account like well
enough to spend the whole of my life in travelling abroad,
if I could anywhere borrow another life to spend afterwards at
home !

ON THE PROSE-STYLE OF POETS.

"Do you read or sing?   If you sing, you sing very ill.

I HAVE but an indifferent opinion of the prose-style of poets : not that it is not sometimes good, nay, excellent ; but it is never the better, and generally the worse, from the habit of writing verse. Poets are winged animals, and can cleave the air, like birds, with ease to themselves and delight to the beholders ; but like those "feathered, two-legged things," when they light upon the ground of prose and matter-of-fact, they seem not to have the same use of their feet.

What is a little extraordinary, there is a want of *rhythmus* and cadence in what they write without the help of metrical rules. Like persons who have been accustomed to sing to music, they are at a loss in the absence of the habitual accompaniment and guide to their judgment. Their style halts, totters, is loose, disjointed, and without expressive pauses or rapid movements. The measured cadence and regular *sing-song* of rhyme or blank verse have destroyed, as it were, their natural ear for the mere characteristic harmony which ought to subsist between the sound and the sense. I should almost guess the Author of *Waverley* to be a writer of ambling verses from the desultory vacillation and want of firmness in the march of his style. There is neither *momentum* nor elasticity in it ; I mean as to the *score*, or effect upon the ear. He has improved since in his other works : to be sure, he has had practice enough. Poets either get into this incoherent, undetermined, shuffling style, made up of "unpleasing flats and sharps," of unaccountable starts and pauses, of doubtful odds and ends, flirted about like straws in a gust of wind ; or, to avoid it and steady themselves, mount into a sustained and measured prose (like the translation of Ossian's *Poems*, or some parts of Shaftes-bury's *Characteristics*) which is more odious still, and as bad as being at sea in a calm. Dr. Johnson's style (particularly in his *Rambler*) is not free from the last objection. There is a tone in it, a mechanical recurrence of the same rise and fall in the clauses of his sentences, independent of any reference to the meaning of the text, or progress or inflection of the sense. There is the alternate roll of his cumbrous cargo of words ; his periods complete their revolutions at certain stated intervals, let the matter be longer or shorter, rough or smooth, round or square, different or the same. This monotonous and balanced mode of composition may be compared to that species of portrait-painting which prevailed about a century ago, in which each face was cast in a regular and preconceived mould. The eyebrows were arched mathematically as if with a pair of com-passes, and the distances between the nose and mouth, the forehead and chin, determined according to a " foregone con-clusion," and the features of the identical individual were after-wards accommodated to them, how they could !*

Horne Tooke used to maintain that no one could write a good prose style who was not accustomed to express himself *vivâ voce*, or to talk in company. He argued that this was the fault of Addison's prose, and that its smooth, equable uniformity, and want of sharpness and spirit, arose from his not having familiarised his ear to the sound of his own voice, or at least only among his friends and admirers, where there was but little collision, dramatic fluctuation, or sudden contrariety of opinion to provoke animated discussion, and give birth to different intonations and lively transitions of speech. His style (in this view of it) was not indented, nor did it project from the surface. There was no stress laid on one word more than another—it did not hurry on or stop short, or sink or swell with the occasion :

* See the portraits of Kneller, Richardson, and others.

it was throughout equally insipid, flowing, and harmonious, and had the effect of a studied recitation rather than of a natural discourse.   This would not have happened (so the Member for Old Sarum contended) had Addison laid himself out to argue at his club, or to speak in public ; for then his ear would have caught the necessary modulations of sound arising out of the feeling of the moment, and he would have transferred them unconsciously to paper.   Much might be said on both sides of this question :* but Mr. Tooke was himself an unintentional confirmation of his own argument ; for the tone of his written compositions is as flat and unraised as his manner of speaking was hard and dry.   Of the poet it is said by some one, that

> " He murmurs by the running brooks
> A music sweeter than their own. "

On the contrary, the celebrated person just alluded to might be said to grind the sentences between his teeth which he after-wards committed to paper, and threw out crusts to the critics, or *bon-mots* to the Electors of Westminster (as we throw bones to the dogs) without altering a muscle, and without the smallest tremulousness of voice or eye !†   I certainly so far agree with the above theory as to conceive that no style is worth a farthing that is not calculated to be read out, or that is not allied to spirited conversation : but I at the same time think the process of modulation and inflection may be quite as complete, or more so, without the external enunciation ; and that an author had better try the effect of his sentences on his stomach than on his

---

* Goldsmith was not a talker, though he blurted out his good things now and then : yet his style is gay and voluble enough.   Pope was also a silent man ; and his prose is timid and constrained, and his verse inclining to the monotonous.

† As a singular example of steadiness of nerves, Mr. Tooke on one occasion had got upon the table at a public dinner to return thanks for his health having been drunk.   He held a bumper of wine in his hand, but he was received with considerable opposition by one party, and at the end of the disturbance, which lasted for a quarter of an hour, he found the wine glass still full to the brim.

ear. He may be deceived by the last, not by the first. No
person, I imagine, can dictate a good style, or spout his own
compositions with impunity. In the former case, he will
flounder on before the sense or words are ready, sooner than
suspend his voice in air ; and in the latter, he can supply what
intonation he pleases, without consulting his readers. Parliamentary speeches sometimes read well aloud ; but we do not
find, when such persons sit down to write, that the prose-
style of public speakers and great orators is the best, most
natural, or varied of all others. It has almost always either
a professional twang, a mechanical rounding off, or else
is stunted and unequal. Charles Fox was the most rapid
and even *hurried* of speakers ; but his written style halts and
creeps slowly along the ground.* A speaker is necessarily kept
within bounds in expressing certain things, or in pronouncing a
certain number of words, by the limits of the breath or power of
respiration : certain sounds are observed to join in harmoniously
or happily with others : an emphatic phrase must not be placed
where the power of utterance is enfeebled or exhausted, etc.
All this must be attended to in writing (and will be so unconsciously by a practised hand), or there will be *hiatus in*

* I have been told, that when Sheridan was first introduced to Mr.
Fox, what cemented an immediate intimacy between them was the
following circumstance. Mr. Sheridan had been the night before to
the House of Commons; and being asked what his impression was,
said he had been principally struck with the difference of manner
between Mr. Fox and Lord Stormont. The latter began by declaring
in a slow, solemn, drawling, nasal tone that "when he considered the
enormity and the unconstitutional tendency of the measures just proposed, he was hurried away in a torrent of passion and a whirlwind of
impetuosity," pausing between every word and syllable; while the first
said (speaking with the rapidity of lightning, and with breathless
anxiety and impatience), that "such was the magnitude, such the
importance, such the vital interest of this question, that he could not
help imploring, he could not help adjuring the House to come to it
with the utmost calmness, the utmost coolness, the utmost deliberation." This trait of discrimination instantly won Mr. Fox's heart.

manuscriptis. The words must be so arranged, in order to make an efficient readable style, as " to come trippingly off the tongue." Hence it seems that there is a natural measure of prose in the feeling of the subject and the power of expression in the voice, as there is an artificial one of verse in the number and co-ordination of the syllables ; and I conceive that the trammels of the last do not (where they have been long worn) greatly assist the freedom or the exactness of the first.

Again, in poetry, from the restraints in many respects, a greater number of inversions, or a latitude in the transposition of words is allowed, which is not conformable to the strict laws of prose. Consequently, a poet will be at a loss, and flounder about for the common or (as we understand it) *natural* order of words in prose-composition. Dr. Johnson endeavoured to give an air of dignity and novelty to his diction by affecting the order of words usual in poetry. Milton's prose has not only this drawback, but it has also the disadvantage of being formed on a classic model. It is like a fine translation from the Latin ; and indeed, he wrote originally in Latin. The frequency of epithets and ornaments, too, is a resource for which the poet finds it difficult to obtain an equivalent. A direct, or simple prose-style seems to him bald and flat ; and instead of forcing an interest in the subject by severity of description and reasoning, he is repelled from it altogether by the absence of those obvious and meretricious allurements by which his senses and his imagination have been hitherto stimulated and dazzled. Thus there is often at the same time a want of splendour and a want of energy in what he writes, without the invocation of the Muse—*invita Minervâ.* It is like setting a rope-dancer to perform a tumbler's tricks—the hardness of the ground jars his nerves ; or it is the same thing as a painter's attempting to carve a block of marble for the first time—the coldness chills him, the colourless uniformity distracts him, the precision of form demanded disheartens him. So in prose writing, the severity of composition required damps the enthusiasm, and cuts off the resources of the poet. He is looking for beauty when he should be seeking for truth ; and aims at pleasure, which he can only communicate by increasing the sense of power in the reader. The poet spreads the colours of fancy, the illusions of his own mind, round every object, *ad libitum;* the prose-writer is compelled to extract his materials patiently, and bit by bit, from his subject. What he adds of ornament, what he borrows from the pencil, must be sparing, and judiciously inserted. The first pretends to nothing but the immediate indulgence of his feelings : the last has a remote practical purpose. The one strolls out into the adjoining fields or groves to gather flowers : the other has a journey to go, sometimes through dirty roads, and at others through untrodden and difficult ways. It is this effeminacy, this immersion in sensual ideas, or craving after continual excitement, that spoils the poet for his prose-tasks. He cannot wait till the effect comes of itself, or arises out of the occasion : he must force it upon all occasions, or his spirit droops and flags under a supposed imputation of dulness. He can never drift with the current, but is always hoisting sail, and has his streamers flying. He has got a striking simile on hand; he *lugs* it in with the first opportunity, and with little connexion, and so defeats his object. He has a story to tell : he tells it in the first page, and where it would come in well, has nothing to say ; like Goldsmith, who having to wait upon a Noble Lord, was so full of himself and of the figure he should make, that he addressed a set speech, which he had studied for the occasion, to his Lordship's butler, and had just ended as the nobleman made his appearance. The prose-ornaments of the poet are frequently beautiful in themselves, but do not assist the subject. They are pleasing excrescences—hindrances, not helps in an argument. The reason is, his embellishments in his own walk grow out of the subject by natural association ; that is, beauty gives birth to kindred beauty, grandeur leads the mind on to greater grandeur. But in treating a common subject, the link is truth, force of illustration, weight of argument, not a graceful harmony in the immediate ideas ; and hence the obvious and habitual clue which before guided him is gone, and he hangs on his patchwork, tinsel finery at random, in despair, without propriety, and without effect. The poetical prose-writer stops to describe an object, if he admires it, or thinks it will bear to be dwelt on : the genuine prose-writer only alludes to or characterises it in passing, and with reference to his subject. The prose-writer is master of his materials : the poet is the slave of his style. Everything showy, everything extraneous tempts him, and he reposes idly on it : he is bent on pleasure, not on business. He aims at effect, at captivating the reader, and yet is contented with commonplace ornaments, rather than none. Indeed, this last result must necessarily follow, where there is an ambition to shine, without the effort to dig for jewels in the mine of truth. The habits of a poet's mind are not those of industry or research : his images come to him, he does not go to them ; and in prose-subjects, and dry matters-of-fact and close reasoning, the natural stimulus that at other times warms and rouses, deserts him altogether. He sees no unhallowed visions, he is inspired by no day-dreams. All is tame, literal, and barren, without the Nine. Nor does he collect his strength to strike fire from the flint by the sharpness of collison, by the eagerness of his blows. He gathers roses, he steals colours from the rainbow. He lives on nectar and ambrosia. He "treads the primrose path of dalliance," or ascends "the highest heaven of invention," or falls flat to the ground. *He is nothing, if not fanciful!*

I shall proceed to explain these remarks, as well as I can, by a few instances in point.

It has always appeared to me that the most perfect prose-style, the most powerful, the most dazzling, the most daring, that which went the nearest to the verge of poetry, and yet never fell over, was Burke's. It has the solidity and sparkling effect of the diamond : all other *fine writing* is like French paste or Bristol-stones in the comparison. Burke's style is airy, flighty, adventurous, but it never loses sight of the subject ; nay, is always in contact with, and derives its increased or varying impulse from it. It may be said to pass yawning gulfs "on the unsteadfast footing of a spear;" still it has an actual resting-place and tangible support under it—it is not suspended on nothing. It differs from poetry, as I conceive, like the chamois from the eagle; it climbs to an almost equal height, touches upon a cloud, overlooks a precipice, is picturesque, sublime—but all the while, instead of soaring through the air, it stands upon a rocky cliff, clambers up by abrupt and intricate ways, and browses on the roughest bark, or crops the tender flower. The principle which guides his pen is truth, not beauty—not pleasure, but power. He has no choice, no selection of subject to flatter the reader's idle taste, or assist his own fancy: he must take what comes, and make the most of it. He works the most striking effects out of the most unpromising materials, by the mere activity of his mind. He rises with the lofty, descends with the mean, luxuriates in beauty, gloats over deformity It is all the same to him, so that he loses no particle of the exact, characteristic, extreme impression of the thing he writes about, and that he communicates this to the reader, after exhausting every possible mode of illustration, plain or abstracted, figurative or literal. Whatever stamps the original image more distinctly on the mind is welcome. The nature of his task precludes continual beauty; but it does not preclude continual ingenuity, force, originality. He had to treat of political questions, mixed modes, abstract ideas, and his fancy (or poetry, if you will) was ingrafted on these artificially, and as it might sometimes be thought, violently, instead of growing naturally out of them, as it would spring of its own accord from individual objects and feelings. There is a resistance in the *matter* to the illustration applied to it—the concrete and abstract are hardly co-ordinate; and therefore it is that, when the first difficulty is overcome, they must agree more closely in the essential qualities, in order that the coincidence may be complete. Otherwise, it is good for nothing; and you justly charge the author's style with being loose, vague, flaccid, and imbecile. The poet has been said

> "To make us heirs
> Of truth and pure delight in endless lays.'

Not so the prose-writer, who always mingles clay with his gold, and often separates truth from mere pleasure. He can only arrive at the last through the first. In poetry, one pleasing or striking image obviously suggests another : the increasing the sense of beauty or grandeur is the principle of composition : in prose, the professed object is to impart conviction, and nothing can be admitted by way of ornament or relief that does not add new force or clearness to the original conception. The two classes of ideas brought together by the orator or impassioned prose-writer, to wit, the general subject and the particular image, are so far incompatible, and the identity must be more strict, more marked, more determinate, to make them coalesce to any practical purpose. Every word should be a blow : every thought should instantly grapple with its fellow. There must be a weight, a precision, a conformity from association in the tropes and figures of animated prose to fit them to their place in the argument, and make them *tell,* which may be dispensed with in poetry, where there is something much more congenial between the subject-matter and the illustration—

"Like beauty making beautiful old rime !"

What can be more remote, for instance, and at the same time more apposite, more *the same,* than the following comparison of the English Constitution to "the proud Keep of Windsor," in the celebrated *Letter to a Noble Lord?*

"Such are *their* ideas ; such *their* religion, and such *their* law. But as to *our* country and *our* race, as long as the well-compacted structure of our Church and State, the sanctuary, the holy of holies of that ancient law, defended by reverence, defended by power—a fortress at once and a temple*—shall stand inviolate on the brow of the British Zion ; as long as the British Monarchy—not more limited than fenced by the orders of the State—shall, like the proud Keep of Windsor, rising in the majesty of proportion, and girt with the double belt of its

---

* "Templum in modum arcis."
      —*Tacitus, of the Temple of Jerusalem.*

kindred and coeval towers ; as long as this awful structure shall oversee and guard the subjected land, so long the mounds and dykes of the low, fat, Bedford level will have nothing to fear from all the pickaxes of all the levellers of France. As long as our Sovereign Lord the King, and his faithful subjects, the Lords and Commons of this realm—the triple cord which no man can break ; the solemn, sworn, constitutional frank-pledge of this nation ; the firm guarantees of each other's being, and each other's rights ; the joint and several securities, each in its place and order, for every kind, and every quality of property and of dignity—as long as these endure, so long the Duke of Bedford is safe : and we are all safe together—the high from the blights of envy and the spoliations of rapacity ; the low from the iron hand of oppression and the insolent spurn of contempt. Amen ! and so be it : and so it will be,

'Dum domus Æneæ Capitoli immobile saxum
Accolet ; imperiumque pater Romanus habebit.' "

Nothing can well be more impracticable to a simile than the vague and complicated idea which is here embodied in one ; yet how finely, how nobly it stands out, in natural grandeur, in royal state, with double barriers round it to answer for its identity, with "buttress, frieze, and coigne of 'vantage" for the imagination to "make its pendant bed and procreant cradle," till the idea is confounded with the object representing it—the wonder of a kingdom ; and then how striking, how determined the descent, "at one fell swoop," to the "low, fat, Bedford level !" Poetry would have been bound to maintain a certain decorum, a regular balance between these two ideas ; sterling prose throws aside all such idle respect to appearances, and with its pen, like a sword, "sharp and sweet," lays open the naked truth ! The poet's Muse is like a mistress, whom we keep only while she is young and beautiful, *durante bene placito ;* the Muse of prose is like a wife, whom we take during life, *for better for worse.* Burke's execution, like that of all good prose, savours of the texture of what he describes, and his pen slides or drags over the ground of his subject, like the painter's pencil. The most rigid fidelity and the most fanciful extravagance meet, and are reconciled in his pages. I never pass Windsor but I think of this passage in Burke, and hardly know to which I am indebted most for enriching my moral sense, that, or the fine picturesque stanza in Gray,

> " From Windsor's heights the expanse below
> Of mead, of lawn, of wood survey," etc.

I might mention that the so-much-admired description, in one of the India speeches, of Hyder Ally's army (I think it is) which "now hung like a cloud upon the mountain, and now burst upon the plain like a thunderbolt," would do equally well for poetry or prose. It is a bold and striking illustration of a naturally impressive object. This is not the case with the Abbe Sieyes's far-famed "pigeon-holes," nor with the comparison of the Duke of Bedford to "the Leviathan, tumbling about his unwieldy bulk in the ocean of royal bounty." Nothing here saves the description but the force of the invective ; the startling truth, the vehemence, the remoteness, the aptitude, the perfect peculiarity and coincidence of the allusion. No writer would ever have thought of it but himself ; no reader can ever forget it. What is there in common, one might say, between a Peer of the Realm, and "that sea-beast," of those

> "Created hugest that swim the ocean-stream?"

Yet Burke has knit the two ideas together, and no man can put them asunder. No matter how slight and precarious the connection, the length of line it is necessary for the fancy to give out in keeping hold of the object on which it has fastened, he seems to have "put his hook in the nostrils" of this enormous creature of the crown, that empurples all its track through the glittering expanse of a profound and restless imagination !

To my taste, the Author of *Rimini*, and Editor of the *Examiner*, is among the best and least corrupted of our poetical prose-writers. In his light but well-supported columns we find the raciness, the sharpness, and sparkling effect of poetry, with little that is extravagant or far-fetched, and no turgidity or pompous pretension. Perhaps there is too much the appearance of relaxation and trifling (as if he had escaped the shackles of rhyme), a caprice, a levity, and a disposition to innovate in words and ideas. Still the genuine master-spirit of the prose-writer is there ; the tone of lively, sensible conversation ; and this may in part arise from the author's being himself an animated talker. Mr. Hunt wants something of the heat and earnestness of the political partisan ; but his familiar and miscellaneous papers have all the ease, grace, and point of the best style of Essay-writing. Many of his effusions in the *Indicator* show, that if he had devoted himself exclusively to that mode of writing, he inherits more of the spirit of Steele than any man since his time.

Lord Byron's prose is bad ; that is to say, heavy, laboured, and coarse : he tries to knock some one down with the butt-end of every line, which defeats his object—and the style of the Author of *Waverley* (if he comes fairly into this discussion) as mere style is villainous. It is pretty plain he is a poet ; for the sound of names runs mechanically in his ears, and he rings the changes unconsciously on the same words in a sentence, like the same rhymes in a couplet.

Not to spin out this discussion too much, I would conclude by observing, that some of the old English prose-writers (who were not poets) are the best, and, at the same time, the most *poetical* in the favourable sense. Among these we may reckon some of the old divines, and Jeremy Taylor at the head of them. There is a flush like the dawn over his writings ; the sweetness of the rose, the freshness of the morning dew. There is a softness in his style, proceeding from the tenderness of his heart : but his head is firm, and his hand is free. His materials are as finely wrought up as they are original and attractive in themselves. Milton's prose-style savours too much of poetry, and, as I have already hinted, of an imitation of the Latin. Dryden's is perfectly unexceptionable, and a model, in simplicity, strength, and perspicuity, for the subjects he treated of.

WHETHER GENIUS IS CONSCIOUS OF ITS POWERS?

No really great man ever thought himself so. The idea of greatness in the mind answers but ill to our knowledge—or to our ignorance of ourselves. What living prose-writer, for instance, would think of comparing himself with Burke? Yet would it not have been equal presumption or egotism in him to fancy himself equal to those who had gone before him— Bolingbroke, or Johnson, or Sir William Temple? Because his rank in letters is become a settled point with us, we conclude that it must have been quite as self-evident to him, and that he must have been perfectly conscious of his vast superiority to the rest of the world. Alas! not so. No man is truly himself but in the idea which others entertain of him. The mind, as well as the eye, "sees not itself, but by reflection from some other thing." What parity can there be between the effect of habitual composition on the mind of the individual, and the surprise occasioned by first reading a fine passage in an admired author; between what we do with ease, and what we thought it next to impossible ever to have done; between the reverential awe we have for years encouraged, without seeing reason to alter it, for distinguished genius, and the slow, reluctant, unwelcome conviction that after infinite toil and repeated disappointments, and when it is too late and to little purpose, we have ourselves at length accomplished what we at first proposed; between the insignificance of our petty, personal pretensions, and the vastness and splendour which the atmosphere of imagination lends to an illustrious name? He who

comes up to his own idea of greatness must always have
had a very low standard of it in his mind. "What a pity,"
said some one, "that Milton had not the pleasure of reading 'Paradise Lost!'" He could not read it as we do,
with the weight of impression that a hundred years of admiration have added to it—"a phœnix gazed by all"—with the
sense of the number of editions it has passed through with
still increasing reputation, with the tone of solidity, time-proof,
which it has received from the breath of cold, envious
maligners, with the sound which the voice of Fame has lent
to every line of it! The writer of an ephemeral production
may be as much dazzled with it as the public: it may sparkle
in his own eyes for a moment, and be soon forgotten by every
one else. But no one can anticipate the suffrages of posterity.
Every man, in judging of himself, is his own contemporary.
He may feel the gale of popularity, but he cannot tell how long
it will last. His opinion of himself wants distance, wants time,
wants numbers, to set it off and confirm it. He must be
indifferent to his own merits before he can feel a confidence
in them. Besides, everyone must be sensible of a thousand
weaknesses and deficiencies in himself; whereas Genius only
leaves behind it the monuments of its strength. A great name
is an abstraction of some one excellence: but whoever fancies
himself an abstraction of excellence, so far from being great,
may be sure that he is a blockhead, equally ignorant of
excellence or defect, of himself or others. Mr. Burke, besides
being the author of the *Reflections*, and the *Letter to a Noble
Lord*, had a wife and son; and had to think as much about
them as we do about him. The imagination gains nothing by
the minute details of personal knowledge.

On the other hand, it may be said that no man knows so well
as the author of any performance what it has cost him, and the
length of time and study devoted to it. This is one, among
other reasons, why no man can pronounce an opinion upon
himself. The happiness of the result bears no proportion
to the difficulties overcome or the pains taken. *Materiam
superabat opus* (the workmanship surpasses the materials) is

an old and fatal complaint. The definition of genius is that it acts unconsciously; and those who have produced immortal works have done so without knowing how or why. The greatest power operates unseen, and executes its appointed task with as little ostentation as difficulty. Whatever is done best is done from the natural bent and disposition of the mind. It is only where our incapacity begins that we begin to feel the obstacles, and to set an undue value on our triumph over them. Correggio, Michael Angelo, Rembrandt, did what they did without premeditation or effort—their works came from their minds as a natural birth—if you had asked them why they adopted this or that style, they would have answered, *because they could not help it*, and because they knew of no other. So Shakespeare says :—

> " Our poesy is as a gum which oozes
> From whence 'tis nourished : the fire i' the flint
> Shows not till it be struck : our gentle flame
> Provokes itself; and, like the current, flies
> Each bound it chafes."

Shakespeare himself was an example of his own rule, and appears to have owed almost everything to industry or design. His poetry flashes from him like the lightning from the summer-cloud, or the stroke from the sun-flower. When we look at the admirable comic designs of Hogarth, they seem from the unfinished state in which they are left, and from the freedom of the pencilling, to have cost him little trouble ; whereas the " Sigismunda " is a very laboured and comparatively feeble performance, and he accordingly set great store by it. He also thought highly of his portraits, and boasted that " he could paint equal to Vandyke, give him his time, and let him choose his subject." This was the very reason why he could not. Vandyke's excellence consisted in this, that he could paint a fine portrait of anyone at sight : let him take ever so much pains or choose ever so bad a subject, he could not help making something of it. His eye, his mind, his hand was cast in the mould of grace and delicacy. Milton, again, is understood to

have preferred "Paradise Regained" to his other works. This,
if so, was either because he himself was conscious of having
failed in it, or because others thought he had. We are willing to
think well of that which we know wants our favourable opinion,
and to prop the rickety bantling. Every step taken, *invitâ
Minerva*, costs us something, and is set down to account ;
whereas we are borne on the full tide of genius and success into
the very haven of our desires almost imperceptibly. The
strength of the impulse by which we are carried along prevents
the sense of difficulty or resistance : the true inspiration of the
Muse is soft and balmy as the air we breathe ; and indeed
leaves us little to boast of, for the effect hardly seems to be our
own.

There are two persons who always appear to me to have
worked under this involuntary, silent impulse more than any
others ; I mean Rembrandt and Correggio. It is not known
that Correggio ever saw a picture of any great master. He
lived and died obscurely in an obscure village. We have few of
his works, but they are all perfect. What truth, what grace,
what angelic sweetness are there ! Not one line or tone that is
not divinely soft or exquisitely fair ; the painter's mind rejecting,
by a natural process, all that is discordant, coarse, or unpleasing.
The whole is an emanation of pure thought. The work grew
under his hand as if of itself, and came out without a flaw, like
the diamond from the rock. He knew not what he did ; and
looked at each modest grace as it stole from the canvas with
anxious delight and wonder. Ah ! gracious God ! not he alone ;
how many more in all time have looked at their works with the
same feelings, not knowing but they too may have done something divine, immortal, and finding in that sole doubt ample
amends for pining solitude, for want, neglect, and an untimely
fate. Oh ! for one hour of that uneasy rapture, when the mind
first thinks that it has struck out something that may last for
ever ; when the germ of excellence bursts from nothing on the
startled sight ! Take, take away the gaudy triumphs of the
world, the long deathless shout of fame, and give back that
heartfelt sigh with which the youthful enthusiast first weds

immortality as his secret bride! And thou too, Rembrandt! Thou wert a man of genius if ever painter was a man of genius!—did this dream hang over you as you painted that strange picture of "Jacob's Ladder?" Did your eye strain over those gradual dusky clouds into futurity, or did those white-vested, beaked figures babble to you of fame as they approached? Did you know what you were about, or did you not paint much as it happened? Oh! if you had thought once about yourself, or anything but the subject, it would have been all over with "the glory, the intuition, the amenity," the dream had fled, the spell had been broken. The hills would not have looked like those we see in sleep—that tatterdemalion figure of Jacob, thrown on one side, would not have slept as if the breath was fairly taken out of his body. So much do Rembrandt's pictures savour of the soul and body of reality, that the thoughts seem identical with the objects—if there had been the least question what he should have done, or how he should do it, or how far he had succeeded, it would have spoiled everything. Lumps of light hung upon his pencil and fell upon his canvas like dew-drops: the shadowy veil was drawn over his backgrounds by the dull, obtuse finger of night, making darkness visible by still greater darkness that could only be felt!

Cervantes is another instance of a man of genius, whose work may be said to have sprung from his mind, like Minerva from the head of Jupiter. Don Quixote and Sancho were a kind of twins; and the jests of the latter, as he says, fell from him like drops of rain when he least thought of it. Shakespeare's creations were more multiform, but equally natural and un-studied. Raphael and Milton seem partial exceptions to this rule. Their productions were the *composite order;* and those of the latter sometimes even amount to centos. Accordingly, we find Milton quoted among those authors who have left proofs of their entertaining a high opinion of themselves, and of cherishing a strong aspiration after fame. Some of Shakespeare's sonnets have been also cited to the same purpose; but they seem rather to convey wayward and dissatisfied complaints of his untoward fortune than anything like a triumphant and confident reliance on his future renown. He appears to have stood more alone and to have thought less about himself than any living being. One reason for this indifference may have been, that as a writer he was tolerably successful in his life-time, and no doubt produced his works with very great facility.

I hardly know whether to class Claude Lorraine as among those who succeeded most "through happiness or pains." It is certain that he imitated no one, and has had no successful imitator. The perfection of his landscapes seems to have been owing to an inherent quality of harmony, to an exquisite sense of delicacy in his mind. His monotony has been complained of, which is apparently produced from a preconceived idea in his mind ; and not long ago I heard a person, not more distinguished for the subtilty than the *naïveté* of his sarcasms, remark, "Oh ! I never look at Claude : if one has seen one of his pictures, one has seen them all ; they are every one alike : there is the same sky, the same climate, the same time of day, the same tree, and that tree is like a cabbage. To be sure, they say he did pretty well ; but when a man is always doing one thing, he ought to do it pretty well." There is no occasion to write the name under this criticism, and the best answer to it is that it is true—his pictures always are the same, but we never wish them to be otherwise. Perfection is one thing. I confess I think that Claude knew this, and felt that his were the finest landscapes in the world—that ever had been, or would ever be.

I am not in the humour to pursue this argument any farther at present, but to write a digression. If the reader is not already apprised of it, he will please to take notice that I write this at Winterslow. My style there is apt to be redundant and excursive. At other times it may be cramped, dry, abrupt ; but here it flows like a river, and overspreads its banks. I have not to seek for thoughts or hunt for images : they come of themselves, I inhale them with the breeze, and the silent groves are vocal with a thousand recollections—

" And visions, as poetic eyes avow,
  Hang on each leaf, and cling to ev'ry bough."

Here I came fifteen years ago, a willing exile; and as I trod the lengthened greensward by the low woodside, repeated the old line,

"My mind to me a kingdom is!"

I found it so then, before, and since; and shall I faint, now that I have poured out the spirit of that mind to the world, and treated many subjects with truth, with freedom, and power, because I have been followed with one cry of abuse ever since *for not being a Government tool?* Here I returned a few years after to finish some works I had undertaken, doubtful of the event, but determined to do my best; and wrote that character of Millimant which was once transcribed by fingers fairer than Aurora's, but no notice was taken of it, because I was not a Government tool, and must be supposed devoid of taste and elegance by all who aspired to these qualities in their own persons. Here I sketched my account of that old honest Signior Orlando Friscobaldo, which with its fine, racy, acrid tone that old crab-apple, Gifford, would have relished or pretended to relish, had I been a Government tool! Here, too, I have written *Table-Talks* without number, and as yet without a falling-off, till now that they are nearly done, or I should not make this boast. I could swear (were they not mine) the thoughts in many of them are founded as the rock, free as air, the tone like an Italian picture. What then? Had the style been like polished steel, as firm and as bright, it would have availed me nothing, for I am not a Government tool! I had endeavoured to guide the taste of the English people to the best old English writers; but I had said that English kings did not reign by right divine, and that his present Majesty was descended from an Elector of Hanover in a right line; and no loyal subject would after this look into Webster or Decker because I had pointed them out. I had done something (more than anyone except Schlegel) to vindicate the *Characters of Shakespeare's Plays* from the stigma of French criticism: but our Anti-Jacobin and Anti-Gallican writers soon found out that I had said and written that Frenchmen, Englishmen, men were not slaves by birthright. This was enough to *damn* the work. Such has been the head and front of my offending. While my friend Leigh Hunt was writing the *Descent of Liberty*, and strewing the march of the Allied Sovereigns with flowers, I sat by the waters of Babylon and hung my harp upon the willows. I knew all along there was but one alternative—the cause of kings or of mankind. This I foresaw, this I feared ; the world would see it now, when it is too late. Therefore I lamented, and would take no comfort when the mighty fell, because we, all men, fell with him, like lightning from heaven, to grovel in the grave of Liberty, in the style of Legitimacy ! There is but one question in the hearts of monarchs—whether mankind are their property or not. There was but this one question in mine. I had made an abstract, metaphysical principle of this question. I was not the dupe of the voice of the charmers. By my hatred of tyrants I knew what their hatred of the freeborn spirit of man must be, of the semblance, of the very name of Liberty and Humanity. And while others bowed their heads to the image of the BEAST, I spat upon it and buffeted it, and made mouths at it, and pointed at it, and drew aside the veil that then half concealed it but has been since thrown off, and named it by its right name ; and it is not to be supposed that my having penetrated their mystery would go unrequited by those whose darling and whose delight the idol, half-brute, half-demon, was, and who were ashamed to acknowledge the image and superscription as their own ! Two half-friends of mine, who would not make a whole one between them, agreed the other day that the indiscriminate, incessant abuse of what I write was mere prejudice and party spirit, and that what I do in periodicals and without a name does well, pays well, and is " cried out upon in the top of the compass." It is this indeed that has saved my shallow skiff from quite foundering on Tory spite and rancour ; for when people have been reading and approving an article in a miscellaneous journal, it does not do to say when they discover the author afterwards (whatever might have been the case before) it is written by a blockhead ; and even Mr. Jerdan recommends the

volume of *Characteristics* as an excellent little work, because it
has no cabalistic name in the title-page, and swears "there is
a first-rate article of forty pages in the last number of the
Edinburgh from Jeffrey's own hand," though when he learns
against his will that it is mine, he devotes three successive
numbers of the *Literary Gazette* to abuse "that *strange* article
in the last number of the *Edinburgh Review.*" Others who
had not this advantage have fallen a sacrifice to the obloquy
attached to the suspicion of doubting, or of being acquainted
with anyone who is known to doubt, the divinity of kings.
Poor Keats paid the forfeit of this *lezè majesté* with his health
and life.   What, though his verses were like the breath of
spring, and many of his thoughts like flowers—would this, with
the circle of critics that beset a throne, lessen the crime of their
having been praised in the *Examiner?*   The lively and most
agreeable editor of that paper has in like manner been driven
from his country and his friends who delighted in him, for no
other reason than having written the *Story of Rimini*, and
asserted ten years ago, "that the most accomplished prince in
Europe was an Adonis of fifty!"

> "Return, Alpheus, the dread voice is past
> That shrunk thy streams ; return Sicilian Muse !"

I look out of my window and see that a shower has just fallen :
the fields look green after it, and a rosy cloud hangs over the
brow of the hill ; a lily expands its petals in the moisture,
dressed in its lovely green and white ; a shepherd boy has just
brought some pieces of turf with daisies and grass for his young
mistress to make a bed for her skylark, not doomed to dip his
wings in the dappled dawn—my cloudy thoughts draw off, the
storm of angry politics has blown over—Mr. Blackwood, I am
yours—Mr. Croker, my service to you—Mr. T. Moore, I am
alive and well—Really, it is wonderful how little the worse I
am for fifteen years' wear and tear, how I came upon my legs
again on the ground of truth and nature, and "look abroad into
universality," forgetting that there is any such person as myself
in the world !

I have let this passage stand (however critical) because it may serve as a practical illustration to show what authors really think of themselves when put upon the defensive—(I confess, the subject has nothing to do with the title at the head of the Essay I)—and as a warning to those' who may reckon upon their fair portion of popularity, as the reward of the exercise of an independent spirit and such talents as they possess. It sometimes seems at first sight as if the low scurrility and jargon of abuse by which it is attempted tó overlay all common sense and decency by the 'tissue of lies and nicknames everlastingly repeated and applied indiscriminately to all those who are not of the regular Government party, was peculiar to the present time, and the anomalous growth of modern criticism ; but if we look back, we shall find the same system acted upon as often as power, prejudice, dulness, and spite found their account in playing the game into one another's hands—in decrying popular efforts, and in giving currency to every species of base metal that had their own conventional stamp upon it. The names of Pope and Dryden were assailed with daily and unsparing abuse ; the epithet A. P. E. was levelled at the sacred head of the former ; and if even men like these, having to deal with the consciousness of their own infirmities and the insolence and spurns of wanton enmity, must have found it hard to possess their souls in patience, any living writer amidst such contradictory evidence can scarcely expect to retain much calm, steady conviction of his own merits, or build himself a secure reversion in immortality.

However one may in a fit of spleen and impatience turn round and assert one's claims in the face of low-bred, hireling malice, I will here repeat what I set out with saying, that there never yet was a man of sense and proper spirit who would not decline rather than court a comparison with any of those names whose reputation he really emulates—who would not be sorry to suppose that any of the great heirs of memory had as many foibles as he knows himself to possess—and who would not shrink from including himself or being included by others in the same praise that was offered to long-established and

universally-acknowledged merits, as a kind of profanation.
Those who are ready to fancy themselves Raphaels and
Homers are very inferior men indeed—they have not even an
idea of the mighty names that "they take in vain." They are
as deficient in pride as in modesty, and have not so much as
served an apprenticeship to a true and honourable ambition.
They mistake a momentary popularity for lasting renown, and
a sanguine temperament for the inspirations of genius. The
love of fame is too high and delicate a feeling in the mind to be
mixed up with realities—it is a solitary abstraction, the secret
sigh of the soul —

> " It is all one as we should love
> A bright particular star, and think to wed it."

A name "fast-anchored in the deep abyss of time" is like a
star twinkling in the firmament, cold, silent, distant, but eternal
and sublime ; and our transmitting one to posterity is as if we
should contemplate our translation to the skies. If we are not
contented with this feeling on the subject, we shall never sit in
Cassiopeia's chair, nor will our names, studding Ariadne's
crown or streaming with Berenice's locks, ever make

> " the face of heaven so bright,
> That birds shall sing, and think it were not night."

Those who are in love only with noise and show, instead of
devoting themselves to a life of study, had better hire a booth
at Bartlemy Fair, or march at the head of a recruiting regiment
with drums beating and colours flying !

It has been urged, that however little we may be disposed to
indulge the reflection at other times or out of mere self-
complacency, yet the mind cannot help being conscious of the
effort required for any great work while it is about it, of

> " The high endeavour and the glad success."

I grant that there is a sense of power in such cases, with the
exception before stated ; but then this very effort and state
of excitement engrosses the mind at the time, and leaves it

listless and exhausted afterwards. The energy we exert, or the high state of enjoyment we feel, puts us out of conceit with ourselves at other times : compared to what we are in the act of composition, we seem dull, commonplace people, generally speaking ; and what we have been able to perform is rather matter of wonder than of self-congratulation to us. The stimulus of writing is like the stimulus of intoxication, with which we can hardly sympathise in our sober moments, when we are no longer under the inspiration of the demon, or when the virtue is gone out of us. While we are engaged in any work, we are thinking of the subject, and cannot stop to admire ourselves ; and when it is done, we look at it with comparative indifference. I will venture to say, that no one but a pedant ever read his own works regularly through. They are not *his*—they are become mere words, waste-paper, and have none of the glow, the creative enthusiasm, the vehemence, and natural spirit with which he wrote them. When we have once committed our thoughts to paper, written them fairly out, and seen that they are right in the printing, if we are in our right wits, we have done with them for ever. I sometimes try to read an article I have written in some magazine or review—(for when they are bound up in a volume, I dread the very sight of them) —but stop after a sentence or two, and never recur to the task. I know pretty well what I have to say on the subject, and do not want to go to school to myself. It is the worst instance of the *bis repetita crambe* in the world. I do not think that even painters have much delight in looking at their works after they are done. While they are in progress, there is a great degree of satisfaction in considering what has been done, or what is still to do—but this is hope, is reverie, and ceases with the completion of our efforts. I should not imagine Raphael or Correggio would have much pleasure in looking at their former works, though they might recollect the pleasure they had had in painting them ; they might spy defects in them (for the idea of unattainable perfection still keeps pace with our actual approaches to it), and fancy that they were not worthy of immortality. The greatest portrait-painter the world ever saw used to write under his pictures, " *Titianus faciebat*," signifying that they were imperfect ; and in his letter to Charles V. accompanying one of his most admired works, he only spoke of the time he had been about it. Annibal Caracci boasted that he could do like Titian and Correggio, and, like most boasters, was wrong.*

The greatest pleasure in life is that of reading, while we are young. I have had as much of this pleasure as perhaps anyone. As I grow older, it fades ; or else, the stronger stimulus of writing takes off the edge of it. At present, I have neither time nor inclination for it : yet I should like to devote a year's entire leisure to a course of the English Novelists ; and perhaps clap on that sly old knave, Sir Walter, to the end of the list. It is astonishing how I used formerly to relish the style of certain authors, at a time when I myself despaired of ever writing a single line. Probably this was the reason. It is not in mental as in natural ascent—intellectual objects seem higher when we survey them from below, than when we look down from any given elevation above the common level. My three favourite writers about the time I speak of were Burke, Junius, and Rousseau. I was never weary of admiring and wondering at the felicities of the style, the turns of expression, the refinements of thought and sentiment. I laid the book down to find out the secret of so much strength and beauty, and I took it up again in despair, to read on and admire. So I passed whole days, months, and I may add, years ; and have only this to say now, that as my life began, so I could wish that it may end. The last time I tasted this luxury in its full perfection was one day after a sultry day's walk in summer between Farnham and Alton. I was fairly tired out ; I walked into an inn-yard (I think at the latter place) ; I was shown by the waiter to what looked at first like common out-houses at the other end of it, but they

* See his spirited Letter to his cousin Ludovico, on seeing the pictures at Parma.

turned out to be a suite of rooms, probably a hundred years old—the one I entered opened into an old-fashioned garden, embellished with beds of larkspur and a leaden Mercury; it was wainscoted, and there was a grave-looking, dark-coloured portrait of Charles II. hanging over the tiled chimney-piece. I had *Love for Love* in my pocket, and began to read; coffee was brought in in a silver coffee-pot; the cream, the bread and butter, everything was excellent, and the flavour of Congreve's style prevailed over all. I prolonged the entertainment till a late hour, and relished this divine comedy better even than when I used to see it played by Miss Mellon, as Miss Prue; Bob Palmer, as Tattle; and Bannister, as honest Ben. This circumstance happened just five years ago, and it seems like yesterday. If I count my life so by lustres, it will soon glide away; yet I shall not have to repine, if, while it lasts, it is enriched with a few such recollections!

ON THE CONVERSATION OF AUTHORS.

In general, wit shines only by reflection. You must take your cue from your company—must rise as they rise, and sink as they fall. You must see that your good things, your knowing allusions, are not flung away, like the pearls in the adage. What a check it is to be asked a foolish question ; to find that the first principles are not understood! You are thrown on your back immediately ; the conversation is stopped like a country-dance by those who do not know the figure. But when a set of adepts, of *illuminati*, get about a question, it is worth while to hear them talk. They may snarl and quarrel over it, like dogs ; but they pick it bare to the bone—they masticate it thoroughly.

This was the case formerly at Lamb's—where we used to have many lively skirmishes at their Thursday evening parties. I doubt whether the small-coal man's musical parties could exceed them. Oh ! for the pen of John Buncle to consecrate a *petit souvenir* to their memory ! There was Lamb himself, the most delightful, the most provoking, the most witty and sensible of men. He always made the best pun, and the best remark in the course of the evening. His serious conversation, like his serious writing, is his best. No one ever stammered out such fine, piquant, deep, eloquent things in half-a-dozen half-sentences as he does. His jests scald like tears ; and he probes a question with a play upon words. What a keen, laughing, hair-brained vein of home-felt truth ! What choice venom ! How often did we cut into the haunch of letters, while we discussed the haunch of mutton on the table! How we skimmed the cream of criticism! How we got into the heart of controversy! How we picked out the marrow of authors! "And, in our flowing cups, many a good name and true was freshly remembered." Recollect (most sage and critical reader) that in all this I was but a guest! Need I go over the names? They were but the old everlasting set— Milton and Shakespeare, Pope and Dryden, Steele and Addison, Swift and Gay, Fielding, Smollett, Sterne, Richardson, Hogarth's prints, Claude's landscapes, the cartoons at Hampton Court, and all those things that, having once been, must ever be. The Scotch novels had not then been heard of : so we said nothing about them. In general, we were hard upon the moderns. The author of the *Rambler* was only tolerated in Boswell's *Life* of him ; and it was as much as anyone could do to edge in a word for *Junius*. Lamb could not bear *Gil Blas*. This was a fault. I remember the greatest triumph I ever had was in persuading him, after some years' difficulty, that Fielding was better than Smollett. On one occasion, he was for making out a list of persons famous in history that one would wish to see again—at the head of whom were Pontius Pilate, Sir Thomas Browne, and Dr. Faustus—but we blackballed most of his list! But with what a gusto would he describe his favourite authors, Donne, or Sir Philip Sidney, and call their most crabbed passages *delicious!* He tried them on his palate as epicures taste olives, and his observations had a smack in them, like a roughness on the tongue. With what discrimination he hinted a defect in what he admired most—as in saying that the display of the sumptuous banquet in "Paradise Regained" was not in true keeping, as the simplest fare was all that was necessary to tempt the extremity of hunger—and stating that Adam and Eve in "Paradise Lost" were too much like married people. He has furnished many a text for Coleridge to preach upon. There was no fuss or cant about him : nor were his sweets or his sours ever diluted with one particle of affectation. I cannot say that the party at Lamb's were all of one description. There were honorary members, lay-brothers. Wit and good fellowship was the motto inscribed over the door. When a stranger came in, it was not asked, "Has he written anything?"—we were above that pedantry; but we waited to see what he could do. If he could take a hand at piquet, he was welcome to sit down. If a person liked anything, if he took snuff heartily, it was sufficient. He could understand, by analogy, the pungency of other things besides Irish blackguard or Scotch rappee. A character was good anywhere, in a room or on paper. But we abhorred insipidity, affectation, and fine gentlemen. There was one of our party who never failed to mark "two for his Nob" at cribbage, and he was thought no mean person. This was Ned Phillips, and a better fellow in his way breathes not. There was ——, who asserted some incredible matter-of-fact as a likely paradox, and settled all controversies by an *ipse dixit*, a *fiat* of his will, hammering out many a hard theory on the anvil of his brain—the Baron Munchausen of politics and practical philosophy; there was Captain Burney, who had you at an advantage by never understanding you—there was Jem White, the Author of *Falstaff's Letters*, who the other day left this dull world to go in search of more kindred spirits, "turning like the latter end of a lover's lute"—there was Ayrton, who sometimes dropped in, the Will Honeycomb of our set—and Mrs. Reynolds, who being of a quiet turn, loved to hear a noisy debate. An utterly uninformed person might have supposed this a scene of vulgar confusion and uproar. While the most critical question was pending, while the most difficult problem in philosophy was solving, Phillips cried out, "That's game," and Martin Burney muttered a quotation over the last remains of a veal-pie at a side-table. Once, and once only, the literary interest overcame the general. For Coleridge was riding the high German horse, and demonstrating the Categories of the Transcendental Philosophy to the Author of the *Road to Ruin*, who insisted on his knowledge of German, and German metaphysics, having read the *Critique of Pure Reason* in the original. "My dear Mr. Holcroft," said Coleridge, in a tone of infinitely provoking conciliation, "you really put me in mind of a sweet, pretty German girl, about fifteen, that I met with in the Hartz forest in Germany—and who one day, as I was reading the *Limits of the Knowable and the Unknowable*, the profoundest of all his works, with great attention, came behind my chair, and leaning over, said, ' What, *you* read Kant ? Why, *I* that am a German born don't understand him !'" This was too much to bear, and Holcroft, starting up, called out in no measured tone, " Mr. Coleridge, you are the most eloquent man I ever met with, and the most troublesome with your eloquence !" Philips held the cribbage-peg that was to mark him game, suspended in his hand ; and the whist table was silent for a moment. I saw Holcroft downstairs, and, on coming to the landing-place at Mitre Court, he stopped me to observe, that "he thought Mr. Coleridge a very clever man, with a great command of language, but that he feared he did not always affix very precise ideas to the words he used." After he was gone, we had our laugh out, and went on with the argument on the nature of Reason, the Imagination, and the Will. I wish I could find a publisher for it : it would make a supplement to the *Biographia Literaria* in a volume-and-a-half octavo.

Those days are over ! An event, the name of which I wish never to mention, broke up our party, like a bomb-shell thrown into the room : and now we seldom meet——

" Like angels' visits, short and far between."

There is no longer the same set of persons, nor of associations. Lamb does not live where he did. By shifting his abode, his notions seem less fixed. He does not wear his old snuff-coloured coat and breeches. It looks like an alteration in his style. An author and a wit should have a separate costume, a particular cloth : he should present something positive and singular to the mind, like Mr. Douce of the Museum. Our faith in the religion of letters will not bear to be taken to pieces, and put together again by caprice or accident. Leigh Hunt goes there sometimes. He has a fine vinous spirit about him, and tropical blood in his veins : but he is better at his own table. He has a great

flow of pleasantry and delightful animal spirits : but his hits do
not tell like Lamb's; you cannot repeat them the next day. He
requires not only to be appreciated but to have a select circle of
admirers and devotees, to feel himself quite at home. He sits
at the head of a party with great gaiety and grace; has an
elegant manner and turn of features ; is never at a loss—
aliquando sufflaminandus erat—has continual sportive sallies
of wit or fancy; tells a story capitally ; mimics an actor or an
acquaintance to admiration ; laughs with great glee and good-
humour at his own or other people's jokes ; understands the
point of an equivoque, or an observation immediately; has a
taste and knowledge of books, of music, of medals ; 'manages
an argument adroitly ; is genteel and gallant, and has a set of
bye-phrases and quaint allusions always at hand to produce a
laugh :—if he has a fault, it is that he does not listen so well as
he speaks, is impatient of interruption, and is fond of being
looked up to, without considering by whom. I believe, however,
he has pretty well seen the folly of this. Neither is his ready
display of personal accomplishment and variety of resources an
advantage to his writings. They sometimes present a desultory
and slipshod appearance, owing to this very circumstance. The
same things that tell, perhaps, best to a private circle round the
fireside, are not always intelligible to the public, nor does he
take pains to make them so. He is too confident and secure of
his audience. That which may be entertaining enough with the
assistance of a certain liveliness of manner, may read very flat
on paper, because it is abstracted from all the circumstances
that had set it off to advantage. A writer should recollect that
he has only to trust to the immediate impression of words, like
a musician who sings without the accompaniment of an instrument. There is nothing to help out, or slubber over, the defects
of the voice in the one case, nor of the style in the other. The
reader may, if he pleases, get a very good idea of Leigh Hunt's
conversation from a very agreeable paper he has lately published, called the *Indicator*, than which nothing can be more
happily conceived or executed.

The art of conversation is the art of hearing as well as of

being heard. Authors in general are not good listeners. Some of the best talkers are, on this account, the worst company ; and some who are very indifferent, but very great talkers, are as bad. It is sometimes wonderful to see how a person, who has been entertaining or tiring a company by the hour together, drops his countenance as if he had been shot, or had been seized with a sudden lockjaw, the moment anyone interposes a single observation. The best converser I know is, however, the best listener. I mean Mr. Northcote, the painter. Painters by their profession are not bound to shine in conversation, and they shine the more. He lends his ear to an observation as if you had brought him a piece of news, and enters into it with as much avidity and earnestness as if it interested himself personally. If he repeats an old remark or story, it is with the same freshness and point as for the first time. It always arises out of the occasion, and has the stamp of originality. There is no parroting of himself. His look is a continual, ever-varying history-piece of what passes in his mind. His face is a book. There need no marks of interjection or interrogation to what he says. His manner is quite picturesque. There is an excess of character and *naïveté* that never tires. His thoughts bubble up and sparkle like beads on old wine. The fund of anecdote, the collection of curious particulars, is enough to set up any common retailer of jests that dines out every day ; but these are not strung together like a row of galley-slaves, but are always introduced to illustrate some argument or bring out some fine distinction of character. The mixture of spleen adds to the sharpness of the point, like poisoned arrows. Mr. Northcote enlarges with enthusiasm on the old painters, and tells good things of the new. The only thing he ever vexed me in was his liking the *Catalogue Raisonnée.* I had almost as soon hear him talk of Titian's pictures (which he does with tears in his eyes, and looking just like them) as see the originals, and I had rather hear him talk of Sir Joshua's than see them. He is the last of that school who knew Goldsmith and Johnson. How finely he describes Pope ! His elegance of mind, his figure, his character were not unlike his own. He does not resemble a modern Englishman, but puts one in mind of a Roman cardinal or a Spanish inquisitor. I never ate or drank with Mr. Northcote ; but I have lived on his conversation with undiminished relish ever since I can remember—and when I leave it, I come out into the street with feelings lighter and more ethereal than I have at any other time. One of his *tete-à-tetes* would at any time make an Essay ; but he cannot write himself, because he loses himself, in the connecting passages, is fearful to the effect, and wants the habit of bringing his ideas into one focus or view. A *lens* is necessary to collect the diverging rays, the refracted and broken angular lights of conversation on paper. Contradiction is half the battle in talking—the being startled by what others say, and having to answer on the spot. You have to defend yourself, paragraph by paragraph, parenthesis within parenthesis. Perhaps it might be supposed that a person who excels in conversation and cannot write, would succeed better in dialogue. But the stimulus, the immediate irritation would be wanting ; and the work would read flatter than ever, from not having the very thing it pretended to have.

Lively sallies and connected discourse are very different things. There are many persons of that impatient and restless turn of mind, that they cannot wait a moment for a conclusion, or follow up the thread of any argument. In the hurry of conversation their ideas are somehow huddled into sense ; but in the intervals of thought, leave a great gap between. Montesquieu said, he often lost an idea before he could find words for it : yet he dictated, by way of saving time, to an amanuensis. This last is, in my opinion, a vile method, and a solecism in authorship. Horne Tooke, among other paradoxes, used to maintain that no one could write a good style who was not in the habit of talking and hearing the sound of his own voice. He might as well have said that no one could relish a good style without reading it aloud, as we find common people do to assist their apprehension. But there is a method of trying periods on the ear, or weighing them with the scales of the breath, without any articulate sound. Authors, as they write, may be said to "hear a sound so fine, there's nothing lives 'twixt it and silence." Even musicians generally compose in their heads. I agree that no style is good that is not fit to be spoken or read aloud with effect. This holds true not only of emphasis and cadence, but also with regard to natural idiom and colloquial freedom. Sterne's was in this respect the best style that ever was written. You fancy that you hear the people talking. For a contrary reason, no college-man writes a good style, or understands it when written. Fine writing is with him all verbiage and monotony—a translation into classical centos or hexameter-lines.

That which I have just mentioned is among many instances I could give of ingenious absurdities advanced by Mr. Tooke in the heat and pride of controversy. A person who knew him well, and greatly admired his talents, said of him that he never (to his recollection) heard him defend an opinion which he thought right, or in which he believed him to be himself sincere. He indeed provoked his antagonists into the toils by the very extravagance of his assertions, and the teasing sophistry by which he rendered them plausible. His temper was prompter to his skill. He had the manners of a man of the world, with great scholastic resources. He flung everyone else off his guard, and was himself immovable. I never knew anyone who did not admit his superiority in this kind of warfare. He put a full-stop to one of Coleridge's long-winded prefatory apologies for his youth and inexperience, by saying abruptly, "Speak up, young man!" and, at another time, silenced a learned professor by desiring an explanation of a word which the other frequently used, and which, he said, he had been many years trying to get at the meaning of—the copulative Is! He was the best intellectual fencer of his day. He made strange havoc of Fuseli's fantastic hieroglyphics, violent humours, and oddity of dialect. Curran, who was sometimes of the same party, was lively and animated in convivial conversation, but dull in argument; nay, averse to anything like reasoning or serious observation, and had the worse taste I ever knew. His favourite critical topics were to abuse Milton's " Paradise Lost," and " Romeo and Juliet." Indeed, he confessed a want of sufficient acquaintance with books when he found himself in literary society in London. He and Sheridan once dined at John Kemble's with Mrs. Inchbald and Mary Woolstonecroft, when the discourse almost wholly turned on Love "from noon to dewy eve, a summer's day !" What a subject ! What speakers, and what hearers ! What would I not give to have been there, had I not learned it all from the bright eyes of Amaryllis, and may one day make a *Table-talk* of it ! Peter Pindar was rich in anecdote and grotesque humour, and profound in technical knowledge both of music, poetry, and painting, but he was gross and overbearing. Wordsworth sometimes talks like a man inspired on subjects of poetry (his own out of the question)—Coleridge well on every subject, and Godwin on none. To finish this subject—Mrs. Montagu's conversation is as fine-cut as her features, and I like to sit in the room with that sort of coronet face. What she says leaves a flavour, like fine green tea. Hunt's is like champagne, and Northcote's like anchovy sandwiches. Haydon's is like a game at trap-ball : Lamb's like snap-dragon : and my own (if I do not mistake the matter) is not very much unlike a game at ninepins ! . . . One source of the conversation of authors is the character of other authors, and on that they are rich indeed. What things they say ! What stories they tell of one another, more particularly of their friends ! If I durst only give some of these confidential communications ! . . . The reader may perhaps think the foregoing a specimen of them—but indeed he is mistaken.

I do not know of any greater impertinence than for an obscure individual to set about pumping a character of celebrity. "Bring him to me," said a Doctor Tronchin, speaking of Rousseau, "that I may see whether he has anything in him." Before you can take measure of the capacity of others, you ought to be sure that they have not taken measure of yours. They may think you a spy on them, and may not like their company. If you really want to know whether another person can talk well, begin by saying a good thing yourself, and you will have a right to look for a rejoinder. "The best tennis-players," says Sir Fopling Flutter, "make the best matches."

> " ————————————For wit is like a rest
> Held up at tennis, which men do the best
> With the best players."

We hear it often said of a great author, or a great actress, that they are very stupid people in private. But he was a fool that said so. *Tell me your company, and I'll tell you your manners.* In conversation, as in other things, the action and reaction should bear a certain proportion to each other. Authors may, in some sense, be looked upon as foreigners, who are not naturalised even in their native soil. Lamb once came down into the country to see us. He was "like the most capricious poet Ovid among the Goths." The country people thought him an oddity, and did not understand his jokes. It would be strange if they had ; for he did not make any while he stayed. But when he crossed the country to Oxford, then he spoke a little. He and the old colleges were "hail-fellow well met ;" and in the quadrangles, he "walked gowned."

There is a character of a gentleman ; so there is a character of a scholar, which is no less easily recognised. The one has an air of books about him, as the other has of good-breeding. The one wears his thoughts as the other does his clothes, gracefully ; and even if they are a little old-fashioned, they are not ridiculous : they have had their day. The gentleman shows, by his manner, that he has been used to respect from others : the scholar that he lays claim to self-respect and to a certain independence of opinion. The one has been accustomed to the best company ; the other has passed his time in cultivating an intimacy with the best authors. There is nothing forward or vulgar in the behaviour of the one ; nothing shrewd or petulant in the observations of the other, as if he should astonish the bystanders, or was astonished himself at his own discoveries. Good taste and good sense, like common politeness, are, or are supposed to be, matters of course. One is distinguished by an appearance of marked attention to every one present ; the other manifests an habitual air of abstraction and absence of mind. The one is not an upstart, with all the self-important airs of the founder of his own fortune ; nor the other a self-taught man, with the repulsive self-sufficiency which arises from an ignorance of what hundreds have known before him. We must excuse perhaps a little conscious family pride in the one, and a little harmless pedantry in the other. As there is a class of the first character which sinks into the mere gentleman, that is, which has nothing but this sense of respectability and propriety to support it—so the character of a scholar not unfrequently dwindles down into the shadow of a shade, till nothing is left of it but the mere bookworm. There is often something amiable as well as enviable in this last character. I know one such instance, at least. The person I mean has an admiration for learning, if he is only dazzled by its light. He lives among old authors, if he does not enter much into their spirit. He handles the covers, and turns over the page, and is familiar with the names and dates. He is busy and self-involved. He hangs like a film and cobweb upon letters, or is like the dust upon the outside of knowledge, which should not be rudely brushed aside. He follows learning as its shadow ; but as such, he is respectable. He browses on the husk and leaves of books, as the young fawn browses on the bark and leaves of trees. Such a one lives all his life in a dream of learning, and has never once had his sleep broken by a real sense of things. He believes implicitly in genius, truth, virtue, liberty, because he finds the names of these things in books. He thinks that love and friendship are the finest things imaginable, both in practice and theory. The legend of good women is to him no fiction. When he steals from the twilight of his cell, the scene breaks upon him like an illuminated missal, and all the people he sees are but so many figures in a *camera obscura*. He reads the world, like a favourite volume, only to find beauties in it, or like an edition of some old work which he is preparing for the press, only to make emendations in it, and correct the errors that have inadvertently slipt in. He and his dog Tray are much the same honest, simple-hearted, faithful, affectionate creatures—if Tray could but read! His mind cannot take the impression of vice : but the gentleness of his nature turns gall to milk. He would not hurt a fly. He draws the picture of mankind from the guileless simplicity of his own heart : and when he dies, his spirit will take its smiling leave, without having ever had an ill thought of others, or the consciousness of one in itself!

ON READING NEW BOOKS.

"And what of this new book, that the whole world make such a rout about?"—STERNE.

I CANNOT understand the rage manifested by the greater part of the world for reading New Books. If the public had read all those that have gone before, I can conceive how they should not wish to read the same work twice over; but when I consider the countless volumes that lie unopened, unregarded, unread, and unthought-of, I cannot enter into the pathetic complaints that I hear made that Sir Walter writes no more—that the press is idle—that Lord Byron is dead. If I have not read a book before, it is, to all intents and purposes, new to me, whether it was printed yesterday or three hundred years ago. If it be urged that it has no modern, passing incidents, and is out of date and old-fashioned, then it is so much the newer; it is farther removed from other works that I have lately read, from the familiar routine of ordinary life, and makes so much more addition to my knowledge. But many people would as soon think of putting on old armour as of taking up a book not published within the last month, or year at the utmost. There is a fashion in reading as well as in dress, which lasts only for the season. One would imagine that books were, like women, the worse for being old;* that they have a pleasure in being read for the first time; that they open their leaves more

* "Laws are not like women, the worse for being old."—*The Duke of Buckingham's Speech in the House of Lords, in Charles the Second's time.*

cordially ; that the spirit of enjoyment wears out with the spirit of novelty ; and that, after a certain age, it is high time to put them on the shelf. This conceit seems to be followed up in practice. What is it to me that another—that hundreds or thousands have in all ages read a work? Is it on this account the less likely to give me pleasure, because it has delighted so many others? Or can I taste this pleasure by proxy? Or am I in any degree the wiser for their knowledge? Yet this might appear to be the inference. *Their* having read the work may be said to act upon us by sympathy, and the knowledge which so many other persons have of its contents deadens our curiosity and interest altogether. We set aside the subject as one on which others have made up their minds for us (as if we really could have ideas in their heads), and are quite on the alert for the next new work, teeming hot from the press, which we shall be the first to read, criticise, and pass an opinion on. Oh, delightful! To cut open the leaves, to inhale the fragrance of the scarcely dry paper, to examine the type to see who is the printer (which is some clue to the value that is set upon the work), to launch out into regions of thought and invention never trod till now, and to explore characters that never met a human eye before—this is a luxury worth sacrificing a dinner-party, or a few hours of a spare morning to. Who, indeed, when the work is critical and full of expectation, would venture to dine out, or to face a coterie of blue-stockings in the evening, without having gone through this ordeal, or at least without hastily turning over a few of the first pages, while dressing, to be able to say that the beginning does not promise much, or to tell the name of the heroine ?

A new work is something in our power : we mount the bench, and sit in judgment on it ; we can damn or recommend it to others at pleasure, can decry or extol it to the skies, and can give an answer to those who have not yet read it and expect an account of it ; and thus show our shrewdness and the inde-pendence of our taste before the world have had time to form an opinion. If we cannot write ourselves, we become, by busying ourselves about it, a kind of *accessories after the fact.*

Though not the parent of the bantling that " has just come into this breathing world, scarce half made up," without the aid of criticism and puffing, yet we are the gossips and foster-nurses on the occasion, with all the mysterious significance and self-importance of the tribe. If we wait, we must take our report from others; if we make haste, we may dictate ours to them. It is not a race, then, for priority of information, but for precedence in tattling and dogmatising. The work last out is the first that people talk and inquire about. It is the subject on the *tapis*—the cause that is pending. It is the last candidate for success (other claims have been disposed of), and appeals for this success to us, and us alone. Our predecessors can have nothing to say to this question, however they may have anticipated us on others; future ages, in all probability, will not trouble their heads about it; we are the panel. How hard, then, not to avail ourselves of our immediate privilege to give sentence of life or death—to seem in ignorance of what every one else is full of—to be behind-hand with the polite, the knowing, and fashionable part of mankind—to be at a loss and dumbfounded, when all around us are in their glory, and figuring away, on no other ground than that of having read a work that we have not! Books that are to be written hereafter cannot be criticised by us; those that were written formerly have been criticised long ago : but a new book is the property, the prey of ephemeral criticism, which it darts triumphantly upon; there is a raw thin air of ignorance and uncertainty about it, not filled up by any recorded opinion ; and curiosity, impertinence, and vanity rush eagerly into the vacuum. A new book is the fair field for petulance and cox-combry to gather laurels in—the butt set up for removing opinion to aim at. Can we wonder, then, that the circulating libraries are besieged by literary dowagers and their grand-daughters, when a new novel is announced? That Mail-Coach copies of the *Edinburgh Review* are or were coveted? That the Manuscript of the *Waverley Romances* is sent abroad in time for the French, German, or even Italian translation to appear on the same day as the original work, so that the longing Continental public may not be kept waiting an instant longer than their fellow-readers in the English metropolis, which would be as tantalising and insupportable as a little girl being kept without her new frock, when her sister's is just come home and is the talk and admiration of every one in the house? To be sure, there is something in the taste of the times; a modern work is expressly adapted to modern readers. It appeals to our direct experience, and to well-known subjects; it is part and parcel of the world around us, and is drawn from the same sources as our daily thoughts. There is, therefore, so far, a natural or habitual sympathy between us and the literature of the day, though this is a different consideration from the mere circumstance of novelty. An author now alive has a right to calculate upon the living public: he cannot count upon the dead, nor look forward with much confidence to those that are unborn. Neither, however, is it true that we are eager to read all new books alike: we turn from them with a certain feeling of distaste and distrust, unless they are recommended to us by some peculiar feature or obvious distinction. Only young ladies from the boarding-school, or milliners' girls, read all the new novels that come out. It must be spoken of or against; the writer's name must be well known or a great secret; it must be a topic of discourse and a mark for criticism —that is, it must be likely to bring us into notice in some way —or we take no notice of it. There is a mutual and tacit understanding on this head. We can no more read all the new books that appear, than we can read all the old ones that have disappeared from time to time. A question may be started here, and pursued as far as needful, whether, if an old and worm-eaten Manuscript were discovered at the present moment, it would be sought after with the same avidity as a new and hot-pressed poem, or other popular work? Not generally, certainly, though by a few with perhaps greater zeal. For it would not affect present interests, or amuse present fancies, or touch on present manners, or fall in with the public *egotism* in any way: it would be the work either of some obscure author— in which case it would want the principle of excitement; or of some illustrious name, whose style and manner would be already familiar to those most versed in the subject, and his fame established—so that, as a matter of comment and controversy, it would only go to account on the old score : there would be no room for learned feuds and heart-burnings. Was there not a Manuscript of Cicero's talked of as having been discovered about a year ago? But we have heard no more of it. There have been several other cases, more or less in point, in our time or near it. A Noble Duke (which may serve to show at least the interest taken in books *not for being new*) some time ago gave £2260 for a copy of the first edition of the *Decameron :* but did he read it ? It has been a fashion also of late for noble and wealthy persons to go to a considerable expense in ordering reprints of the old Chronicles and black-letter works. Does not this rather prove that the books did not circulate very rapidly or extensively, or such extraordinary patronage and liberality would not have been necessary ? Mr. Thomas Taylor, at the instance, I believe, of the old Duke of Norfolk, printed fifty copies in quarto of a translation of the works of Plato and Aristotle. He did not choose that a larger impression should be struck off, lest these authors should get into the hands of the vulgar. There was no danger of a run in that way. I tried to read some of the Dialogues in the translation of Plato, but, I confess, could make nothing of it : "the logic was so different from ours !"* A

---

* An expression borrowed from a voluble German scholar, who gave this as an excuse for not translating the *Critique of Pure Reason* into English. He might as well have said seriously, that the *Rule of Three* in German was different from ours. Mr. Taylor (the Platonist, as he was called) was a singular instance of a person in our time believing in the heathen mythology. He had a very beautiful wife. An impudent Frenchman, who came over to London, and lodged in the same house, made love to her, by pretending to worship her as Venus, and so thought to turn the tables on our philosopher. I once spent an evening with this gentleman at George Dyer's chambers, in Clifford's Inn, where there was no exclusion of persons or opinions. I remember he showed with some triumph two of his fingers, which had been bent so

startling experiment was made on this sort of retrospective curiosity, in the case of Ireland's celebrated Shakespeare forgery. The public there certainly manifested no backward-ness nor lukewarmness : the enthusiasm was equal to the folly. But then the spirit exhibited on this occasion was partly critical and polemical, and it is a problem whether an actual and undoubted play of Shakespeare's would have excited the same ferment ; and, on the other hand, Shakespeare is an essential modern. People read and go to see his real plays, as well as his pretended ones. The *fuss* made about Ossian is another test to refer to. It was its being the supposed revival of an old work (known only by scattered fragments or lingering tradition) which gave it its chief interest, though there was also a good deal of mystery and quackery concerned along with the din and stir of national jealousy and pretension. Who reads Ossian now ? It is one of the reproaches brought against Buonaparte that he was fond of it when young. I

that he had lost the use of them, in copying out the manuscripts of Proclus and Plotinus in a fine Greek hand. Such are the trophies of human pride ! It would be well if our deep studies often produced no other crookedness and deformity ! I endeavoured (but in vain) to learn something from the heathen philosopher as to Plato's doctrine of abstract ideas being the foundation of particular ones, which I suspect has more truth in it than we moderns are willing to admit. Another friend of mine once breakfasted with Mr. Dyer (the most amiable and absent of hosts), when there was no butter, no knife to cut the loaf with, and the tea-pot was without a spout. My friend, after a few immaterial ceremonies, adjourned to Peele's coffee-house, close by, where he regaled himself on buttered toast, coffee, and the newspaper of the day (a newspaper possessed some interest when we were young) ; and the only interruption to his satisfaction was the fear that his host might suddenly enter, and be shocked at his imperfect hospitality. He would probably forget the circumstance altogether. I am afraid that this veteran of the old school has not received many proofs of the *archaism* of the prevailing taste ; and that the corrections in his *History of the University of Cambridge* have cost him more than the public will ever repay him for.

cannot for myself see the objection. There is no doubt an antiquarian spirit always at work, and opposed to the spirit of novelty-hunting; but, though opposed, it is scarcely a match for it in a general and popular point of view. It is not long ago that I happened to be suggesting a new translation of *Don Quixote* to an enterprising bookseller; and his answer was—"We want new Don Quixotes." I believe I deprived the same active-minded person of a night's rest, by telling him there was the beginning of another novel by Goldsmith in existence. This, if it could be procured, would satisfy both tastes for the new and the old at once. I fear it is but a fragment, and that we must wait till a new Goldsmith appears. We may observe of late a strong craving after Memoirs and Lives of the Dead. But these, it may be remarked, savour so much of the real and familiar, that the persons described differ from us only in being dead, which is a reflection to our advantage: or, if remote and romantic in their interest and adventures, they require to be bolstered up in some measure by the embellishments of modern style and criticism. The accounts of Petrarch and Laura, of Abelard and Eloise, have a lusciousness and warmth in the subject which contrast quaintly and pointedly with the coldness of the grave; and, after all, we prefer Pope's "Eloise and Abelard," with the modern dress and flourishes, to the sublime and affecting simplicity of the original Letters.

In some very just and agreeable reflections on the story of *Abelard and Eloise,* in a late number of a contemporary publication, there is a quotation of some lines from Lucan, which Eloise is said to have repeated in broken accents as she was advancing to the altar to receive the veil.

> 'O maxime conjux!
> O thalamis indigne meis! Hoc juris habebat
> In tantum fortuna caput? Cur impia nupsi,
> Si miserum factura fui? Nunc accipe pœnas,
> Sed quas sponte luam."

" Ah ! my once greatest lord ! ah, cruel hour !
Is thy victorious head in fortune's power?
Since miseries my baneful love pursue,
Why did I wed thee, only to undo?
But see, to death my willing neck I bow ;
Atone the angry gods by one kind blow."
—ROWE'S TRANSLATION.

This speech, quoted by another person, on such an occasion,
might seem cold and pedantic; but from the mouth of the
passionate and unaffected Eloise it cannot bear that interpretation. What sounding lines ! What a pomp, and yet what
a familiar boldness in their application—" proud as when
blue Iris bends !" The reading this account brought forcibly
to mind what has struck me often before—the unreason-
ableness of the complaint we constantly hear of the ignorance
and barbarism of former ages, and the folly of restricting
all refinement and literary elegance to our own. We are,
indeed, indebted to the ages that have gone before us, and
could not well do without them. But in all ages there will be
found still others that have gone before with nearly equal lustre
and advantage, though, by distance and the intervention of
multiplied excellence, this lustre may be dimmed or forgotten.
Had it then no existence? We might, with the same reason,
suppose that the horizon is the last boundary and verge of the
round earth. Still, as we advance, it recedes from us ; and so
time from its storehouse pours out an endless succession of the
productions of art and genius ; and the farther we explore the
obscurity, other trophies and other land-marks rise up. It is
only our ignorance that fixes a limit—as the mist gathered
round the mountain's brow makes us fancy we are treading the
edge of the universe ! Here was Eloise living at a period when
monkish indolence and superstition were at their height—in one
of those that are emphatically called the *dark ages ;* and yet,
as she is led to the altar to make her last fatal vow, expressing
her feelings in language quite natural to her, but from which
the most accomplished and heroic of our modern females would
shrink back with pretty and affected wonder and affright. The

glowing and impetuous lines which she murmured, as she passed on, with spontaneous and rising enthusiasm, were engraven on her heart, familiar to her as her daily thoughts; her mind must have been full of them to overflowing, and at the same time enriched with other stores and sources of knowledge equally elegant and impressive; and we persist, notwithstanding this and a thousand similar circumstances, in indulging our surprise how people could exist, and see, and feel, in those days, without having access to our opportunities and acquirements, and how Shakespeare wrote long after, *in a barbarous age!* The mystery in this case is of our own making. We are struck with astonishment at finding a fine moral sentiment or a noble image nervously expressed in an author of the age of Queen Elizabeth; not considering that, independently of nature and feeling, which are the same in all periods, the writers of that day, who were generally men of education and learning, had such models before them as the one that has been just referred to—were thoroughly acquainted with those masters of classic thought and language, compared with whom, in all that relates to the artificial graces of composition, the most studied of the moderns are little better than Goths and Vandals. It is true, we have lost sight of, and neglected the former, because the latter have, in a great degree, superseded them, as the elevations nearest to us intercept those farthest off; but our not availing ourselves of this vantage ground is no reason why our forefathers should not (who had not our superfluity of choice), and most assuredly they did study and cherish the precious fragments of antiquity, collected together in their time, "like sunken wreck and sumless treasuries;"* and while they did this, we need be at no loss to account for any examples of grace, of force, or dignity in their writings, if these must always be traced back to a previous source. One age cannot understand how another could subsist without its lights, as one country thinks every other must be poor for want of its physical productions. This is a narrow and superficial view of the subject: we should by all means rise above it. I am not for devoting the whole of our time to the study of the classics, or of any other set of writers, to the exclusion and neglect of nature ; but I think we should turn our thoughts enough that way to convince us of the existence of genius and learning before our time, and to cure us of an overweening conceit of ourselves, and of a contemptuous opinion of the world at large. Every civilised age and country (and of these there is not one, but a hundred) has its literature, its arts, its comforts, large and ample though we may know nothing of them ; nor is it (except for our own sakes) important that we should.

Books have been so multiplied in our days (like the Vanity Fair of knowledge), and we have made such progress beyond ourselves in some points, that it seems at first glance as if we had monopolised every possible advantage, and the rest of the world must be left destitute and in darkness. This is the *cockneyism* (with leave be it spoken) of the nineteenth century. There is a tone of smartness and piquancy in modern writing, to which former examples may, in one sense, appear flat and pedantic. Our allusions are more pointed and personal : the ancients are, in this respect, formal and prosaic personages. Some one, not long ago, in this vulgar, shallow spirit of criticism (which sees everything from its own point of view), said that the tragedies of Sophocles and Æschylus were about as good as the pieces brought out at Sadler's Wells or the Adelphi Theatre. An oration of Demosthenes is thought dry and meagre, because it is not "full of wise saws and modern instances : " one of Cicero's is objected to as flimsy and extravagant, for the same reason. There is a style in one age which does not fall in with the taste of the public in another, as it requires greater effeminacy and softness, greater severity or simplicity, greater force or refinement. Guido was more admired than Raphael in his day, because the manners were grown softer without the strength : Sir Peter Lely was thought in his to have eclipsed Vandyke—an opinion that no one holds at present : Holbein's faces must be allowed to be very different from Sir Thomas Lawrence's—yet the one was the favourite painter of Henry VIII., as the other is of George IV. What should we say in our time to the *euphuism* of the age of Elizabeth, when style was made a riddle and the court talked in conundrums? This, as a novelty and a trial of the wits, might take for a while : afterwards, it could only seem absurd. We must always make some allowance for a change of style, which those who are accustomed to read none but works written within the last twenty years neither can nor will make. When a whole generation read, they will read none but contemporary productions. The taste for literature becomes superficial, as it becomes universal, and is spread over a larger space. When ten thousand boarding-school girls, who have learnt to play on the piano, are brought out in the same season, Rossini will be preferred to Mozart, as the last new composer. I remember a very genteel young couple in the boxes of Drury Lane being very much scandalised some years ago at the phrase in " A New Way to Pay Old Debts "—" an insolent piece of paper "— applied to the contents of a letter ; it wanted the modern lightness and indifference. Let an old book be ever so good, it treats (generally speaking) of topics that are stale, in a style that has grown "somewhat musty;" of manners that are exploded, probably by the very ridicule thus cast upon them ; of persons that no longer figure on the stage ; and of interests that have long since given place to others in the infinite fluctuations of human affairs. Longinus complains of the want of interest in the *Odyssey*, because it does not, like the *Iliad*, treat of war. The very complaint we make against the latter is that it treats of nothing else ; or that, as Fuseli expresses it, everything is seen "through the blaze of war." Books of devotion are no longer read (if we read Irving's *Orations*, it is merely that we may go as a *lounge* to see the man) : even attacks on religion are out of date and insipid. Voltaire's jests and the *Jew's Letters* in answer (equal in wit, and more than equal in learning), repose quietly on the shelf together. We want something in England about Rent and the Poor-Laws, and something in France about the Charter—or Lord Byron. With the attempts, however, to revive superstition and intolerance, a spirit of

opposition has been excited, and Pascal's *Provincial Letters*
have been once more enlisted into the service. In France you
meet with no one who can read the *New Eloise:* the *Princess
of Cleves* is not even mentioned in these degenerate days. Is it
not provoking with us to see the "Beggars' Opera" cut down to
two acts, because some of the allusions are too broad, and
others not understood? And in America this sterling satire is
hooted off the stage, because, fortunately, they have no such
state of matters as it describes before their eyes ; and because,
unfortunately, they have no conception of anything but what
they see. America is singularly and awkwardly situated in this
respect. It is a new country with an old language ; and while
everything about them is of a day's growth, they are constantly
applying to us to know what to think of it, and taking their
opinions from our books and newspapers with a strange mixture
of servility and of the spirit of contradiction. They are an
independent state in politics : in literature they are still a
colony from us—not out of their leading strings, and strangely
puzzled how to determine between the *Edinburgh* and *Quarterly
Reviews.* We have naturalised some of their writers, who had
formed themselves upon us. · This is at once a compliment to
them and to ourselves. Amidst the scramble and lottery for
fame in the present day, besides puffing, which may be regarded
as the hot-bed of reputation, another mode has been attempted
by *transplanting* it ; and writers who are set down as drivellers
at home, shoot up great authors on the other side of the water ;
pack up their all—a title-page and sufficient impudence ; and a
work, of which the *flocci-nauci-nihili-pili-fication*, in Shenstone's
phrase, is well known to every competent judge, is *placarded*
into eminence, and "flames in the forehead of the morning sky"
on the walls of Paris or St. Petersburgh. I dare not mention
the instances, but so it is. Some reputations last only while
the possessors live, from which one might suppose that they
gave themselves a character for genius : others are cried up by
their gossiping acquaintances, as long as they give dinners, and
make their houses places of polite resort ; and, in general, in
our time, a book may be considered to have passed the ordeal

that is mentioned at all three months after it is printed. Immortality is not even a dream—a boy's conceit; and posthumous fame is no more regarded by the author than by his bookseller.

This idle, dissipated turn seems to be a set-off to, or the obvious reaction of, the exclusive admiration of the ancients, which was formerly the fashion : as if the sun of human intellect rose and set at Rome and Athens, and the mind of man had never exerted itself to any purpose since. The ignorant, as well as the adept, were charmed only with what was obsolete and far-fetched, wrapped up in technical terms and in a learned tongue. Those who spoke and wrote a language which hardly any one at present even understood, most of course be wiser than we. Time, that brings so many reputations to decay, had embalmed others and rendered them sacred. From an implicit faith and overstrained homage paid to antiquity, we of the modern school have taken too strong a bias to what is new ; and divide all wisdom and worth between ourselves and posterity—not a very formidable rival to our self-love, as we attribute all its advantages to ourselves, though we pretend to owe little or nothing to our predecessors. About the time of the French Revolution, it was agreed that the world had hitherto been in its dotage or its infancy ; and that Mr. Godwin, Condorcet, and others were to begin a new race of men—a new epoch in society. Everything up to that period was to be set aside as puerile or barbarous ; or, if there were any traces of thought and manliness now and then discoverable, they were to be regarded with wonder as prodigies—as irregular and fitful starts in that long sleep of reason and night of philosophy. In this liberal spirit Mr. Godwin composed an Essay to prove that, till the publication of *The Inquiry Concerning Political Justice*, no one knew how to write a word of common grammar, or a style that was not utterly uncouth, incongruous, and feeble. Addison, Swift, and Junius were included in this censure. The English language itself might be supposed to owe its stability and consistency, its roundness and polish, to the whirling motion of the French Revolution. Those who had gone before us were, like our grandfathers and grandmothers, decrepit, superannuated people, blind and dull; poor creatures, like flies in winter, without pith or marrow in them. The past was barren of interest—had neither thought nor object worthy to arrest our attention; and the future would be equally a senseless void, except as we projected ourselves and our theories into it. There is nothing I hate more than I do this exclusive, upstart spirit.

> " By Heavens, I'd rather be
> A pagan suckled in a creed outworn,
> So might I, standing on some pleasant lea,
> Catch glimpses that might make me less forlorn,
> Have sight of Proteus coming from the sea.
> Or hear Old Triton blow his wreathed horn."

Neither do I see the good of it even in a personal and interested point of view. By despising all that has preceded us, we teach others to despise ourselves. Where there is no established scale nor rooted faith in excellence, all superiority—our own as well as that of others—soon comes to the ground. By applying the wrong end of the magnifying glass to all objects indiscriminately, the most respectable dwindle into insignificance, and the best are confounded with the worst. Learning, no longer supported by opinion, or genius by fame, is cast into the mire, and "trampled under the hoofs of a swinish multitude." I would rather endure the most blind and bigoted respect for great and illustrious names, than that pitiful, grovelling humour which has no pride in intellectual excellence, and no pleasure but in decrying those who have given proofs of it, and reducing them to its own level. If, with the diffusion of knowledge, we do not gain an enlargement and elevation of views, where is the benefit? If, by tearing asunder names from things, we do not leave even the name or shadow of excellence, it is better to let them remain as they were; for it is better to have something to admire than nothing—names, if not things—the shadow, if not the substance—the tinsel, if not the gold. All can now read and write equally; and, it is therefore presumed, equally well.

Anything short of this sweeping conclusion is an invidious distinction ; and those who claim it for themselves or others are *exclusionists* in letters. Every one at least can call names—can invent a falsehood, or repeat a story against those who have galled their pragmatical pretensions by really adding to the stock of general amusement or instruction. Every one in a crowd has the power to throw dirt ; nine out of ten have the inclination. It is curious that, in an age when the most universally-admitted claim to public distinction is literary merit, the attaining this distinction is almost a sure title to public contempt and obloquy.* They cry you up because you are unknown, and do not excite their jealousy ; and run you down, when they have thus distinguished you, out of envy and spleen at the very idol they have set up. A public favourite is "kept like an apple in the jaw of an ape—first mouthed, to be afterwards swallowed. When they need what you have gleaned, it is but squeezing you, and, sponge, you shall be dry again." At first they think only of the pleasure or advantage they receive : but, on reflection, they are mortified at the superiority implied in this involuntary concession, and are determined to be even with you the very first opportunity. What is the prevailing spirit of modern literature ? To defame men of letters. What are the publications that succeed ? Those that pretend to teach the public that the persons they have been accustomed unwittingly to look up to as the lights of the earth are no better than themselves, or a set of vagabonds, miscreants that should be hunted out of society. Hence men of letters, losing their self-respect, become government tools, and prostitute their talents to the most infamous purposes, or turn *dandy scribblers*, and set up for gentlemen authors in their own defence. I like the Order of the Jesuits better than this ; they made themselves respected by the laity, kept their own secret, and did not prey on one another. Resume then, oh ! Learning, thy robe pontifical ;

---

* Is not this partly owing to the disappointment of the public at finding any defect in their idol ?

clothe thyself in pride and purple; join the sacred to the profane; wield both worlds; instead of twopenny trash and mechanics' magazines, issue bulls and decretals; say not, let there be light, but darkness visible; draw a bandage over the eyes of the ignorant and unlettered; hang the terrors of superstition and despotism over them;—and for thy pains they will bless thee; children will pull off their caps as thou dost pass; women will courtesy; the old will wipe their beards; and thou wilt rule once more over the base serving people, clowns, and nobles, with a rod of iron!

ON READING OLD BOOKS.

I HATE to read new books.   There are twenty or thirty volumes that I have read over and over again, and these are the only ones that I have any desire ever to read at all.   It was a long time before I could bring myself to sit down to the *Tales of My Landlord,* but now that author's works have made a considerable addition to my scanty library.   I am told that some of Lady Morgan's are good, and have been recommended to look into *Anastasius;* but I have not yet ventured upon that task.   A lady, the other day, could not refrain from expressing her surprise to a friend, who said he had been reading *Delphine:* —she asked,—If it had not been published some time back? Women judge of books as they do of fashions or complexions, which are admired only " in their newest gloss." That is not my way.   I am not one of those who trouble the circulating libraries much, or pester the booksellers for mail-coach copies of standard periodical publications.   I cannot say that I am greatly addicted to black-letter, but I profess myself well versed in the marble bindings of Andrew Millar, in the middle of the last century; nor does my taste revolt at Thurlow's *State Papers,* in russia leather; or an ample impression of Sir William Temple's *Essays,* with a portrait after Sir Godfrey Kneller in front.   I do not think altogether the worse of a book for having survived the author a generation or two.   I have more confidence in the dead than the living.   Contemporary writers may generally be divided into two classes—one's friends or one's foes. Of the first we are compelled to think too well, and of the last we are disposed to think too ill, to receive much genuine pleasure from the perusal, or to judge fairly of the merits of either. One candidate for literary fame, who happens to be of our acquaintance, writes finely, and like a man of genius ; but unfortunately has a foolish face, which spoils a delicate passage ; another inspires us with the highest respect for his personal talents and character, but does not quite come up to our expectations in print. All these contradictions and petty details interrupt the calm current of our reflections. If you want to know what any of the authors were who lived before our time, and are still objects of anxious inquiry, you have only to look into their works. But the dust and smoke and noise of modern literature have nothing in common with the pure, silent air of immortality.

When I take up a work that I have read before (the oftener the better), I know what I have to expect. The satisfaction is not lessened by being anticipated. When the entertainment is altogether new, I sit down to it as I should to a strange dish— turn and pick out a bit here and there, and am in doubt what to think of the composition. There is a want of confidence and security to second appetite. New-fangled books are also like made-dishes in this respect, that they are generally little else than hashes and *rifaccimenti* of what has been served up entire and in a more natural state at other times. Besides, in thus turning to a well-known author, there is not only an assurance that my time will not be thrown away, or my palate nauseated with the most insipid or vilest trash, but I shake hands with, and look an old, tried, and valued friend in the face, compare notes, and chat the hours away. It is true, we form dear friendships with such ideal guests—dearer, alas ! and more lasting, than those with our most intimate acquaint- ance. In reading a book which is an old favourite with me (say the first novel I ever read) I not only have the pleasure of imagination and of a critical relish of the work, but the pleasures of memory added to it. It recalls the same feelings and associations which I had in first reading it, and which I can never have again in any other way. Standard productions of this kind are links in the chain of our conscious being. They bind together the different scattered divisions of our personal identity. They are landmarks and guides . in our journey through life. They are pegs and loops on which we can hang up, or from which we can take down, at pleasure, the wardrobe of a moral imagination, the relics of our best affections, the tokens and records of our happiest hours. They are "for thoughts and for remembrance!" They are like Fortunatus's Wishing Cap—they give us the best riches—those of Fancy; and transport us, not over half the globe, but (which is better) over half our lives, at a word's notice !

My father Shandy solaced himself with Bruscambille. Give me for this purpose a volume of *Peregrine Pickle* or *Tom Jones.* Open either of them anywhere—at the Memoirs of Lady Vane, or the adventures at the masquerade with Lady Bellaston, or the disputes between Thwackum and Square, or the escape of Molly Seagrim, or the incident of Sophia and her muff, or the edifying prolixity of her aunt's lecture—and there I find the same delightful, busy, bustling scene as ever, and feel myself the same as when I was first introduced into the midst of it. Nay, sometimes the sight of an odd volume of these good old English authors on a stall, or the name lettered on the back among others on the shelves of a library, answers the purpose, revives the whole train of ideas, and sets " the puppets dallying." Twenty years are struck off the list, and I am a child again. A sage philosopher, who was not a very wise man, said, that he should like very well to be young again, if he could take his experience along with him. This ingenious person did not seem to be aware, by the gravity of his remark, that the great advantage of being young is to be without this weight of experience, which he would fain place upon the shoulders of youth, and which never comes too late with years. Oh! what a privilege to be able to let this bump, like Christian's burthen, drop from off one's back, and transport oneself, by the help of a little musty duodecimo, to the time when "ignorance was bliss,"

and when we first got a peep at the raree-show of the world,
through the glass of fiction—gazing at mankind, as we do at
wild beasts in a menagerie, through the bars of their cages—
or at curiosities in a museum, that we must not touch ! For
myself, not only are the old ideas of the contents of the work
brought back to my mind in all their vividness, but the old
associations of the faces and persons of those I then knew,
as they were in their lifetime—the place where I sat to read
the volume, the day when I got it, the feeling of the air,
the fields, the sky—return, and all my early impressions with
them. This is better to me—those places, those times, those
persons, and those feelings that come across me as I retrace the
story and devour the page, are to me better far than the wet
sheets of the last new novel from the Ballantyne press, to say
nothing of the Minerva press in Leadenhall Street. It is like
visiting the scenes of early youth. I think of the time " when
I was in my father's house, and my path ran down with butter
and honey "—when I was a little, thoughtless child, and had no
other wish or care but to con my daily task, and be happy !
Tom Jones, I remember, was the first work that broke the spell.
It came down in numbers once a fortnight, in Cooke's pocket-
edition, embellished with cuts. I had hitherto read only in
school-books, and a tiresome ecclesiastical history (with the
exception of Mrs. Radcliffe's *Romance of the Forest*): but this
had a different relish with it—"sweet in the mouth," though
not "bitter in the belly." It smacked of the world I lived in,
and in which I was to live—and showed me groups, "gay
creatures" not "of the element," but of the earth ; not "living in
the clouds," but travelling the same road that I did ;—some
that had passed on before me, and others that might soon overtake me. My heart had palpitated at the thoughts of a boarding-school ball, or gala-day at Midsummer or Christmas : but
the world I had found out in Cooke's edition of the *British
Novelists* was to me a dance through life, a perpetual gala-day.
The sixpenny numbers of this work regularly contrived to leave
off just in the middle of a sentence, and in the nick of a story,
where Tom Jones discovers Square behind the blanket : or

where Parson Adams, in the inextricable confusion of events, very undesignedly gets to bed to Mrs. Slip-slop. Let me caution the reader against this impression of Joseph Andrews ; for there is a picture of Fanny in it which he should not set his heart on, lest he should never meet with anything like it ; or if he should, it would, perhaps, be better for him that he had not. It was just like —— —— | With what eagerness I used to look forward to the next number, and open the prints | Ah | never again shall I feel the enthusiastic delight with which I gazed at the figures, and anticipated the story and adventures of Major Bath and Commodore Trunnion, of Trim and my Uncle Toby, of Don Quixote and Sancho and Dapple, of Gil Blas and Dame Lorenza Sephora, of Laura and the fair Lucretia, whose lips open and shut like buds of roses. To what nameless ideas did they give rise—with what airy delights I filled up the outlines, as I hung in silence over the page | Let me still recall them, that they may breathe fresh life into me, and that I may live that birthday of thought and romantic pleasure over again | Talk of the *ideal !* This is the only true ideal—the heavenly tints of Fancy reflected in the bubbles that float upon the spring-tide of human life.

> " O Memory | shield me from the world's poor strife,
> And give those scenes thine everlasting life !"

The paradox with which I set out is, I hope, less startling than it was ; the reader will, by this time, have been let into my secret. Much about the same time, or I believe rather earlier, I took a particular satisfaction in reading Chubb's *Tracts*, and I often think I will get them again to wade through. There is a high gusto of polemical divinity in them ; and you fancy that you hear a club of shoemakers at Salisbury debating a disputable text from one of St. Paul's Epistles in a workmanlike style, with equal shrewdness and pertinacity. I cannot say much for my metaphysical studies, into which I launched shortly after with great ardour, so as to make a toil of a pleasure. I was presently entangled in the briars and thorns of subtle distinctions—of " fate, free-will, fore-knowledge absolute," though

I cannot add that "in their wandering mazes I found no end;" for I did arrive at some very satisfactory and potent conclusions; nor will I go so far, however ungrateful the subject might seem, as to exclaim with Marlowe's Faustus—"Would I had never seen Wittenberg, never read book"—that is, never studied such authors as Hartley, Hume, Berkeley, etc. Locke's *Essay on the Human Understanding* is, however, a work from which I never derived either pleasure or profit ; and Hobbes, dry and powerful as he is, I did not read till long afterwards. I read a few poets, which did not much hit my taste—for I would have the reader understand, I am deficient in the faculty of imagination ; but I fell early upon French romances and philosophy, and devoured them tooth-and-nail. Many a dainty repast have I made of the *New Eloise;*—the description of the kiss ; the excursion on the water ; the letter of St. Preux, recalling the time of their first loves ; and the account of Julia's death ; these I read over and over again with unspeakable delight and wonder. Some years after, when I met with this work again, I found I had lost nearly my whole relish for it (except some few parts), and was, I remember, very much mortified with the change in my taste, which I sought to attribute to the smallness and gilt edges of the edition I had bought, and its being perfumed with rose-leaves. Nothing could exceed the gravity, the solemnity with which I carried home and read the Dedication to the *Social Contract*, with some other pieces of the same author, which I had picked up at a stall in a coarse leathern cover. Of the *Confessions* I have spoken elsewhere, and may repeat what I have said—"Sweet is the dew of their memory, and pleasant the balm of their recollection!" Their beauties are not "scattered like stray-gifts o'er the earth," but sown thick on the page, rich and rare. I wish I had never read the *Emilius*, or read it with implicit faith. I had no occasion to pamper my natural aversion to affectation or pretence, by romantic and artificial means. I had better have formed myself on the model of Sir Fopling Flutter. There is a class of persons whose virtues and most shining qualities sink in, and are concealed by, an absorbent ground of modesty and

reserve ; and such a one I do, without vanity, profess myself.*
Now these are the very persons who are likely to attach themselves to the character of Emilius, and of whom it is sure to be
the bane. This dull, phlegmatic, retiring humour is not in a
fair way to be corrected, but confirmed and rendered desperate,
by being in that work held up as an object of imitation, as an
example of simplicity and magnanimity—by coming upon us
with all the recommendations of novelty, surprise, and superiority
to the prejudices of the world—by being stuck upon a pedestal,
made amiable, dazzling, a *leurre de dupe!* The reliance on
solid worth which it inculcates, the preference of sober truth to
gaudy tinsel, hangs like a mill-stone round the neck of the
imagination—" a load to sink a navy "—impedes our progress,
and blocks up every prospect in life. A man, to get on, to be
successful, conspicuous, applauded, should not retire upon the
centre of his conscious resources, but be always at the circumference of appearances. He must envelop himself in a halo of
mystery—he must ride in an equipage of opinion—he must
walk with a train of self-conceit following him—he must not
strip himself to a buff-jerkin, to the doublet and hose of his
real merits, but must surround himself with a *cortège* of
prejudices, like the signs of the Zodiac—he must seem anything
but what he is, and then he may pass for anything he pleases.
The world love to be amused by hollow professions, to be
deceived by flattering appearances, to live in a state of hallucination ; and can forgive everything but the plain, downright,
simple, honest truth—such as we see it chalked out in the
character of Emilius. To return from this digression, which is
a little out of place here.

Books have in a great measure lost their power over me ;
nor can I revive the same interest in them as formerly. I
perceive when a thing is good, rather than feel it. It is true,

* Nearly the same sentiment was wittily and happily expressed by a
friend, who had some lottery puffs, which he had been employed to
write, returned on his hands for their too great severity of thought and
classical terseness of style, and who observed on that occasion, that
' Modest merit never can succeed ! "

" Marcian Colonna is a dainty book ; "

and the reading of Mr. Keats's *Eve of St. Agnes* lately made me regret that I was not young again. The beautiful and tender images there conjured up, "come like shadows—so depart." The "tiger-moth's wings," which he has spread over his rich poetic blazonry, just flit across my fancy ; the gorgeous twilight window which he has painted over again in his verse, to me "blushes" almost in vain "with blood of queens and kings." I know how I should have felt at one time in reading such passages ; and that is all. The sharp luscious flavour, the fine *aroma* is fled, and nothing but the stalk, the bran, the husk of literature is left. If any one were to ask me what I read now, I might answer with my Lord Hamlet in the play— "Words, words, words."—"What is the matter?"—"*Nothing !*" —They have scarce a meaning. But it was not always so. There was a time when to my thinking, every word was a flower or a pearl, like those which dropped from the mouth of the little peasant-girl in the Fairy tale, or like those that fall from the great preacher in the Caledonian Chapel ! I drank of the stream of knowledge that tempted, but did not mock my lips, as of the river of life, freely. How eagerly I slaked my thirst of German sentiment, "as the hart that panteth for the water-springs ;" how I bathed and revelled, and added my floods of tears to Göethe's *Sorrows of Werter*, and to Schiller's *Robbers*—

"Giving my stock of more to that which had too much !"

I read and assented with all my soul to Coleridge's fine Sonnet, beginning—

"Schiller ! that hour I would have wish'd to die,
If through the shuddering midnight I had sent,
From the dark dungeon of the tow'r time-rent,
That fearful voice, a famish'd father's cry !"

I believe I may date my insight into the mysteries of poetry from the commencement of my acquaintance with the Authors of the *Lyrical Ballads;* at least, my discrimination of the higher sorts—not my predilection for such writers as Goldsmith or

Pope: nor do I imagine they will say I got my liking for the
Novelists, or the comic writers—for the characters of Valentine,
Tattle, or Miss Prue—from them. If so, I must have got from
them what they never had themselves. In points where poetic
diction and conception are concerned, I may be at a loss, and
liable to be imposed upon: but in forming an estimate of
passages relating to common life and manners, I cannot think I
am a plagiarist from any man. I there " know my cue without
a prompter." I may say of such studies, *Intus et in cute.* I am
just able to admire those literal touches of observation and
description which persons of loftier pretensions overlook and
despise. I think I comprehend something of the characteristic
part of Shakespeare; and in him indeed all is characteristic,
even the nonsense and poetry. I believe it was the celebrated
Sir Humphry Davy who used to say, that Shakespeare was
rather a metaphysician than a poet. At any rate, it was not ill
said. I wish that I had sooner known the dramatic writers
contemporary with Shakespeare; for in looking them over
about a year ago, I almost revived my old passion for reading,
and my old delight in books, though they were very nearly new
to me. The Periodical Essayists I read long ago. The *Spectator* I liked extremely: but the *Tatler* took my fancy most. I
read the others soon after, the *Rambler*, the *Adventurer*, the
World, the *Connoisseur.* I was not sorry to get to the end of
them, and have no desire to go regularly through them again.
I consider myself a thorough adept in Richardson. I like the
longest of his novels best, and think no part of them tedious;
nor should I ask to have anything better to do than to read
them from beginning to end, to take them up when I chose, and
lay them down when I was tired, in some old family mansion in
the country, till every word and syllable relating to the bright
Clarissa, the divine Clementina, the beautiful Pamela, " with
every trick and line of their sweet favour," were once more
"graven in my heart's table."* I have a sneaking kindness for

* During the peace of Amiens, a young English officer, of the name
of Lovelace, was presented at Buonaparte's levee. Instead of the usual

Mackenzie's *Julia de Roubigné*—for the deserted mansion, and straggling gilliflowers on the mouldering garden-wall ; and still more for his *Man of Feeling ;* not that it is better, nor so good ; but at the time I read it, I sometimes thought of the heroine, Miss Walton, and of Miss —— together, and "that ligament, fine as it was, was never broken !"—One of the poets that I have always read with most pleasure, and can wander about in for ever with a sort of voluptuous indolence, is Spenser ; and I like Chaucer even better. The only writer among the Italians I can pretend to any knowledge of, is Boccaccio, and of him I cannot express half my admiration. His story of the Hawk I could read and think of from day to day, just as I would look at a picture of Titian's !

I remember, as long ago as the year 1798, going to a neighbouring town (Shrewsbury, where Farquhar has laid the plot of his *Recruiting Officer*) and bringing home with me, "at one proud swoop," a copy of Milton's *Paradise Lost*, and another of Burke's *Reflections on the French Revolution*—both which I have still ; and I still recollect, when I see the covers, the pleasure with which I dipped into them as I returned with my double prize. I was set up for one while. That time is past "with all its giddy raptures :" but I am still anxious to preserve its memory, "embalmed with odours."—With respect to the first of these works, I would be permitted to remark here in passing, that it is a sufficient answer to the German criticism which has since been started against the character of Satan (viz., that it is not one of disgusting deformity, or pure, defecated malice), to say that Milton has there drawn, not the abstract principle of evil, not a devil incarnate, but a fallen angel. This

question, "Where have you served, Sir?" the First Consul immediately addressed him, "I perceive your name, Sir, is the same as that of the hero of Richardson's Romance !" Here was a Consul. The young man's uncle, who was called Lovelace, told me this anecdote while we were stopping together at Calais. I had also been thinking that his was the same name as that of the hero of Richardson's Romance. This is one of my reasons for liking Buonaparte.

is the Scriptural account, and the poet has followed it. We may safely retain such passages as that well-known one—

> "—— His form had not yet lost
> All her original brightness ; nor appear'd
> Less than archangel ruin'd ; and the excess
> Of glory obscur'd "—

for the theory, which is opposed to them, "falls flat upon the grunsel edge, and shames its worshippers." Let us hear no more, then, of this monkish cant, and bigoted outcry for the restoration of the horns and tail of the devil !—Again, as to the other work, Burke's *Reflections*, I took a particular pride and pleasure in it, and read it to myself and others for months afterwards. I had reason for my prejudice in favour of this author. To understand an adversary is some praise : to admire him is more. I thought I did both : I knew I did one. From the first time I ever cast my eyes on anything of Burke's (which was an extract from his "Letter to a Noble Lord" in a three-times-a-week paper, the *St. James's Chronicle*, in 1796), I said to myself, "This is true eloquence : this is a man pouring out his mind on paper." All other style seemed to me pedantic and impertinent. Dr. Johnson's was walking on stilts ; and even Junius's (who was at that time a favourite with me), with all his terseness, shrunk up into little antithetic points and well-trimmed sentences. But Burke's style was forked and playful as the lightning, crested like the serpent. He delivered plain things on a plain ground ; but when he rose, there was no end of his flights and circumgyrations—and in this very Letter, "he, like an eagle in a dove-cot, fluttered *his* Volscians," (the Duke of Bedford and the Earl of Lauderdale) "in Corioli." I did not care for his doctrines. I was then, and am still, proof against their contagion ; but I admired the author, and was considered as not a very staunch partisan of the opposite side, though I thought myself that an abstract proposition was one thing—a masterly transition, a brilliant metaphor, another. I conceived, too, that he might be wrong in his main argument, and yet deliver fifty truths in arriving at a false conclusion. I remember

Coleridge assuring me, as a poetical and political set-off to my sceptical admiration, that Wordsworth had written an "Essay on Marriage," which, for manly thought and nervous expression, he deemed incomparably superior. As I had not, at that time, seen any specimens of Mr. Wordsworth's prose style, I could not express my doubts on the subject. If there are greater prose-writers than Burke, they either lie out of my course of study, or are beyond my sphere of comprehension. I am too old to be a convert to a new mythology of genius. The niches are occupied, the tables are full. If such is still my admiration of this man's misapplied powers, what must it have been at a time when I myself was in vain trying, year after year, to write a single essay, nay, a single page or sentence ; when I regarded the wonders of his pen with the longing eyes of one who was dumb and a changeling ; and when to be able to convey the slightest conception of my meaning to others in words, was the height of an almost hopeless ambition ! But I never measured others' excellences by my own defects : though a sense of my own incapacity, and of the steep, impassable ascent from me to them, made me regard them with greater awe and fondness. I have thus run through most of my early studies and favourite authors, some of whom I have since criticised more at' large. Whether those observations will survive me, I neither know nor do I much care : but to the works themselves, "worthy of all acceptation," and to the feelings they have always excited in me since I could distinguish a meaning in language, nothing shall ever prevent me from looking back with gratitude and triumph. To have lived in the cultivation of an intimacy with such works, and to have familiarly relished such names, is not to have lived quite in vain.

There are other authors whom I have never read, and yet whom I have frequently had a great desire to read, from some circumstance relating to them. Among these is Lord Clarendon's *History of the Grand Rebellion*, after which I have a hankering, from hearing it spoken of by good judges—from my interest in the events, and knowledge of the characters from other sources, and from having seen fine portraits of most of them. I like to read a well-penned character, and Clarendon is said to have been a master in his way. I should like to read Froissart's *Chronicles,* Holinshed and Stowe, and Fuller's *Worthies.* I intend, whenever I can, to read Beaumont and Fletcher all through. There are fifty-two of their plays, and I have only read a dozen or fourteen of them. "A Wife for a Month" and "Thierry and Theodoret" are, I am told, delicious, and I can believe it. I should like to read the speeches in *Thucydides,* and Guicciardini's *History of Florence,* and *Don Quixote* in the original. I have often thought of reading the *Loves of Persiles and Sigismunda,* and the *Galatea* of the same author. But I somehow reserve them like "another Yarrow." I should also like to read the last new novel (if I could be sure it was so) of the author of *Waverley:*—no one would be more glad than I to find it the best!

THE FIGHT.

> "——The *fight*, the *fight*'s the thing,
> Wherein I'll catch the conscience of the king."

Where there's a will there's a way.—I said so to myself, as I walked down Chancery Lane, about half-past six o'clock on Monday, the 10th of December, to inquire at Jack Randall's where the fight the next day was to be ; and I found the proverb nothing "musty" in the present instance. I was determined to see this fight, come what would, and see it I did, in great style. It was my *first fight*, yet it more than answered my expectations. Ladies ! it is to you I dedicate this description ; nor let it seem out of character for the fair to notice the exploits of the brave. Courage and modesty are the old English virtues ; and may they never look cold and askance on one another ! Think, ye fairest of the fair, loveliest of the lovely kind, ye practisers of soft enchantment, how many more ye kill with poisoned baits than ever fell in the ring ; and listen with subdued air and without shuddering, to a tale tragic only in appearance, and sacred to the FANCY !

I was going down Chancery Lane, thinking to ask at Jack Randall's where the fight was to be, when looking through the glass-door of the *Hole in the Wall*, I heard a gentleman asking the same question *at* Mrs. Randall, as the author of *Waverley* would express it. Now Mrs. Randall stood answering the gentleman's question, with all the authenticity of the lady of the Champion of the Light Weights. Thinks I, I'll wait till this person comes out, and learn from him how it is. For to say a

truth, I was not fond of going into this house of call for heroes
and philosophers, ever since the owner of it (for Jack is no
gentleman) threatened once upon a time to kick me out of
doors for wanting a mutton-chop at his hospitable board, when
the conqueror in thirteen battles was more full of *blue ruin* than
of good manners. I was the more mortified at this repulse,
inasmuch as I had heard Mr. James Simpkins, hosier in the
Strand, one day when the character of the *Hole in the Wall*
was brought in question, observe—"The house is a very good
house, and the company quite genteel; I have been there
myself!" Remembering this unkind treatment of mine host,
to which mine hostess was also a party, and not wishing to put
her in unquiet thoughts at a time jubilant like the present, I
waited at the door, when, who should issue forth but my friend
Joe P——s, and, seeing him turn suddenly up Chancery Lane
with that quick jerk and impatient stride which distinguish a
lover of the FANCY, I said, "I'll be hanged if that fellow is not
going to the fight, and is on his way to get me to go with him."
So it proved in effect, and we agreed to adjourn to my lodgings
to discuss measures with that cordiality which makes old
friends like new, and new friends like old, on great occasions.
We are cold to others only when we are dull in ourselves, and
have neither thoughts nor feelings to impart to them. Give a
man a topic in his head, a throb of pleasure in his heart, and he
will be glad to share it with the first person he meets. Joe and
I, though we seldom meet, were an *alter idem* on this
memorable occasion, and had not an idea that we did not
candidly impart; and "so carelessly did we fleet the time," that
I wish no better, when there is another fight, than to have him
for a companion on my journey down, and to return with my
friend Jack Pigott, talking of what was to happen or of what
did happen, with a noble subject always at hand, and liberty to
digress to others whenever they offered. Indeed, on my
repeating the lines from Spenser in an involuntary fit of
enthusiasm,

What more felicity can fall to creature,
Than to enjoy delight with liberty?"

my last-named ingenious friend stopped me by saying that this, translated into the vulgate, meant "*Going to see a fight.*"

Joe and I could not settle about the method of going down. He said there was a caravan, he understood, to start from Tom Belcher's at two, which would go there *right out* and back again the next day. Now, I never travel all night, and said I should get a cast to Newbury by one of the mails. Joe swore the thing was impossible, and I could only answer that I had made up my mind to it. In short, he seemed to me to waver, said he only came to see if I was going, had letters to write, a cause coming on the day after, and faintly said at parting (for I was bent on setting out that moment)—"Well, we meet at Philippi?" I made the best of my way to Piccadilly. The mail-coach stand was bare. "They are all gone," said I—"this is always the way with me—in the instant I lose the future—if I had not stayed to pour out that last cup of tea, I should have been just in time;"—and cursing my folly and ill-luck together, without inquiring at the coach-office whether the mails were gone or not, I walked on in despite, and to punish my own dilatoriness and want of determination. At any rate, I would not turn back : I might get to Hounslow, or perhaps farther, to be on my road the next morning. I passed Hyde Park corner (my Rubicon), and trusted to fortune. Suddenly I heard the clattering of a Brentford stage, and the fight rushed full upon my fancy. I argued (not unwisely) that even a Brentford coachman was better company than my own thoughts (such as they were just then), and at his invitation mounted the box with him. I immediately stated my case to him—namely, my quarrel with myself for missing the Bath or Bristol mail, and my determination to get on in consequence as well as I could, without any disparagement or insulting comparison between longer or shorter stages. It is a maxim with me that stage-coaches, and consequently stage-coachmen, are respectable in proportion to the distance they have to travel : so I said nothing on that subject to my Brentford friend. Any incipient tendency to an abstract proposition, or (as he might have construed it) to a personal reflection of this kind, was however nipped in the bud ; for I had no sooner declared indignantly that I had missed the mails, than he flatly denied that they were gone along, and lo ! at the instant three of them drove by in rapid, provoking, orderly succession, as if they would devour the ground before them. Here again I seemed in the contradictory situation of the man in Dryden who exclaims,

"I follow Fate, which does too hard pursue !"

If I had stopped to inquire at the White Horse Cellar, which would not have taken me a minute, I should now have been driving down the road in all the dignified unconcern and *ideal* perfection of mechanical conveyance. The Bath mail I had set my mind upon, and I had missed it, as I miss everything else, by my own absurdity, in putting the will for the deed, and aiming at ends without employing means. "Sir," said he of the Brentford, "the Bath mail will be up presently, my brother-in-law drives it, and I will engage to stop him if there is a place empty." I almost doubted my good genius ; but, sure enough, up it drove like lightning, and stopped directly at the call of the Brentford Jehu. I would not have believed this possible, but the brother-in-law of a mail-coach driver is himself no mean man. I was transferred without loss of time from the top of one coach to that of the other, desired the guard to pay my fare to the Brentford coachman for me as I had no change, was accommodated with a great coat, put up my umbrella to keep off a drizzling mist, and we began to cut through the air like an arrow. The mile-stones disappeared one after another, the rain kept off; Tom Turtle* the trainer sat before me on the coach-box, with whom I exchanged civilities as a gentleman going to the fight ; the passion that had transported me an hour before was subdued to pensive regret and conjectural musing on the next day's battle ; I was promised a place inside at Reading, and upon the whole, I thought myself a lucky fellow. Such is the force of imagination ! On the outside of any other coach on the 10th of December, with a Scotch mist

---

* John Thurtell, to wit.

drizzling through the cloudy moonlight air, I should have been cold, comfortless, impatient, and, no doubt, wet through ; but seated on the Royal mail, I felt warm and comfortable, the air did me good, the ride did me good, I was pleased with the progress we had made, and confident that all would go well through the journey. When I got inside at Reading, I found Turtle and a stout valetudinarian, whose costume bespoke him one of the FANCY, and who had risen from a three months' sick bed to get into the mail to see the fight. They were intimate, and we fell into a lively discourse. My friend the trainer was confined in his topics to fighting dogs and men, to bears and badgers ; beyond this he was "quite chap-fallen," had not a word to throw at a dog, or indeed very wisely fell asleep, when any other game was started. The whole art of training (I, however, learnt from him) consists in two things, exercise and abstinence, abstinence and exercise, repeated alternately and without end. A yolk of an egg with a spoonful of rum in it is the first thing in a morning, and then a walk of six miles till breakfast. This meal consists of a plentiful supply of tea and toast and beef-steaks. Then another six or seven miles till dinner-time, and another supply of solid beef or mutton with a pint of porter, and perhaps, at the utmost, a couple of glasses of sherry. Martin trains on water, but this increases his infirmity on another very dangerous side. The Gasman takes now and then a chirping glass (under the rose) to console him, during a six weeks' probation, for the absence of Mrs. Hickman—an agreeable woman, with (I under-stand) a pretty fortune of two hundred pounds. How matter presses on me ! What stubborn things are facts ! How inex-haustible is nature and art ! "It is well," as I once heard Mr. Richmond observe, "to see a variety." He was speaking of cock-fighting as an edifying spectacle. I cannot deny but that one learns more of what *is* (I do not say of what *ought to be*) in this desultory mode of practical study, than from reading the same book twice over, even though it should be a moral treatise. Where was I ? I was sitting at dinner with the candidate for the honours of the ring, " where good digestion waits on appetite, and health on both." Then follows an hour of social chat and native glee ; and afterwards, to another breathing over heathy hill or dale. Back to supper, and then to bed, and up by six again—our hero

> " Follows so the ever-running sun,
> With profitable *ardour*"—

to the day that brings him victory or defeat in the green fairy circle. Is not this life more sweet than mine? I was going to say ; but I will not libel any life by comparing it to mine, which is (at the date of these presents) bitter as coloquintida and the dregs of aconitum !

The invalid in the Bath mail soared a pitch above the trainer, and did not sleep so sound, because he had "more figures and more fantasies." We talked the hours away merrily. He had faith in surgery, for he had three ribs set right, that had been broken in a *turn-up* at Belcher's, but thought physicians old women, for they had no antidote in their catalogue for brandy. An indigestion is an excellent commonplace for two people that never met before. By way of ingratiating myself, I told him the story of my doctor, who, on my earnestly representing to him that I thought his regimen had done me harm, assured me that the whole pharmacopeia contained nothing comparable to the prescription he had given me ; and, as a proof of its undoubted efficacy, said, that "he had had one gentleman with my complaint under his hands for the last fifteen years." This anecdote made my companion shake the rough sides of his three greatcoats with boisterous laughter ; and Turtle, starting out of his sleep, swore he knew how the fight would go, for he had had a dream about it. Sure enough the rascal told us how the three first rounds went off, but "his dream" like others, "denoted a foregone conclusion." He knew his men. The moon now rose in silver state, and I ventured, with some hesitation, to point out this object of placid beauty, with the blue serene beyond, to the man of science, to which his ear he "seriously inclined," the more as it gave promise *d'un beau jour* for the morrow, and showed the ring undrenched by

envious showers, arrayed in sunny smiles. Just then, all going
on well, I thought on my friend Joe, whom I had left behind,
and said innocently, "There was a blockhead of a fellow
I left in town, who said there was no possibility of getting down
by the mail, and talked of going by a caravan from Belcher's
at two in the morning, after he had written some letters."
"Why," said he of the lapels, "I should not wonder if that
was the very person we saw running about like mad from one
coach-door to another, and asking if any one had seen a friend
of his, a gentleman going to the fight, whom he had missed
stupidly enough by staying to write a note." "Pray, sir," said
my fellow-traveller, "had he a plaid-cloak on?" "Why, no,"
said I, "not at the time I left him, but he very well might afterwards, for he offered to lend me one." The plaid-cloak and the
letter decided the thing. Joe, sure enough, was in the Bristol
mail, which preceded us by about fifty yards. This was droll
enough. We had now but a few miles to our place of destination, and the first thing I did on alighting at Newbury, both
coaches stopping at the same time, was to call out, "Pray is
there a gentleman in that mail of the name of P——s?" "No,"
said Joe, borrowing something of the vein of Gilpin, "for I
have just got out." "Well!" says he, "this is lucky; but you
don't know how vexed I was to miss you; for," added he,
lowering his voice, "do you know when I left you I went to
Belcher's to ask about the caravan, and Mrs. Belcher said very
obligingly, she couldn't tell about that, but there were two gentlemen who had taken places by the mail and were gone on in
a landau, and she could frank us. It's a pity I didn't meet with
you; we could then have got down for nothing. But *mum's the
word.*" It's the devil for any one to tell me a secret, for it is
sure to come out in print. I do not care so much to gratify a
friend, but the public ear is too great a temptation to me.

Our present business was to get beds and supper at an inn;
but this was no easy task. The public-houses were full, and
where you saw a light at a private house, and people poking
their heads out of the casement to see what was going on, they
instantly put them in and shut the window, the moment you

seemed advancing with a suspicious overture for accommoda-
tion. Our guard and coachman thundered away at the outer
gate of the Crown for some time without effect—such was the
greater noise within ; and when the doors were unbarred, and
we got admittance, we found a party assembled in the kitchen
round a good hospitable fire, some sleeping, others drinking,
others talking on politics and on the fight. A tall English
yeoman (something like Matthews in the face, and quite as
great a wag)—

        " A lusty man to ben an abbot able "—

was making such a prodigious noise about rent and taxes, and
the price of corn now and formerly, that he had prevented us
from being heard at the gate. The first thing I heard him say
was to a shuffling fellow who wanted to be off a bet for a
shilling glass of brandy and water—"Confound it, man, don't
be *insipid!*" Thinks I, that is a good phrase. It was a good
omen. He kept it up so all night, nor flinched with the
approach of morning. He was a fine fellow, with sense, wit,
and spirit, a hearty body and a joyous mind, free-spoken, frank,
convivial—one of that true English breed that went with Harry
the Fifth to the siege of Harfleur—"standing like greyhounds
in the slips," etc. We ordered tea and eggs (beds were soon
found to be out of the question), and this fellow's conversation
was *sauce piquante.* It did one's heart good to see him
brandish his oaken towel and to hear him talk. He made
mince-meat of a drunken, stupid, red-faced, quarrelsome,
frowsy farmer, whose nose "he moralised into a thousand
similes," making it out a firebrand like Bardolph's. "I'll tell
you what, my friend," says he, "the landlady has only to
keep you here to save fire and candle. If one was to touch
your nose, it would go off like a piece of charcoal." At this the
other only grinned like an idiot, the sole variety in his purple
face being his little peering grey eyes and yellow teeth, called
for another glass, swore he would not stand it, and after many
attempts to provoke his humorous antagonist to single combat,
which the other turned off (after working him up to a ludicrous

pitch of choler) with great adroitness, he fell quietly asleep with a glass of liquor in his hand, which he could not lift to his head. His laughing persecutor made a speech over him, and turning to the opposite side of the room, where they were all sleeping in the midst of this "loud and furious fun," said—"There's a scene, by G—d, for Hogarth to paint. I think he and Shakespeare were our two best men at copying life." This confirmed me in my good opinion of him. Hogarth, Shakespeare, and Nature, were just enough for him (indeed for any man) to know. I said, "You read Cobbett, don't you? At least," says I, "you talk just as well as he writes." He seemed to doubt this. But I said, "We have an hour to spare: if you'll get pen, ink, and paper, and keep on talking, I'll write down what you say; and if it doesn't make a capital *Political Register*, I'll forfeit my head. You have kept me alive to-night, however. I don't know what I should have done without you." He did not dislike this view of the thing, nor my asking if he was not about the size of Jem Belcher; and told me soon afterwards, in the confidence of friendship, that "the circumstance which had given him nearly the greatest concern in his life, was Cribb's beating Jem after he had lost his eye by racket-playing."—The morning dawns; that dim but yet clear light appears, which weighs like solid bars of metal on the sleepless eyelids; the guests dropped down from their chambers one by one—but it was too late to think of going to bed now (the clock was on the stroke of seven), we had nothing for it but to find a barber's (the pole that glittered in the morning sun lighted us to his shop), and then a nine miles' march to Hungerford. The day was fine, the sky was blue, the mists were retiring from the marshy ground, the path was tolerably dry, the sitting-up all night had not done us much harm—at least the cause was good; we talked of this and that with amicable difference, roving and sipping of many subjects, but still invariably we returned to the fight. At length, a mile to the left of Hungerford, on a gentle eminence, we saw the ring surrounded by covered carts, gigs, and carriages, of which hundreds had passed us on the road; Joe gave a youthful shout, and' we hastened down a narrow lane to the scene of action.

Reader, have you ever seen a fight? If not, you have a pleasure to come, at least if it is a fight like that between the Gasman and Bill Neate. The crowd was very great when we arrived on the spot ; open carriages were coming up, with streamers flying and music playing, and the country-people were pouring in over hedge and ditch in all directions, to see their hero beat or be beaten. The odds were still on Gas, but only about five to four. Gully had been down to try Neate, and had backed him considerably, which was a damper to the sanguine confidence of the adverse party. About £200,000 were pending. Gas says he has lost £3000, which were promised him by different gentlemen if he had won. He had presumed too much on himself, which had made others presume on him. This spirited and formidable young fellow seems to have taken for his motto, the old maxim, that "there are three things necessary to success in life—*Impudence! Impudence! Impudence!*" It is so in matters of opinion, but not in the *Fancy*, which is the most practical of all things, though even here confidence is half the battle, but only half. Our friend had vapoured and swaggered too much, as if he wanted to grin and bully his adversary out of the fight. "Alas ! the Bristol man was not so tamed !"—"This is the *grave-digger*" (would Tom Hickman exclaim in the moments of intoxication from gin and success, showing his tremendous right hand), "this will send many of them to their long homes ; I haven't done with them yet !" Why should he—though he had licked four of the best men within the hour—why should he threaten to inflict dishonourable chastisement on my old master Richmond, a veteran going off the stage, and who has borne his sable honours meekly ? Magnanimity, my dear Tom, and bravery, should be inseparable. Or why should he go up to his antagonist, the first time he ever saw him at the Fives Court, and measuring him from head to foot with a glance of contempt, as Achilles surveyed Hector, say to him, "What, are you Bill Neate? I'll knock more blood out of that great carcase of thine, this day fortnight, than you ever knock'd out of a bullock's!" It was not manly—'twas not fighter-like. If he was sure of the victory (as he was not), the less said about it the better. Modesty should accompany the *Fancy* as its shadow. The best men were always the best behaved. Jem Belcher, the Game Chicken (before whom the Gasman could not have lived) were civil, silent men. So is Cribb; so is Tom Belcher, the most elegant of sparrers, and not a man for every one to take by the nose. I enlarged on this topic in the mail (while Turtle was asleep), and said very wisely (as I thought) that impertinence was a part of no profession. A boxer was bound to beat his man, but not to thrust his fist, either actually or by implication, in every one's face. Even a highwayman, in the way of trade, may blow out your brains, but if he uses foul language at the same time, I should say he was no gentleman. A boxer, I would infer, need not be a blackguard or a coxcomb, more than another. Perhaps I press this point too much on a fallen man—Mr. Thomas Hickman has by this time learnt that first of all lessons, "That man was made to mourn." He has lost nothing by the late fight but his presumption; and that every man may do as well without! By an over display of this quality, however, the public had been prejudiced against him, and the *knowing ones* were taken in. Few but those who had bet on him wished Gas to win. With my own prepossessions on the subject, the result of the 11th of December appeared to me as fine a piece of poetical justice as I had ever witnessed. The difference of weight between the two combatants (14 stones to 12) was nothing to the sporting men. Great, heavy, clumsy, long-armed Bill Neate kicked the beam in the scale of the Gasman's vanity. The amateurs were frightened at his big words, and thought they would make up for the difference of six feet and five feet nine. Truly, the *Fancy* are not men of imagination. They judge of what has been, and cannot conceive of anything that is to be. The Gasman had won hitherto; therefore he must beat a man half as big again as himself—and that to a certainty. Besides, there are as many feuds, factions, prejudices, pedantic notions in the

Fancy as in the state or in the schools. Mr. Gully is almost
the only cool, sensible man among them, who exercises an
unbiassed discretion, and is not a slave to his passions in these
matters. But enough of reflections, and to our tale. The
day, as I have said, was fine for a December morning. The
grass was wet, and the ground miry, and ploughed up with
multitudinous feet, except that, within the ring itself, there was
a spot of virgin-green, closed in and unprofaned by vulgar
tread, that shone with dazzling brightness in the mid-day sun.
For it was now noon, and we had an hour to wait. This is the
trying time. It is then the heart sickens, as you think what the
two champions are about, and how short a time will determine
their fate. After the first blow is struck, there is no opportunity
for nervous apprehensions; you are swallowed up in the
immediate interest of the scene—but

> "Between the acting of a dreadful thing
> And the first motion, all the interim is
> Like a phantasma, or a hideous dream."

I found it so as I felt the sun's rays clinging to my back, and
saw the white wintry clouds sink below the verge of the horizon.
"So," I thought, "my fairest hopes have faded from my sight!
—so will the Gasman's glory, or that of his adversary, vanish in
an hour." The *swells* were parading in their white box-coats,
the outer ring was cleared with some bruises on the heads and
shins of the rustic assembly (for the *cockneys* had been distanced
by the sixty-six miles); the time drew near; I had got a good
stand; a bustle, a buzz, ran through the crowd; and from the
opposite side entered Neate, between his second and bottle-
holder. He rolled along, swathed in his loose greatcoat, his
knock-knees bending under his huge bulk; and, with a modest,
cheerful air, threw his hat into the ring. He then just looked
round, and begun quietly to undress; when from the other side
there was a similar rush and an opening made, and the Gasman
came forward with a conscious air of anticipated triumph, too
much like the cock-of-the-walk. He strutted about more than
became a hero, sucked oranges with a supercilious air, and

threw away the skin with a toss of his head, and went up and looked at Neate, which was an act of supererogation. The only sensible thing he did was, as he strode away from the modern Ajax, to fling out his arms, as if he wanted to try whether they would do their work that day. By this time they had stripped, and presented a strong contrast in appearance. If Neate was like Ajax, "with Atlantean shoulders, fit to bear" the pugilistic reputation of all Bristol, Hickman might be compared to Diomed, light, vigorous, elastic, and his back glistened in the sun, as he moved about, like a panther's hide. There was now a dead pause—attention was awe-struck. Who at that moment, big with a great event, did not draw his breath short—did not feel his heart throb? All was ready. They tossed up for the sun, and the Gasman won. They were led up to the *scratch*—shook hands, and went at it.

In the first round every one thought it was all over. After making play a short time, the Gasman flew at his adversary like a tiger, struck five blows in as many seconds, three first, and then following him as he staggered back, two more, right and left, and down he fell, a mighty ruin. There was a shout, and I said, "There is no standing this." Neate seemed like a lifeless lump of flesh and bone, round which the Gasman's blows played with the rapidity of electricity or lightning, and you imagined he would only be lifted up to be knocked down again. It was as if Hickman held a sword or a fire in that right hand of his, and directed it against an unarmed body. They met again, and Neate seemed, not cowed, but particularly cautious. I saw his teeth clenched together and his brows knit close against the sun. He held out both his arms at full length straight before him, like two sledge hammers, and raised his left an inch or two higher. The Gasman could not get over this guard—they struck mutually and fell, but without advantage on either side. It was the same in the next round ; but the balance of power was thus restored—the fate of the battle was suspended. No one could tell how it would end. This was the only moment in which opinion was divided ; for, in the next, the Gasman aiming a mortal blow at his adversary's neck, with his right hand, and failing from the length he had to reach, the other returned it with his left at full swing, planted a tremendous blow on his cheek-bone and eyebrow, and made a red ruin of that side of his face. The Gasman went down, and there was another shout—a roar of triumph as the waves of fortune rolled tumultuously from side to side. This was a settler. Hickman got up, and "grinned horrible a ghastly smile," yet he was evidently dashed in his opinion of himself; it was the first time he had ever been so punished; all one side of his face was perfect scarlet, and his right eye was closed in dingy blackness, as he advanced to the fight, less confident, but still determined. After one or two rounds, not receiving another such remembrancer, he rallied and went at it with his former impetuosity. But in vain. His strength had been weakened—his blows could not tell at such a distance—he was obliged to fling himself at his adversary, and could not strike from his feet; and almost as regularly as he flew at him with his right hand, Neate warded the blow, or drew back out of its reach, and felled him with the return of his left. There was little cautious sparring—no half-hits—no tapping and trifling, none of the *petit-maitreship* of the art—they were almost all knock-down blows :—the fight was a good stand-up fight. The wonder was the half-minute time. If there had been a minute or more allowed between each round, it would have been intelligible how they should by degrees recover strength and resolution ; but to see two men smashed to the ground, smeared with gore, stunned, senseless, the breath beaten out of their bodies ; and then, before you recover from the shock, to see them rise up with new strength and courage, stand ready to inflict or receive mortal offence, and rush upon each other "like two clouds over the Caspian"—this is the most astonishing thing of all :—this is the high and heroic state of man ! From this time forward the event became more certain every round ; and about the twelfth it seemed as if it must have been over. Hickman generally stood with his back to me ; but in the scuffle, he had changed positions, and Neate just then made a tremendous lunge at him, and hit him full in the face. It was doubtful whether he would fall backwards or forwards; he hung suspended for a minute or two, and then fell back, throwing his hands in the air, and with his face lifted up to the sky. I never saw anything more terrific than his aspect just before he fell. All traces of life, of natural expression, were gone from him. His face was like a human skull, a death's head spouting blood. The eyes were filled with blood, the nose streamed with blood, the mouth gaped blood. He was not like an actual man, but like a preternatural, spectral appearance, or like one of the figures in Dante's *Inferno.* Yet he fought on after this for several rounds, still striking the first desperate blow, and Neate standing on the defensive, and using the same cautious guard to the last, as if he had still all his work to do; and it was not till the Gasman was so stunned in the seventeenth or eighteenth round, that his senses forsook him, and he could not come to time, that the battle was declared over.* Ye who despise the Fancy, do something to show as much *pluck*, or as much self-possession as this, before you assume a superiority which you have never given a single proof of by any one action in the whole course of your lives!—When the Gasman came to himself, the first words he uttered were, "Where am I? What is the matter?" "Nothing is the matter, Tom,—you have lost the battle, but you are the bravest man alive." And Jackson whispered to him, "I am collecting a purse for you, Tom."—Vain sounds, and unheard at that moment! Neate instantly went up and shook him cordially by the hand, and seeing some old acquaintance, began to flourish with his fists, calling out, "Ah! you always said I couldn't fight—what do you think now?" But all in good-humour, and without any appearance of arrogance; only it was evident Bill Neate was pleased that he had won the fight.

* Scroggins said of the Gasman, that he thought he was a man of that courage, that if his hands were cut off he would still fight on with the stumps—like that of Widdrington—

—— "In doleful dumps,
Who, when his legs were smitten off,
Still fought upon his stumps."

When it was over, I asked Cribb if he did not think it was a good one? He said, "*Pretty well!*" The carrier-pigeons now mounted into the air, and one of them flew with the news of her husband's victory to the bosom of Mrs. Neate. Alas, for Mrs. Hickman !

Mais au revoir, as Sir Fopling Flutter says. I went down with Joe P——s ; I returned with Jack Pigott, whom I met on the ground. Toms is a rattle-brain ; Pigott is a sentimentalist. Now, under favour, I am a sentimentalist too—therefore I say nothing, but that the interest of the excursion did not flag as I came back. Pigott and I marched along the causeway leading from Hungerford to Newbury, now observing the effect of a brilliant sun on the tawny meads or moss-coloured cottages, now exulting in the fight, now digressing to some topic of general and elegant literature. My friend was dressed in character for the occasion, or like one of the Fancy ; that is, with a double portion of greatcoats, clogs, and overhauls : and just as we had agreed with a couple of country-lads to carry his superfluous wearing-apparel to the next town, we were over-taken by a return post-chaise, into which I got, Pigott prefer-ring a seat on the bar. There were two strangers already in the chaise, and on their observing they supposed I had been to the fight, I said I had, and concluded they had done the same. They appeared, however, a little shy and sore on the subject ; and it was not till after several hints dropped, and questions put, that it turned out that they had missed it. One of these friends had undertaken to drive the other there in his gig : they had set out, to make sure work, the day before at three in the afternoon. The owner of the one-horse vehicle scorned to ask his way, and drove right on to Bagshot, instead of turning off at Hounslow : there they stopped all night, and set off the next day across the country to Reading, from whence they took coach, and got down within a mile or two of Hungerford, just half-an-hour after the fight was over. This might be safely set down as one of the miseries of human life. We parted with these two gentlemen who had been to see the fight, but had returned as they went, at Wolhampton, where we were promised beds (an irresistible temptation, for Pigott had passed the preceding night at Hungerford as we had done at Newbury), and we turned into an old bow-windowed parlour with a carpet and a snug fire ; and after devouring a quantity of tea, toast, and eggs, sat down to consider, during an hour of philosophic leisure, what we should have for supper.   In the midst of an Epicurean deliberation between a roasted fowl and mutton chops with mashed potatoes, we were interrupted by an inroad of Goths and Vandals—*O procul este profani*—not real flash-men, but interlopers, noisy pretenders, butchers from Tothill Fields, brokers from Whitechapel, who called immediately for pipes and tobacco, hoping it would not be disagreeable to the gentlemen, and began to insist that it was *a cross*.   Pigott withdrew from the smoke and noise into another room, and left me to dispute the point with them for a couple of hours *sans intermission* by the dial.   The next morning we rose refreshed ; and on observing that Jack had a pocket volume in his hand, in which he read in the intervals of our discourse, I inquired what it was, and learned to my particular satisfaction that it was a volume of the *New Eloise.*   Ladies, after this, you will contend that a love for the Fancy is incompatible with the cultivation of sentiment?— We jogged on as before, my friend setting me up in a genteel drab great coat and green silk handkerchief (which I must say became me exceedingly), and after stretching our legs for a few miles, and seeing Jack Randall, Ned Turner, and Scroggins pass on the top of one of the Bath coaches, we engaged with the driver of the second to take us to London for the usual fee.   I got inside, and found three other passengers.   One of them was an old gentleman with an aquiline nose, powdered hair, and a pig-tail, and who looked as if he had played many a rubber at the Bath rooms.   I said to myself, he is very like Mr. Windham ; I wish he would enter into conversation, that I might hear what fine observations would come from those finely-turned features.   However, nothing passed, till, stopping to dine at Reading, some inquiry was made by the company about the fight, and I gave (as (the reader may believe) an eloquent and animated description of it. When we got into the coach again, the old gentleman, after a graceful exordium, said he had, when a boy, been to a fight between the famous Broughton and George Stevenson, who was called the *Fighting Coachman,* in the year 1770, with the late Mr. Windham. This beginning flattered the spirit of prophecy with me, and riveted my attention. He went on—" George Stevenson was coachman to a friend of my father's. He was an old man when I saw him, some years afterwards. He took hold of his own arm and said, 'there was muscle here once, but now it is no more than this young gentleman's.' He added, 'well, no matter ; I have been here long, I am willing to go hence, and I hope I have done no more harm than another man.' Once," said my unknown companion, " I asked him if he had ever beat Broughton ? He said Yes ; that he had fought with him three times, and the last time he fairly beat him, though the world did not allow it. 'I'll tell you how it was, master. When the seconds lifted us up in the last round, we were so exhausted that neither of us could stand, and we fell upon one another, and as Master Broughton fell uppermost, the mob gave it in his favour, and he was said to have won the battle. But the fact was, that as his second (John Cuthbert) lifted him up, he said to him, " I'll fight no more, I've had enough ;" which,' says Stevenson, 'you know gave me the victory. And to prove to you that this was the case, when John Cuthbert was on his death-bed, and they asked him if there was anything on his mind which he wished to confess, he answered, " Yes, that there was one thing he wished to set right, for that certainly Master Stevenson won that last fight with Master Broughton ; for he whispered him as he lifted him up in the last round of all, that he had had enough."' "This," said the Bath gentleman, " was a bit of human nature ;" and I have written this account of the fight on purpose that it might not be lost to the world. He also stated as a proof of the candour of mind in this class of men, that Stevenson acknowledged that Broughton could have beat him in his best day ; but that he (Broughton) was getting old in their last rencounter.

When we stopped in Piccadilly, I wanted to ask the gentleman some questions about the late Mr. Windham, but had not courage. I got out, resigned my coat and green silk handkerchief to Pigott (loth to part with these ornaments of life), and walked home in high spirits.

P.S.—Joe called upon me the next day, to ask me if I did not think the fight was a complete thing? I said I thought it was. I hope he will relish my account of it.

ON THE LOOK OF A GENTLEMAN.

The nobleman-look? Yes, I know what you mean very well: that look which a nobleman should have, rather than what they have generally now. The Duke of Buckingham (Sheffield) was a genteel man, and had a great deal the look you speak of. Wycherley was a very genteel man, and had the nobleman-look as much as the Duke of Buckingham.—POPE.

He instanced it too in Lord Peterborough, Lord Bolingbroke, Lord Hinchinbroke, the Duke of Bolton, and two or three more.—SPENCE'S *Anecdotes of Pope.*

I HAVE chosen the above motto to a very delicate subject, which in prudence I might let alone. I, however, like the title; and will try, at least, to make a sketch of it.

What it is that constitutes the look of a gentleman is more easily felt than described. We all know it when we see it; but we do not know how to account for it, or to explain in what it consists. *Causa latet, res ipsi notassima.* Ease, grace, dignity have been given as the exponents and expressive symbols of this look; but I would rather say, that an habitual self-possession determines the appearance of a gentleman. He should have the complete command, not only over his countenance, but over his limbs and motions. In other words, he should discover in his air and manner a voluntary power over his whole body, which, with every inflection of it, should be under the control of his will. It must be evident that he looks and does as he likes, without any restraint, confusion, or awkwardness. He is, in fact, master of his person, as the professor of any art or science is of a particular instrument ; he directs it to what use he pleases and intends. Wherever this power and facility appear, we recognise the look and deport- ment of the gentleman—that is, of a person who by his habits and situation in life, and in his ordinary intercourse with society, has had little else to do than to study those movements, and that carriage of the body, which were accompanied with most satisfaction to himself, and were calculated to excite the approbation of the beholder. Ease, it might be observed, is not enough ; dignity is too much. There must be a certain *retenu*, a conscious decorum, added to the first—and a certain "familiarity of regard, quenching the austere countenance of control," in the other, to answer to our conception of this character. Perhaps propriety is as near a word as any to denote the manners of the gentleman ; elegance is necessary to the fine gentleman ; dignity is proper to noblemen ; and majesty to kings !

Wherever this constant and decent subjection of the body to the mind is visible in the customary actions of walking, sitting, riding, standing, speaking, etc., we draw the same conclusion as to the individual—whatever may be the impediments or unavoidable defects in the machine of which he has the management. A man may have a mean or disagreeable exterior, may halt in his gait, or have lost the use of half his limbs ; and yet he may show this habitual attention to what is graceful and becoming in the use he makes of all the power he has left—in the "nice conduct" of the most unpromising and impracticable figure. A hump-backed or deformed man does not necessarily look like a clown or a mechanic ; on the contrary, from his care in the adjustment of his appear- ance, and his desire to remedy his defects, he for the most part acquires something of the look of a gentleman. The common nick-name of *My Lord,* applied to such persons, has allusion to this—to their circumspect deportment, and tacit resistance to vulgar prejudice. Lord Ogleby, in the " Clandestine Marriage," is as crazy a piece of elegance and refinement, even after he is "wound up for the day," as can well be imagined; yet in the hands of a genuine actor, his tottering step, his twitches of the gout, his unsuccessful attempts at youth and gaiety, take nothing from the nobleman. He has the *ideal* model in his mind, resents his deviations from it with proper horror, recovers himself from any ungraceful action as soon as possible; does all he can with his limited means, and fails in his just pretensions, not from inadvertence, but necessity. Sir Joseph Banks, who was almost bent double, retained to the last the look of a privy-councillor. There was all the firmness and dignity that could be given by the sense of his own import-ance to so distorted and disabled a trunk. Sir Charles Bunbury, as he saunters down St. James's Street, with a large slouched hat, a lack-lustre eye, and aquiline nose, an old shabby drab-coloured coat, buttoned across his breast without a cape—with old top-boots, and his hands in his waistcoat or breeches pockets, as if he were strolling along his own garden-walks, or over the turf at Newmarket, after having made his bets secure —presents nothing very dazzling, or graceful, or dignified to the imagination; though you can tell infallibly at the first glance, or even a bow-shot off, that he is a gentleman of the first water (the same that sixty years ago married the beautiful Lady Sarah Lennox, with whom the king was in love). What is the clue to this mystery? It is evident that his person costs him no more trouble than an old glove. His limbs are, as it were, left to take care of themselves; they move of their own accord; he does not strut or stand on tip-toe to show

> "—— how tall
> His person is above them all;"—

but he seems to find his own level, and wherever he is, to slide into his place naturally; he is equally at home among lords or gamblers; nothing can discompose his fixed serenity of look and purpose; there is no mark of superciliousness about him, nor does it appear as if anything could meet his eye to startle or throw him off his guard; he neither avoids nor courts notice; but the *archaism* of his dress may be understood to denote a lingering partiality for the costume of the last age, and something like a prescriptive contempt for the finery of this. The old one-eyed Duke of Queensbury is another example that I might quote. As he sat in his bow-window in Piccadilly, erect and emaciated, he seemed like a nobleman framed and glazed, or a well-dressed mummy of the court of George II.

We have few of these precious specimens of the gentleman or nobleman-look now remaining; other considerations have set aside the exclusive importance of the character, and, of course, the jealous attention to the outward expression of it. Where we oftenest meet with it now-a-days is, perhaps, in the butlers in old families, or the valets, and "gentlemen's gentlemen" of the younger branches. The sleek pursy gravity of the one answers to the stately air of some of their *quondam* masters; and the flippancy and finery of our old-fashioned beaux, having been discarded by the heirs to the title and estate, have been retained by their lacqueys. The late Admiral Byron (I have heard Northcote say) had a butler, or steward, who, from constantly observing his master, had so learned to mimic him—the look, the manner, the voice, the bow were so alike—he was so "subdued to the very quality of his lord"—that it was difficult to distinguish them apart. Our modern footmen, as we see them fluttering and lounging in lobbies, or at the doors of ladies' carriages, bedizened in lace and powder, with ivory-headed cane and embroidered gloves, give one the only idea of the fine gentlemen of former periods, as they are still occasionally represented on the stage ; and indeed our theatrical heroes, who top such parts, might be supposed to have copied, as a last resource, from the heroes of the shoulder-knot. We also sometimes meet with straggling personation of this character, got up in common life from pure romantic enthusiasm, and on absolutely ideal principles. I recollect a well-grown comely haberdasher, who made a practice of walking every day from Bishopsgate Street to Pall Mall and Bond Street with the undaunted air and strut of a general-officer ; and also a prim undertaker, who regularly tendered his person, whenever the weather would permit, from the neighbourhood of Camberwell into the favourite promenades of the City with

a mincing gait that would have become a gentleman-usher of
the black-rod. What a strange infatuation to live in a dream
of being taken for what one is not—in deceiving others, and at
the same time ourselves ; for no doubt these persons believed
that they thus appeared to the world in their true characters,
and that their assumed pretensions did no more than justice to
their real merits.

> "*Dress* makes the man, and want of it the fellow :
> The rest is all but leather and prunella."

I confess, however, that I admire this look of a gentleman
more when it rises from the level of common life, and bears the
stamp of intellect, than when it is formed out of the mould of
adventitious circumstances. I think more highly of Wycherley
than I do of Lord Hinchinbroke, for looking like a lord. In
the one it was the effect of native genius, grace, and spirit ; in
the other, comparatively speaking, of pride or custom. A
visitor complimenting Voltaire on the growth and flourishing
condition of some trees in his grounds, "Ay," said the French
wit, "they have nothing else to do !" A lord has nothing to do
but to look like a lord : our comic poet had something else to
do, and did it ! *

Though the disadvantages of nature or accident do not act as
obstacles to the look of a gentleman, those of education and
employment do. A shoemaker who is bent in two over his
daily task ; a tailor who sits crossed-legged all day ; a plough-
man who wears clog-shoes over the furrowed miry soil, and can
hardly drag his feet after him ; a scholar who has pored all his
life over books—are not likely to possess that natural freedom
and ease, or to pay that strict attention to personal appearances,
that the look of a gentleman implies. I might add, that a man-
milliner behind a counter, who is compelled to show every mark
of complaisance to his customers, but hardly expects common
civility from them in return ; or a sheriff's officer, who has a consciousness of power, but none of good-will to or from anybody,

---

* Wycherley was a great favourite with the Duchess of Cleveland.

are equally remote from the *beau-idéal* of this character. A man who is awkward from bashfulness is a clown—as one who is showing off a number of impertinent airs and graces at every turn, is a coxcomb or an upstart. Mere awkwardness or rusticity of behaviour may arise either from want of presence of mind in the company of our *betters* (the commonest hind goes about his regular business without any of the *mauvaise honte*), from a deficiency of breeding, as it is called, in not having been taught certain fashionable accomplishments—or from unremitting application to certain sorts of mechanical labour, unfitting the body for general or indifferent uses. (That vulgarity which proceeds from a total disregard of decorum, and want of careful control over the different actions of the body—such as loud speaking, boisterous gesticulations, etc. —is rather rudeness and violence, than awkwardness or uneasy restraint.) Now the gentleman is free from all these causes of ungraceful demeanour. He is independent in his circumstances, and is used to enter into society on equal terms ; he is taught the modes of address and forms of courtesy most commonly practised and most proper to ingratiate him into the good opinion of those he associates with ; and he is relieved from the necessity of following any of those laborious trades or callings which cramp, strain, and distort the human frame. He is not bound to do any one earthly thing ; to use any exertion, or put himself in any posture, that is not perfectly easy and graceful, agreeable and becoming. Neither is he (at the present day) required to excel in any art or science, game or exercise. He is supposed qualified to dance a minuet, not to dance on the tight-rope—to stand upright, not to stand on his head. He has only to sacrifice to the Graces. Alcibiades threw away a flute, because the playing on it discomposed his features. Take the fine gentleman out of the common boarding-school or drawing-room accomplishments, and set him to any ruder or more difficult task, and he will make but a sorry figure. Ferdinand in the "Tempest," when he is put by Prospero to carry logs of wood, does not strike us as a very heroic character, though he loses nothing of the king's son. If a young gallant of the first fashion were asked to shoe a horse, or hold a plough, or fell a tree, he would make a very ridiculous business of the first experiment. I saw a set of young naval officers, very genteel-looking young men, playing at rackets not long ago, and it is impossible to describe the uncouthness of their motions and unaccountable contrivances for hitting the ball. Something effeminate as well as commonplace, then, enters into the composition of the gentleman : he is a little of the *petit-maître* in his pretensions. He is only graceful and accomplished in those things to which he has paid almost his whole attention—such as the carriage of his body, and adjustment of his dress ; and to which he is of sufficient importance in the scale of society to attract the idle attention of others.

A man's manner of presenting himself in company is but a superficial test of his real qualifications. Serjeant Atkinson, we are assured by Fielding, would have marched, at the head of his platoon, up to a masked battery with less apprehension than he came into a room full of pretty women. So we may sometimes see persons look foolish enough on entering a party, or returning a salutation, who instantly feel themselves at home, and recover all their self-possession, as soon as any of that sort of conversation begins from which nine-tenths of the company retire in the extremest trepidation lest they should betray their ignorance or incapacity. A high spirit and stubborn pride are often accompanied with an unprepossessing and unpretending appearance. The greatest heroes do not show it by their looks. There are individuals of a nervous habit, who might be said to abhor their own persons, and to startle at their own appearance, as the peacock tries to hide its legs. They are always shy, uncomfortable, restless ; and all their actions are, in a manner, at cross-purposes with themselves. This, of course, destroys the look we are speaking of, from the want of ease and self-confidence. There is another sort who have too much negligence of manner and contempt for formal punctilios. They take their full swing in whatever they are about, and make it seem almost necessary to get out of their way. Perhaps something of this bold, licentious, slovenly, lounging

character may be objected by a fastidious eye to the appearance
of Lord Castlereagh. It might be said of him, without disparagement, that he looks more like a lord than a gentleman.
We see nothing petty or finical, assuredly—nothing hard-bound
or reined-in—but a flowing outline, a broad, free style. He sits
in the House of Commons, with his hat slouched over his
forehead, and a sort of stoop in his shoulders, as if he cowered
over his antagonists, like a bird of prey over its quarry—
" hatching vain empires." There is an irregular grandeur about
him, an unwieldy power, loose, disjointed, " voluminous and
vast "—coiled up in the folds of its own purposes—cold, death-
like, smooth, and smiling—that is neither quite at ease with
itself, nor safe for others to approach! On the other hand,
there is the Marquis Wellesley, a jewel of a man. He advances
into his place in the House of Lords, with head erect, and his
best foot foremost. The star sparkles on his breast, and the
garter is seen bound tight below his knee. It might be thought
that he still trod a measure on soft carpets, and was surrounded,
not only by spiritual and temporal lords, but

> " Stores of ladies, whose bright eyes
> Rain influence, and judge the prize."

The chivalrous spirit that shines through him, the air of gallantry in his personal as well as rhetorical appeals to the
House, glances a partial lustre on the Woolsack as he addresses
it ; and makes Lord Erskine raise his sunken head from a
dream of transient popularity. His heedless vanity throws
itself unblushingly on the unsuspecting candour of his hearers,
and ravishes mute admiration. You would almost guess of this
nobleman beforehand that he was a marquis—something higher
than an earl, and less important than a duke. Nature has just
fitted him for the niche he fills in the scale of rank or title. He
is a finished miniature-picture set in brilliants : Lord C——
might be compared to a loose sketch in oil, not properly hung.
The character of the one is ease, of the other, elegance.
Elegance is something more than ease ; it is more than a
freedom from awkwardness or restraint. It implies, I conceive,

a precision, a polish, a sparkling effect, spirited yet delicate, which is perfectly exemplified in Lord Wellesley's face and figure.

The greatest contrast to this little lively nobleman was the late Lord Stanhope. Tall above his peers, he presented an appearance something between a Patagonian chief and one of the Long Parliament. With his long black hair, "unkempt and wild"—his black clothes, lank features, strange antics, and screaming voice, he was the Orson of debate.

> " A Satyr that comes staring from the woods
> Cannot at first speak like an orator."

Yet he was both an orator and a wit in his way. His harangues were an odd jumble of logic and mechanics, of the Statutes at Large and Joe Miller jests, of stern principle and sly humour, of shrewdness and absurdity, of method and madness. What is more extraordinary, he was an honest man. He was out of his place in the House of Lords. He particularly delighted, in his eccentric onsets, to make havoc of the bench of bishops. " I like," said he, "to argue with one of my lords the bishops ; and the reason why I do so is, that I generally have the best of the argument." He was altogether a different man from Lord Eldon ; yet his lordship "gave him good *œillades*," as he broke a jest, or argued a moot-point, and, while he spoke, smiles, roguish twinkles, glittered in the Chancellor's eyes.

The look of the gentleman, "the nobleman-look," is little else than the reflection of the looks of the world. We smile at those who smile upon us : we are gracious to those who pay their court to us : we naturally acquire confidence and ease when all goes well with us, when we are encouraged by the blandishments of fortune and the good opinion of mankind. A whole street bowing regularly to a man every time he rides out may teach him how to pull off his hat in return, without supposing a particular genius for bowing (more than for governing, or anything else) born in the family. It has been observed that persons who sit for their pictures improve the character of their countenances, from the desire they have to procure the most favourable representation of themselves. "Tell me, pray, good Mr. Carmine, when you come to the eyes, that I may call up a look," says the Alderman's wife, in Foote's farce of "Taste." Ladies grow handsome by looking at themselves in the glass, and heightening the agreeable airs and expression of features they so much admire there. So the favourites of fortune adjust themselves in the glass of fashion and the flattering illusions of public opinion. Again, the expression of face in the gentleman or thorough-bred man of the world is not that of refinement so much as of flexibility; of sensibility or enthusiasm, so much as of indifference : it argues presence of mind, rather than enlargement of ideas. In this it differs from the heroic and philosophical look. Instead of an intense unity of purpose, wound up to some great occasion, it is dissipated and frittered down into a number of evanescent expressions, fitted for every variety of unimportant occurrences : instead of the expansion of general thought or intellect, you trace chiefly the little, trite, cautious, movable lines of conscious but concealed self-complacency. If Raphael had painted St. Paul as a gentleman, what a figure he would have made of the great Apostle of the Gentiles—occupied with himself, not carried away, raised, inspired with his subject—insinuating his doctrines into his audience, not launching them from him with the tongues of the Holy Spirit, and with looks of fiery, scorching zeal! Gentlemen, luckily, can afford to sit for their own portraits : painters do not trouble them to sit as studies for history. What a difference is there in this respect beween a Madonna of Raphael, and a lady of fashion, even by Vandyke : the former refined and elevated, the latter light and trifling, with no emanation of soul, no depth of feeling—each arch expression playing on the surface, and passing into any other at pleasure—no one thought having its full scope, but checked by some other—soft, careless, insincere, pleased, affected, amiable! The French physiognomy is more cut up and subdivided into petty lines and sharp angles than any other : it does not want for subtlety, or an air of gentility, which last it often has in a remarkable degree—but it is the most unpoetical and the least picturesque of all others. I cannot explain what I mean by this variable telegraphic machinery of polite expression better than by an obvious allusion. Every one by walking the streets of London (or any other populous city) acquires a walk which is easily distinguished from that of strangers ; a quick flexibility of movement, a smart jerk, an aspiring and confident tread, and an air as if on the alert to keep the line of march ; but for all that, there is not much grace or grandeur in this local strut : you see the person is not a country bumpkin, but you would not say he is a hero or a sage—because he is a cockney. So it is in passing through the artificial and thickly-peopled scenes of life. You get the look of a man of the world : you rub off the pedant and the clown ; but you do not make much progress in wisdom or virtue, or in the characteristic expression of either.

The character of a gentleman (I take it) may be explained nearly thus :—A blackguard *(un vaurien)* is a fellow who does not care whom he offends : a clown is a blockhead who does not know when he offends : a gentleman is one who understands and shows every mark of deference to the claims of self-love in others, and exacts it in return from them. Politeness and the pretensions to the character in question have reference almost entirely to this reciprocal manifestation of good-will and good opinion towards each other in casual society. Morality regulates our sentiments and conduct as they have a connection with ultimate and important consequences. Manners, properly speaking, regulate our words and actions in the routine of personal intercourse. They have little to do with real kindness of intention, or practical services, or disinterested sacrifices ; but they put on the garb, and mock the appearance of these, in order to prevent a breach of the peace, and to smooth and varnish over the discordant materials, when any number of individuals are brought in contact together. The conventional compact of good manners does not reach beyond the moment and the company. Say, for instance, that the *rabble*, the labouring and industrious part of the community, are taken up with supplying their own wants, and pining over their own hardships—scrambling for what they can get, and not refining on any of their pleasures, or troubling themselves about the fastidious pretensions of others : again, there are philosophers who are busied in the pursuit of truth—or patriots who are active for the good of their country ; but here, we will suppose, are a knot of people got together, who, having no serious wants of their own, with leisure and independence, and caring little about abstract truth or practical utility, are met for no mortal purpose but to say and to do all manner of obliging things, to pay the greatest possible respect, and show the most delicate and flattering attentions to one another. The politest set of gentlemen and ladies in the world can do no more than this. The laws that regulate this species of select and fantastic society are conformable to its ends and origin. The fine gentleman or lady must not, on any account, say a rude thing to the persons present, but you may turn them into the utmost ridicule the instant they are gone : nay, not to do so is sometimes considered as an indirect slight to the party that remains. You must compliment your bitterest foe to his face, and may slander your dearest friend behind his back. The last may be immoral, but it is not unmannerly. The gallant maintains his title to this character by treating every woman he meets with the same marked and unremitting attention as if she was his mistress : the courtier treats every man with the same professions of esteem and kindness as if he were an accomplice with him in some plot against mankind. Of course, these professions, made only to please, go for nothing in practice. To insist on them afterwards as literal obligations, would be to betray an ignorance of this kind of interlude, or masquerading in real life. To ruin your friend at play is not inconsistent with the character of a gentleman and a man of honour, if it is done with civility ; though to warn him of his danger, so as to imply a doubt of his judgment, or interference with his will, would be to subject yourself to be run through the body with a sword. It is that which wounds the self-love of the individual that is offensive—that which flatters it that is welcome—however salutary the one, or however fatal the other may be. A habit of plain speaking is totally contrary to the tone of good breeding. You must prefer the opinion of the company to your own, and even to truth. I doubt whether a gentleman must not be of the Established Church, and a Tory. A true cavalier can only be a martyr to prejudice or fashion. A Whig lord appears to me as great an anomaly as a patriot king. A sectary is sour and unsociable. A philosopher is quite out of the question. He is in the clouds, and had better not be let down on the floor in a basket, to play the blockhead. He is sure to commit himself in good company, and by dealing always in abstractions, and driving at generalities, to offend against the three proprieties of time, place, and person. Authors are angry, loud, and vehement in argument : the man of more refined breeding, who has been "all tranquillity and smiles," goes away, and tries to ruin the antagonist whom he could not vanquish in a dispute. The manners of a court and of polished life are by no means downright, straightforward, but the contrary. They have something dramatic in them ; each person plays an assumed part ; the affected, overstrained politeness and suppression of real sentiment lead to concealed irony, and the spirit of satire and raillery ; and hence we may account for the perfection of the genteel comedy of the century before the last, when poets were allowed to mingle in the court-circles, and took their cue from the splendid ring

" Of mimic statesmen and their merry king."

The essence of this sort of conversation and intercourse, both on and off the stage, has somehow since evaporated ; the disguises of royalty, nobility, gentry have been in some measure seen through : we have become individually of little importance, compared with greater objects, in the eyes of our neighbours, and even in our own : abstract topics, not personal pretensions, are the order of the day ; so that what remains of the character we have been talking of, is chiefly exotic and provincial, and may be seen still flourishing in country-places, in a wholesome state of vegetable decay !

A man may have the manners of a gentleman without having the look, and he may have the character of a gentleman, in a more abstracted point of view, without the manners. The feelings of a gentleman, in this higher sense, only denote a more refined humanity—a spirit delicate in itself, and unwilling to offend, either in the greatest or the smallest things. This may be coupled with absence of mind, with ignorance of forms, and frequent blunders. But the will is good. The spring of gentle offices and true regards is untainted. A person of this stamp blushes at an impropriety he was guilty of twenty years before, though he is, perhaps, liable to repeat it to-morrow. He never forgives himself for even a slip of the tongue, that implies an assumption of superiority over any one. In proportion to the concessions made to him, he lowers his demands. He gives the wall to a beggar : but does not always bow to great men. This class of character have been called "God Almighty's gentlemen." There are not a great many of them. The *late* George Dyer was one; for we understand that that gentleman was not able to survive some ill-disposed person's having asserted of him that he had mistaken Lord Castlereagh for the Author of *Waverley.*

ON THE CONDUCT OF LIFE; OR, ADVICE TO A SCHOOL-BOY.

MY DEAR LITTLE FELLOW,—You are now going to settle at school, and may consider this as your first entrance into the world. As my health is so indifferent, and I may not be with you long, I wish to leave you some advice (the best I can) for your conduct in life, both that it may be of use to you, and as something to remember me by. I may at least be able to caution you against my own errors, if nothing else.

As we went along to your new place of destination, you often repeated that "You durst say they were a set of stupid, disagreeable people," meaning the people at the school. You were to blame in this. It is a good old rule to hope for the best. Always, my dear, believe things to be right till you find them the contrary; and even then, instead of irritating yourself against them, endeavour to put up with them as well as you can, if you cannot alter them. You said, "You were sure you should not like the school where you were going." This was wrong. What you meant was that you did not like to leave home. But you could not tell whether you should like the school or not, till you had given it a trial. Otherwise, your saying that you should not like it was determining that you would not like it. Never anticipate evils; or, because you cannot have things exactly as you wish, make them out worse than they are, through mere spite and wilfulness.

You seemed at first to take no notice of your school-fellows, or rather to set yourself against them, because they were strangers to you. They knew as little of you as you did of them ; so that this would have been a reason for their keeping aloof from you as well, which you would have felt as a hardship. Learn never to conceive a prejudice against others, because you know nothing of them. It is bad reasoning, and makes enemies of half the world. Do not think ill of them, till they behave ill to you ; and then strive to avoid the faults which you see in them. This will disarm their hostility sooner than pique, or resentment, or complaint.

I thought you were disposed to criticise the dress of some of the boys as not so good as your own. Never despise any one for anything that he cannot help—least of all, for his poverty. I would wish you to keep up appearances yourself as a defence against the idle sneers of the world, but I would not have you value yourself upon them. I hope you will neither be the dupe nor victim of vulgar prejudices. Instead of saying above— "Never despise any one for anything that he cannot help"—I might have said—"Never despise any one at all ;" for contempt implies a triumph over and pleasure in the ill of another. It means that you are glad and congratulate yourself on their failings or misfortunes. The sense of inferiority in others, without this indirect appeal to our self-love, is a painful feeling, and not an exulting one.

You complain since, that the boys laugh at you and do not care about you, and that you are not treated as you were at home. My dear, that is one chief reason for your being sent to school, to inure you betimes to the unavoidable rubs and uncertain reception you may meet with in life. You cannot always be with me, and perhaps it is as well that you cannot. But you must not expect others to show the same concern about you as I should. You have hitherto been a spoiled child, and have been used to have your own way a good deal, both in the house and among your play-fellows, with whom you were too fond of being a leader : but you have good nature and good sense, and will get the better of this in time. You have now got among other boys who are your equals, or bigger and stronger than yourself, and who have something else to attend to besides humouring your whims and fancies, and you feel this as a repulse or piece of injustice.   But the first lesson to learn is that there are other people in the world besides yourself. There are a number of boys in the school where you are, whose amusements and pursuits (whatever they may be) are and ought to be of as much consequence to them as yours can be to you, and to which therefore you must give way in your turn. The more airs of childish self-importance you give yourself, you will only expose yourself to be the more thwarted and laughed at.   True equality is the only true morality or true wisdom. Remember always that you are but one among others, and you can hardly mistake your place in society.   In your father's house you might do as you pleased : in the world, you will find competitors at every turn.   You are not born a king's son, to destroy or dictate to millions : you can only expect to share their fate, or settle your differences amicably with them.   You already find it so at school ; and I wish you to be reconciled to your situation as soon and with as little pain as you can.

It was my misfortune, perhaps, to be bred up among Dissenters, who look with too jaundiced an eye at others, and set too high a value on their own peculiar pretensions. From being proscribed themselves, they learn to proscribe others ; and come in the end to reduce all integrity of principle and soundness of opinion within the pale of their own little communion.   Those who were out of it, and did not belong to the class of *Rational Dissenters*, I was led erroneously to look upon as hardly deserving the name of rational beings.   Being thus satisfied as to the select few who are "the salt of the earth," it is easy to persuade ourselves that we are at the head of them, and to fancy ourselves of more importance in the scale of true desert than all the rest of the world put together, who do not interpret a certain text of Scripture in the manner that we have been taught to do.   You will (from the difference of education) be free from this bigotry, and will, I hope, avoid everything akin to the same exclusive and narrow-minded spirit.   Think that the minds of men are various as their faces —that the modes and employments of life are numberless as they are necessary—that there is more than one class of merit —that though others may be wrong in some things, they are not so in all—and that countless races of men have been born, have lived and died, without ever hearing of any one of those points in which you take a just pride and pleasure—and you will not err on the side of that spiritual pride or intellectual coxcombry which has been so often the bane of the studious and learned !

I observe you have got a way of speaking of your school-fellows as "*that* Hoare, *that* Harris," and so on, as if you meant to mark them out for particular reprobation, or did not think them good enough for you. It is a bad habit to speak disrespectfully of others : for it will lead you to think and feel uncharitably towards them. Ill names beget ill blood. Even where there may be some repeated trifling provocation, it is better to be courteous, mild, and forbearing, than captious, impatient, and fretful. The faults of others too often arise cut of our own ill temper ; or though they should be real, we shall not mend them by exasperating ourselves against them. Treat your playmates as Hamlet advises Polonious to treat the players, "according to your own dignity rather than their deserts." If you fly out at everything in them that you dis-approve or think done on purpose to annoy you, you lie constantly at the mercy of their caprice, rudeness, or ill-nature. You should be more your own master.

Do not begin to quarrel with the world too soon : for, bad as it may be, it is the best we have to live in—here. If railing would have made it better, it would have been reformed long ago : but as this is not to be hoped for at present, the best way is to slide through it as contentedly and innocently as we may. The worst fault it has is want of charity : and calling *knave* and *fool* at every turn will not cure this failing. Consider (as a matter of vanity) that if there were not so many knaves and fools as we find, the wise and honest would not be those rare and shining characters that they are allowed to be ; and (as a matter of philosophy) that if the world be really incorrigible in this respect, it is a reflection to make one sad, not angry. We may laugh or weep at the madness of mankind : we have no right to vilify them, for our own sakes or theirs.   Misanthropy is not the disgust of the mind at human nature, but with itself ; or it is laying its own exaggerated vices and foul blots at the door of others ! Do not, however, mistake what I have here said. I would not have you, when you grow up, adopt the low and sordid fashion of palliating existing abuses or of putting the best face upon the worst things. I only mean that indiscriminate unqualified satire can do little good, and that those who indulge in the most revolting speculations on human nature do not themselves always set the fairest examples, or strive to prevent its lower degradation. They seem rather willing to reduce it to their theoretical standard. For the rest, the very outcry that is made (if sincere) shows that things cannot be quite so bad as they are represented. The abstract hatred and scorn of vice implies the capacity for virtue : the impatience expressed at the most striking instances of deformity proves the innate idea and love of beauty in the human mind. The best antidote I can recommend to you hereafter against the disheartening effect of such writings as those of Rochefoucault, Mandeville, and others, will be to look at the pictures of Raphael and Correggio. You need not be altogether ashamed, my dear little boy, of belonging to a species which could produce such faces as those ; nor despair of doing something worthy of a laudable ambition, when you see what such hands have wrought ! You will, perhaps, one day have reason to thank me for this advice.

As to your studies and school-exercises, I wish you to learn Latin, French, and dancing. I would insist upon the last more particularly, both because it is more likely to be neglected, and because it is of the greatest consequence to your success in life. Everything almost depends upon first impressions ; and these depend (besides *person,* which is not in our power) upon two things, *dress* and *address,* which every one may command with proper attention. These are the small coin in the intercourse of life which are continually in request ; and perhaps you will find at the year's end, or towards the close of life, that the daily insults, coldness, or contempt, to which you have been exposed by a neglect of such superficial recommendations, are hardly atoned for by the few proofs of esteem or admiration which your integrity or talents have been able to extort in the course of it. When we habitually disregard those things which we know will ensure the favourable opinion of others, it shows we set that opinion at defiance, or consider ourselves above it, which no one ever did with impunity. An inattention to our own persons implies a disrespect to others, and may often be traced no less to a want of good-nature than of good sense. The old maxim—*Desire to please, and you will infallibly please*—explains the whole matter. If there is a tendency to vanity and affectation on this side of the question, there is an equal alloy of pride and obstinacy on the opposite one. Slovenliness may at any time be cured by an effort of resolution, but a graceful carriage requires an early habit, and in most cases the aid of the dancing-master. I would not have you, from not knowing how to enter a room properly, stumble at the very threshold in the good graces of those on whom it is possible the fate of your future life may depend. Nothing creates a greater prejudice against anyone than awkwardness. A person who is confused in manner and gesture seems to have done something wrong, or as if he was conscious of no one qualification to build a confidence in himself upon. On the other hand, openness, freedom, self-possession, set others at ease with you by showing that you are on good terms with yourself. Grace in women gains the affections sooner, and secures them longer, than anything else—it is an outward and visible sign of an inward harmony of soul—as the want of it in men, as if the mind and body equally hitched in difficulties and were distracted with doubts, is the greatest impediment in the career of gallantry and road to the female heart. Another thing I would caution you against is not to pore over your books till you are bent almost double—a habit you will never be able to get the better of, and which you will find of serious ill-consequence. *A stoop in the shoulders* sinks a man in public and in private estimation. You are at present straight enough, and you walk with boldness and spirit. Do nothing to take away the use of your limbs, or the spring and elasticity of your muscles. As to all wordly advantages, it is to the full of as much importance that your deportment should be erect and manly as your actions.

You will naturally find out all this, and fall into it, if your attention is drawn out sufficiently to what is passing around you ; and this will be the case, unless you are absorbed too much in books and those sedentary studies,

"Which waste the marrow, and consume the brain."

You are, I think, too fond of reading as it is. As one means of avoiding excess in this way, I would wish you to make it a rule, never to read at meal-times, nor in company when there is any (even the most trivial) conversation going on, nor even to let your eagerness to learn encroach upon your play-hours. Books are but one inlet of knowledge ; and the pores of the mind, like those of the body, should be left open to all impressions. I applied too close to my studies, soon after I was of your age, and hurt myself irreparably by it. Whatever may be the value of learning, health and good spirits are of more.

I would have you, as I said, make yourself master of French, because you may find it of use in the commerce of life ; and I would have you learn Latin, partly because I learnt it myself, and I would not have you without any of the advantages or sources of knowledge that I possessed—it would be a bar of separation between us—and secondly, because there is an atmosphere round this sort of classical ground, to which that of actual life is gross and vulgar. Shut out from this garden of early sweetness, we may well exclaim—

" How shall we part and wander down
Into a lower world, to this obscure
And wild ? How shall we breathe in other air
Less pure, accustom'd to immortal fruits? "

I do not think the classics so indispensable to the cultivation of your intellect as on another account, which I have seen explained elsewhere, and you will have no objection to turn with me to the passages. "The study of the classics is less to be regarded as an exercise of the intellect, than as *a discipline of humanity*. The peculiar advantage of this mode of education consists not so much in strengthening the understanding, as in softening and refining the taste. It gives men liberal views; it accustoms the mind to take an interest in things foreign to itself; to love virtue for its own sake; to prefer fame to life, and glory to riches; and to fix our thoughts on the remote and permanent, instead of narrow and fleeting objects. It teaches us to believe that there is something really great and excellent in the world, surviving all the shocks of accident and fluctuations of opinion, and raises us above that low and servile fear, which bows only to present power and upstart authority. Rome and Athens filled a place in the history of mankind, which can never be occupied again. They were two cities set on a hill, which could not be hid; all eyes have seen them, and their light shines like a mighty sea-mark into the abyss of time.

> '·Still green with bays each ancient altar stands,
> Above the reach of sacrilegious hands;
> Secure from flames, from envy's fiercer rage,
> Destructive war, and all-involving age.
> Hail, bards triumphant, born in happier days,
> Immortal heirs of universal praise !
> Whose honours with increase of ages grow,
> As streams roll down, enlarging as they flow !'

It is this feeling more than anything else which produces a marked difference between the study of the ancient and modern languages, and which, by the weight and importance of the consequences attached to the former, stamps every word with a monumental firmness. By conversing with the *mighty dead*, we imbibe sentiment with knowledge. We become strongly attached to those who can no longer either hurt or serve us, except through the influence which they exert over the mind. We feel the presence of that power which gives immortality to human thoughts and actions, and catch the flame of enthusiasm from all the nations and ages."

Because, however, you have learnt Latin and Greek, and can

speak a different language, do not fancy yourself of a different order of beings from those you ordinarily converse with.   They perhaps know and can do more *things* than you, though you have learnt a greater variety of *names* to express the same thing by.   The great object, indeed, of these studies is, to be "a cure for a narrow and selfish spirit," and to carry the mind out of its petty and local prejudices to the idea of a more general humanity.   Do not fancy, because you are intimate with Homer and Virgil, that your neighbours who can never attain the same posthumous fame are to be despised, like those impudent valets who live in noble families and look down upon every one else.   Though you are master of Cicero's *Orations*, think it possible for a cobbler at a stall to be more eloquent than you.   "But you are a scholar, and he is not."   Well, then, you have that advantage over him, but it does not follow that you are to have every other.   Look at the heads of the celebrated poets and philosophers of antiquity in the collection at Wilton, and you will say they answer to their works ; but you will find others in the same collection whose names have hardly come down to us that are equally fine, and cast in the same classic mould.   Do you imagine that all the thoughts, genius, and capacity of those old and mighty nations are contained in a few odd volumes, to be thumbed by school-boys?   This reflection is not meant to lessen your admiration of the great names to which you will be accustomed to look up, but to direct it to that solid mass of intellect and power of which they were the most shining ornaments.   I would wish you to excel in this sort of learning and to take a pleasure in it, because it is the path that has been chosen for you ; but do not suppose that others do not excel equally in their line of study or exercise of skill, or that there is but one mode of excellence in the art or nature.   You have got on vastly beyond the point at which you set out ; but others have been getting on as well as you in the same or other ways, and have kept pace with you.   What then, you may ask, is the use of all the pains you have taken, if it gives you no superiority over mankind in general ?   It is this—You have reaped all the benefit of improvement and knowledge yourself; and farther, if you had not moved forwards, you would by this time have been left behind. Envy no one, disparage no one, think yourself above no one. Their demerits will not piece out your deficiencies; nor is it a waste of time and labour for you to cultivate your own talents, because you cannot bespeak a monopoly of all advantages. You are more learned than many of your acquaintance who may be more active, healthy, witty, successful in business, or expert in some elegant or useful art than you; but you have no reason to complain, if you have attained the object of your ambition. Or if you should not be able to compass this from a want of genius or parts, yet learn, my child, to be contented with a mediocrity of acquirements. You may still be respectable in your conduct, and enjoy a tranquil obscurity, with more friends and fewer enemies than you might otherwise have had.

There is one almost certain drawback on a course of scholastic study, that it unfits men for active life. The *ideal* is always at variance with the *practical*. The habit of fixing the attention on the imaginary and abstracted deprives the mind equally of energy and fortitude. By indulging our imaginations on fictions and chimeras, where we have it all our own way and are led on only by the pleasure of the prospect, we grow fastidious, effeminate, lapped in idle luxury, impatient of contradiction, and unable to sustain the shock of real adversity when it comes; as by being taken-up with abstract reasoning or remote events in which we are merely passive spectators, we have no resources to provide against it, no readiness, or expedients for the occasion, or spirit to use them, even if they occur. We must think again before we determine, and thus the opportunity for action is lost. While we are considering the very best possible mode of gaining an object, we find that it has slipped through our fingers, or that others have laid rude, fearless hands upon it. The youthful tyro reluctantly discovers that the ways of the world are not his ways, nor their thoughts his thoughts. Perhaps the old monastic institutions were not in this respect unwise, which carried on to the end of life the secluded habits and romantic associations with which

it began, and which created a privileged world for the inhab-
itants, distinct from the common world of men and women.
You will bring with you from your books and solitary reveries
a wrong measure of men and things, unless you correct it by
careful experience and mixed observation. You will raise your
standard of character as much too high at first as from disappointed expectation it will sink too low afterwards. The
best qualifier of this theoretical *mania* and of the dreams of
poets and moralists (who both treat of things as *they ought to
be* and not as *they are*) is in one sense to be found in some of
our own popular writers, such as our Novelists and periodical
Essayists. But you had, after all, better wait and see what
things are, than try to anticipate the results. You know more
of a road by having travelled it than by all the conjectures and
descriptions in the world. You will find the business of life
conducted on a much more varied and individual scale than
you would expect. People will be concerned about a thousand
things that you have no idea of, and will be utterly indifferent
to what you feel the greatest interest in. You will find good
and evil, folly and discretion, more mingled, and the shades of
character running more into each other than they do in the
ethical charts. No one is equally wise or guarded at all points,
and it is seldom that anyone is quite a fool. Do not be surprised,
when you go out into the world, to find men talk exceedingly
well on different subjects, who do not derive their information
immediately from books. In the first place, the light of books
is diffused very much abroad in the world in conversation and
at second-hand ; and besides, common sense is not a monopoly,
and experience and observation are sources of information open
to the man of the world as well as to the retired student. If
you know more of the outline and principles, he knows more of
the details and "*practique* part of life." A man may discuss
very agreeably the adventures of a campaign in which he was
engaged without having read the "Retreat of the Ten
Thousand," or give a singular account of the method of drying
teas in China without being a profound chemist. It is the vice
of scholars to suppose that there is no knowledge in the world

but that of books. Do you avoid it, I conjure you ; and thereby save yourself the pain and mortification that must otherwise ensue from finding out your mistake continually !

Gravity is one great ingredient in the conduct of life, and perhaps a certain share of it is hardly to be dispensed with. Few people can afford to be quite unaffected. At any rate, do not put your worst qualities foremost. Do not seek to distinguish yourself by being ridiculous ; nor entertain that miserable ambition to be the sport and butt of the company. By aiming at a certain standard of behaviour or intellect, you will at least show your taste and value for what is excellent. There are those who *blurt* out their good things with so little heed of what they are about that no one thinks anything of them ; as others by keeping their folly to themselves gain the reputation of wisdom. Do not, however, affect to speak only in oracles, or to deal in *bon-mots :* condescend to the level of the company, and be free and accessible to all persons. Express whatever occurs to you, that cannot offend others or hurt yourself. Keep some opinions to yourself. Say what you please of others, but never repeat what you hear said of them to themselves. If you have nothing yourself to offer, laugh with the witty—assent to the wise : they will not think the worse of you for it. Listen to information on subjects you are acquainted with, instead of always striving to lead the conversation to some favourite one of your own. By the last method you will shine, but will not improve. I am ashamed myself ever to open my lips on any question I have ever written upon. It is much more difficult to be able to converse on an equality with a number of persons in turn, than to soar above their heads, and excite the stupid gaze of all companies by bestriding some senseless topic of your own and con founding the understandings of those who are ignorant of it. Be not too fond of argument. Indeed, by going much into company (which I do not, however, wish you to do) you will be weaned from this practice, if you set out with it. Rather suggest what remarks may have occurred to you on a subject than aim at dictating your opinions to others or at defending

yourself at all points. You will learn more by agreeing in the
main with others and entering into their trains of thinking, than
by contradicting and urging them to extremities. Avoid
singularity of opinion as well as of everything else. Sound
conclusions come with practical knowledge, rather than with
speculative refinements: in what we really understand, we
reason but little. Long-winded disputes fill up the place of
common-sense and candid inquiry. Do not imagine that you
will make people friends by showing your superiority over
them : it is what they will neither admit nor forgive, unless you
have a high and acknowledged reputation beforehand, which
renders this sort of petty vanity more inexcusable. Seek to
gain the good-will of others rather than to extort their
applause ; and to this end, be neither too tenacious of your own
claims, nor inclined to press too hard on their weaknesses.

Do not affect the society of your superiors in rank, nor court
that of the great. There can be no real sympathy in either
case. The first will consider you as a restraint upon them, and
the last as an intruder, or *upon sufferance.* It is not a desirable
distinction to be admitted into company as a man of talents.
You are a mark for invidious observation. If you say nothing,
or merely behave with common propriety and simplicity, you
seem to have no business there. If you make a studied display
of yourself, it is arrogating a consequence you have no right
to. If you are contented to pass as an indifferent person, they
despise you ; if you distinguish yourself, and show more
knowledge, wit, or taste than they do, they hate you for it.
You have no alternative. I would rather be asked out to sing
than to talk. Everyone does not pretend to a fine voice, but
every one fancies he has as much understanding as another.
Indeed, the secret of this sort of intercourse has been pretty
well found out. Literary men are seldom invited to the tables
of the great ; they send for players and musicians, as they keep
monkeys and parrots !

I would not, however, have you run away with a notion
that the rich are knaves, or that lords are fools. They are
for what I know as honest and as wise as other people. But

it is a trick of our self-love, supposing that another has the decided advantage of us in one way, to strike a balance by taking it for granted (as a moral antithesis) that he must be as much beneath us in those qualities on which we plume ourselves, and which we would appropriate almost entirely to our own use. It is hard indeed if others are raised above us not only by the gifts of fortune, but of understanding too. It is not to be credited. People have an unwillingness to admit that the House of Lords can be equal in talent to the House of Commons. So in the other sex, if a woman is handsome, she is an idiot or no better than she should be : in ours, if a man is worth a million of money, he is a miser, a fellow that cannot spell his own name, or a poor creature in some way, to bring him to our level. This is malice, and not truth. Believe all the good you can of every one. Do not measure others by yourself. If they have advantages which you have not, let your liberality keep pace with their good fortune. Envy no one, and you need envy no one. If you have but the magnanimity to allow merit wherever you see it— understanding in a lord or wit in a cobbler—this temper of mind will stand you instead of many accomplishments. Think no man too happy. Raphael died young. Milton had the misfortune to be blind. If any one is vain or proud, it is from folly or ignorance. Those who pique themselves excessively on some one thing have but that one thing to pique themselves upon, as languages, mechanics, etc. I do not say that this is not an enviable delusion, where it is not liable to be disturbed ; but at present knowledge is too much diffused and pretensions come too much into collision for this to be long the case ; and it is better not to form such a prejudice at first than to have it to undo all the rest of one's life. If you learn any two things, though they may put you out of conceit one with the other, they will effectually cure you of any conceit you might have of yourself by showing the variety and scope there is in the human mind beyond the limits you had set to it.

You were convinced the first day that you could not learn Latin, which now you find easy. Be taught from this, not to think other obstacles insurmountable that you may meet with in the course of your life, though they seem so at first sight.

Attend above all things to your health ; or rather, do nothing wilfully to impair it. Use exercise, abstinence, and regular hours. Drink water when you are alone, and wine or very little spirits in company. It is the last that are ruinous by leading to an unlimited excess. There is not the same headlong *impetus* in wine. But one glass of brandy and water makes you want another, that other makes you want a third, and so on in an increased proportion. Therefore no one can stop midway who does not possess the resolution to abstain altogether ; for the inclination is sharpened with its indulgence. Never gamble. Or if you play for anything, never do so for what will give you uneasiness the next day. Be not precise in these matters ; but do not pass certain limits, which it is difficult to recover. Do nothing in the irritation of the moment, but take time to reflect. Because you have done one foolish thing do not do another ; nor throw away your health, or reputation, or comfort, to thwart impertinent advice. Avoid a spirit of contradiction, both in words and actions. Do not aim at what is beyond your reach, but at what is within it. Indulge in calm and pleasing pursuits, rather than violent excitements ; and learn to conquer your own will, instead of striving to obtain the mastery of that of others.

With respect to your friends, I would wish you to choose them neither from caprice nor accident, and to adhere to them as long as you can. Do not make a surfeit of friendship, through over sanguine enthusiasm, nor expect it to last for ever. Always speak well of those with whom you have once been intimate, or take some part of the censure you bestow on them to yourself. Never quarrel with tried friends, or those whom you wish to continue such. Wounds of this kind are sure to open again. When once the prejudice is removed that sheathes defects, familiarity only causes jealousy and distrust. Do not keep on with a mockery of friendship after the substance is gone—but part, while you can part friends. Bury the carcase of friendship : it is not worth embalming.

As to the books you will have to read by choice or for amusement, the best are the commonest. The names of many of them are already familiar to you. Read them as you grow up with all the satisfaction in your power, and make much of them. It is perhaps the greatest pleasure you will have in life, the one you will think of longest, and repent of least. If my life had been more full of calamity than it has been (much more than I hope yours will be) I would live it over again, my poor little boy, to have read the books I did in my youth.

In politics I wish you to be an honest man, but no brawler. Hate injustice and falsehood for your own sake. Be neither a martyr nor a sycophant. Wish well to the world without expecting to see it much better than it is ; and do not gratify the enemies of liberty by putting yourself at their mercy, if it can be avoided with honour.

If you ever marry, I would wish you to marry the woman you like. Do not be guided by the recommendation of friends. Nothing will atone for or overcome an original distaste. It will only increase from intimacy ; and if you are to live separate, it is better not to come together. There is no use in dragging a chain through life unless it binds one to the object we love. No woman ever married into a family above herself that did not try to make all the mischief she could in it. Be not in haste to marry, nor to engage your affections, where there is no probability of a return. Do not fancy every woman you see the heroine of a romance, a Sophia Western, a Clarissa, or a Julia ; and yourself the potential hero of it, Tom Jones, Lovelace, or St. Preux. Avoid this error as you would shrink back from a precipice. All your fine sentiments and romantic notions will (of themselves) make no more impression on one of these delicate creatures than on a piece of marble. Their soft bosoms are steel to your amorous refinements, if you have no other pretensions. It is not what you think of them that determines their choice, but what they think of you. Endeavour, if you would escape lingering torments, and the gnawing of the worm that dies not, to find out this, and to abide by the issue. We trifle with, make sport of, and despise those who are attached to us, and follow those that fly from us. "We hunt the wind—we worship a statue—cry aloud to the desert." Do you, my dear boy, stop short in this career if you find yourself setting out in it, and make up your mind to this—that, if a woman does not like you of her own accord, that is, from involuntary impressions, nothing you can say, or do, or suffer for her sake will make her, but will set her the more against you. So the song goes—

> " Quit, quit for shame; this will not move :
> If of herself she will not love,
> Nothing will make her, the devil take her !"

Your pain is her triumph ; the more she feels you in her power, the worse she will treat you : the more you make it appear you deserve her regard, the more she will resent it as an imputation on her first judgment. Study first impressions above all things, for everything depends on them—in love especially. Women are armed by nature and education with a power of resisting the importunity of men, and they use this power according to their discretion. They enforce it to the utmost rigour of the law against those whom they do not like, and relax their extreme severity proportionably in favour of those that they do like, and who in general care as little about them. Hence we see so many desponding lovers and forlorn damsels. Love in women, at least, is either vanity, or interest, or fancy. It is a merely selfish feeling. It has nothing to do, I am sorry to say, with friendship, or esteem, or even pity. I once asked a girl, the pattern of her sex in shape and mind and attractions, whether she did not think Mr. Coleridge had done wrong in making the heroine of his beautiful ballad story of Geneviève take compassion on her hapless lover—

> " When on the yellow forest-leaves
> A dying man he lay ;"—

and whether she believed that any woman ever fell in love through a sense of compassion, and she made answer—" Not if it was against her inclination !" I would take this lady's word

for a thousand pounds on this point. Pain holds antipathy to
pleasure ; pity is not akin to love ; a dying man has more need
of a nurse than of a mistress. There is no forcing liking. It is
as little to be fostered by reason and good-nature as it can be
controlled by prudence or propriety It is a mere blind, head-
strong impulse. Least of all, flatter yourself that talents or
virtue will recommend you to the favour of the sex in lieu of
exterior advantages. Oh! no. Women care nothing about
poets, or philosophers, or politicians. They go by a man's
looks and manner Richardson calls them "an eye-judging
sex," and I am sure he knew more about them than I can
pretend to do. If you run away with a pedantic notion that
they care a pin's point about your head or your heart, you will
repent it too late. Some blue-stocking may have her vanity
flattered by your reputation, or be edified by the solution of a
metaphysical problem, or a critical remark, or a dissertation on
the state of the nation, and fancy that she has a taste for
intellect and is an epicure in sentiment. No true woman ever
regarded anything but her lover's person and address. Gravity
will here answer all the same purpose without understanding,
gaiety without wit, folly without good-nature, and impudence
without any other pretension. The natural and instinctive
passion of love is excited by qualities not peculiar to artists,
authors, and men of letters. It is not the jest but the
laugh that follows, not the sentiment but the glance that
accompanies it, that *tells*—in a word, the sense of actual
enjoyment that imparts itself to others, and excites mutual
understanding and inclination. Authors, on the other hand,
feel nothing spontaneously. The common incidents and circumstances of life with which others are taken up, make no
alteration in them, nor provoke any of the common expressions
of surprise, joy, admiration, anger, or merriment. Nothing
stirs their blood or accelerates their juices or tickles their veins.
Instead of yielding to the first natural and lively impulses of
things, in which they would find sympathy, they screw themselves up to some far-fetched view of the subject in order to be
unintelligible. Realities are not good enough for them, till

they undergo the process of imagination and reflection.   If you offer them your hand to shake, they will hardly take it ; for this does not amount to a proposition.   If you enter their room suddenly, they testify neither surprise nor satisfaction : no new idea is elicited by it.   Yet if you suppose this to be a repulse you are mistaken.   They will enter into your affairs or combat your ideas with all the warmth and vehemence imaginable as soon as they have a subject started.   But their faculty for thinking must be set in motion, before you can put any soul into them.   They are intellectual dram-drinkers ; and without their necessary stimulus, are torpid, dead, insensible to everything.   They have great life of mind, but none of body.   They do not drift with the stream of company or of passing occurrences, but are straining at some hyberbole, or striking out a bye-path of their own.   Follow them who list.   Their minds are a sort of Herculaneum, full of old, petrified images ;—are set in stereotype, and little fitted to the ordinary occasions of life.

What chance, then, can they have with women, who deal only in the pantomime of discourse, in gesticulation and the flippant bye-play of the senses, " nods and winks and wreathed smiles ;" and to whom to offer a remark is an impertinence, or a reason an affront ?   The only way in which I ever knew mental qualities or distinction tell was in the clerical character ; and women do certainly incline to this with some sort of favourable regard.   Whether it is that the sanctity of pretension piques curiosity, or that the habitual submission of their understandings to their spiritual guides subdues the will, a popular preacher generally has the choice among the *élite* of his female flock.   According to Mrs Inchbald (see her *Simple Story*) there is another reason why religious courtship is not without its charms !   But as I do not intend you for the church, do not, in thinking to study yourself into the good graces of the fair, study yourself out of them, millions of miles.   Do not place thought as a barrier between you and love : do not abstract yourself into the regions of truth, far from the smile of earthly beauty.   Let not the cloud

sit upon your brow : let not the canker sink into your heart.
Look up, laugh loud, talk big, keep the colour in your cheek
and the fire in your eye, adorn your person, maintain your
health, your beauty, and your animal spirits, and you will pass
for a fine man. But should you let your blood stagnate in some
deep metaphysical question, or refine too much in your ideas of
the sex, forgetting yourself in a dream of exalted perfection, you
will want an eye to cheer you, a hand to guide you, a bosom to
lean on, and will stagger into your grave, old before your time,
unloved and unlovely. If you feel that you have not the
necessary advantages of person, confidence, and manner, and
that it is *up-hill* work with you to gain the ear of beauty,
quit the pursuit at once, and seek for other satisfactions and
consolations.

A spider, my dear, the meanest creature that crawls or lives,
has its mate or fellow : but a scholar has no mate or fellow.
For myself, I had courted thought, I had felt pain ; and Love
turned away his face from me. I have gazed along the silent
air for that smile which had lured me to my doom. I no more
heard those accents which would have burst upon me like a
voice from heaven. I loathed the light that shone on my
disgrace. Hours, days, years passed away, and only turned
false hope to fixed despair. And as my frail bark sails down
the stream of time, the God of Love stands on the shore, and as
I stretch out my hands to him in vain, claps his wings, and
mocks me as I pass !

There is but one other point on which I meant to speak
to you, and that is the choice of a profession. This, probably,
had better be left to time or accident or your own inclination.
You have a very fine ear, but I have somehow a prejudice
against men-singers, and indeed against the stage altogether.
It is an uncertain and ungrateful soil. All professions are bad
that depend on reputation, which is "as often got without merit
as lost without deserving." Yet I cannot easily reconcile myself to your being a slave to business, and I shall be hardly
able to leave you an independence. A situation in a public
office is secure, but laborious and mechanical, and without the

two great springs of life, Hope and Fear. Perhaps, however, it might ensure you a competence, and leave you leisure for some other favourite amusement or pursuit. I have said all reputation is hazardous, hard to win, harder to keep. Many never attain a glimpse of what they have all their lives been looking for, and others survive a passing shadow of it. Yet if I were to name one pursuit rather than another, I should wish you to be a good painter, if such a thing could be hoped. I have failed in this myself, and should wish you to be able to do what I have not—to paint like Claude or Rembrandt or Guido or Vandyke, if it were possible. Artists, I think, who have succeeded in their chief object, live to be old, and are agreeable old men. Their minds keep alive to the last. Cosway's spirits never flagged till after ninety, and Nollekins, though nearly blind, passed all his mornings in giving directions about some group or bust in his workshop. You have seen Mr. Northcote, that delightful specimen of the last age. With what avidity he takes up his pencil, or lays it down again to talk of numberless things ! His eye has not lost its lustre, nor "paled its ineffectual fire." His body is a shadow : he himself is a pure spirit. There is a kind of immortality about this sort of ideal and visionary existence that dallies with Fate and baffles the grim monster, Death. If I thought you could make as clever an artist and arrive at such an agreeable old age as Mr. Northcote, I should declare at once for your devoting yourself to this enchanting profession ; and in that reliance, should feel less regret at some of my own disappointments, and little anxiety on your account !

THE INDIAN JUGGLERS.

COMING forward and seating himself on the ground in his
white dress and tightened turban, the chief of the Indian
Jugglers begins with tossing up two brass balls, which is what
any of us could do, and concludes with keeping up four at the
same time, which is what none of us could do to save our lives,
nor if we were to take our whole lives to do it in. Is it then a
trifling power we see at work, or is it not something next to
miraculous? It is the utmost stretch of human ingenuity, which
nothing but the bending the faculties of body and mind to it
from the tenderest infancy with incessant, ever anxious application up to manhood can accomplish or make even a slight
approach to. Man, thou art a wonderful animal, and thy ways
are past finding out! Thou canst do strange things, but thou
turnest them to little account!—To conceive of this effort of
extraordinary dexterity distracts the imagination and makes
admiration breathless. Yet it costs nothing to the performer,
any more than if it were a mere mechanical deception with
which he had nothing to do but to watch and laugh at the
astonishment of the spectators. A single error of a hair's-
breadth, of the smallest conceivable portion of time, would be
fatal: the precision of the movements must be like a mathematical truth, their rapidity is like lightning. To catch four
balls in succession in less than a second of time, and deliver
them back so as to return with seeming consciousness to the
hand again, to make them revolve round him, at certain
intervals, like the planets in their spheres, to make them chase
one another like sparkles of fire, or shoot up like flowers or

meteors, to throw them behind his back and twine them round his neck like ribbons or like serpents, to do what appears an impossibility, and to do it with all the ease, the grace, the carelessness imaginable, to laugh at, to play with the glittering mockeries, to follow them with his eye as if he could fascinate them with its lambent fire, or as if he had only to see that they kept time with the music on the stage—there is something in all this which he who does not admire may be quite sure he never really admired anything in the whole course of his life. It is skill surmounting difficulty, and beauty triumphing over skill. It seems as if the difficulty once mastered naturally resolved itself into ease and grace, and as if to be overcome at all, it must be overcome without an effort. The smallest awkwardness or want of pliancy or self-possession would stop the whole process. It is the work of witchcraft, and yet sport for children. Some of the other feats are quite as curious and wonderful, such as the balancing the artificial tree and shooting a bird from each branch through a quill ; though none of them have the elegance or facility of the keeping up of the brass balls. You are in pain for the result and glad when the experiment is over ; they are not accompanied with the same unmixed, unchecked delight as the former ; and I would not give much to be merely astonished without being pleased at the same time. As to the swallowing of the sword, the police ought to interfere to prevent it. When I saw the Indian Juggler do the same things before, his feet were bare, and he had large rings on his toes, which kept turning round all the time of the performance, as if they moved of themselves.—The hearing a speech in Parliament, drawled or stammered out by the Honourable Member or the Noble Lord, the ringing the changes on their commonplaces, which any one could repeat after them as well as they, stirs me not a jot, shakes not my good opinion of myself ; but the seeing the Indian Jugglers does. It makes me ashamed of myself. I ask what there is that I can do as well as this? Nothing. What have I been doing all my life? Have I been idle, or have I nothing to show for all my labour and pains? Or have I passed my time in pouring words like water into empty sieves, rolling a stone up a hill and then down again, trying to prove an argument in the teeth of facts, and looking for causes in the dark, and not finding them? Is there no one thing in which I can challenge competition, that I can bring as an instance of exact perfection, in which others cannot find a flaw? The utmost I can pretend to is to write a description of what this fellow can do, I can write a book: so can many others who have not even learned to spell. What abortions are these Essays! What errors, what ill-pieced transitions, what crooked reasons, what lame conclusions! How little is made out, and that little how ill! Yet they are the best I can do. I endeavour to recollect all I have ever observed or thought upon a subject, and to express it as nearly as I can. Instead of writing on four subjects at a time, it is as much as I can manage to keep the thread of one discourse clear and unentangled. I have also time on my hands to correct my opinions, and polish my periods: but the one I cannot, and the other I will not do. I am fond of arguing: yet with a good deal of pains and practice it is often as much as I can do to beat my man; though he may be an indifferent hand. A common fencer would disarm his adversary in the twinkling of an eye, unless he were a professor like himself. A stroke of wit will sometimes produce this effect, but there is no such power or superiority in sense or reasoning. There is no complete mastery of execution to be shown there: and you hardly know the professor from the impudent pretender or the mere clown.*

I have always had this feeling of the inefficacy and slow progress of intellectual compared to mechanical excellence, and it has always made me somewhat dissatisfied. It is a great many years since I saw Richer, the famous rope-dancer, perform

* The celebrated Peter Pindar (Dr. Wolcot) first discovered and brought out the talents of the late Mr. Opie, the painter. He was a poor Cornish boy, and was out at work in the fields, when the poet went in search of him. "Well, my lad, can you go and bring me your very best picture?" The other flew like lightning, and soon came back with what he considered as his masterpiece. The stranger

THE INDIAN JUGGLERS.

at Sadler's Wells. He was matchless in his art, and added to
his extraordinary skill exquisite ease, and unaffected, natural
grace. I was at that time employed in copying a half-length
picture of Sir Joshua Reynolds's ; and it put me out of conceit
with it. How ill this part was made out in the drawing! How
heavy, how slovenly this other was painted! I could not help
saying to myself, "If the rope-dancer had performed his task
in this manner, leaving so many gaps and botches in his work,
he would have broken his neck long ago ; I should never have
seen that vigorous elasticity of nerve and precision of movement!"—Is it then so easy an undertaking (comparatively)
to dance on a tight-rope? Let anyone who thinks so get up
and try. There is the thing. It is that which at first we
cannot do at all, which in the end is done to such perfection.
To account for this in some degree, I might observe that
mechanical dexterity is confined to doing some one particular
thing, which you can repeat as often as you please, in which
you know whether you succeed or fail, and where the point
of perfection consists in succeeding in a given undertaking.
—In mechanical efforts, you improve by perpetual practice,
and you do so infallibly, because the object to be attained is
not a matter of taste or fancy or opinion, but of actual experiment, in which you must either do the thing or not do it. If
a man is put to aim at a mark with a bow and arrow, he must
hit it or miss it, that's certain. He cannot deceive himself,
and go on shooting wide or falling short, and still fancy that he
is making progress. The distinction between right and wrong,
between true and false, is here palpable ; and he must either
correct his aim or persevere in his error with his eyes open,
for which there is neither excuse nor temptation. If a man
is learning to dance on a rope, if he does not mind what he

looked at it, and the young artist, after waiting for some time without
his giving any opinion, at length exclaimed eagerly, "Well, what do
you think of it?"—"Think of it?" said Wolcot, "why, I think you
ought to be ashamed of it—that you who might do so well, do no
better!" The same answer would have applied to this artist's latest
performances, that had been suggested by one of his earliest efforts.

is about, he will break his neck. After that, it will be in vain for him to argue that he did not make a false step. His situation is not like that of Goldsmith's pedagogue :—

> " In argument they own'd his wondrous skill,
>   And e'en though vanquish'd, he could argue still."

Danger is a good teacher, and makes apt scholars. So are disgrace, defeat, exposure to immediate scorn and laughter. There is no opportunity in such cases for self-delusion, no idling time away, no being off your guard (or you must take the consequences)—neither is there any room for humour or caprice or prejudice. If the Indian Juggler were to play tricks in throwing up the three case-knives, which keep their positions like the leaves of a crocus in the air, he would cut his fingers. I can make a very bad antithesis without cutting my fingers. The tact of style is more ambiguous than that of double-edged instruments. If the Juggler were told that by flinging himself under the wheels of the Juggernaut, when the idol issues forth on a gaudy day, he would immediately be transported into Paradise, he might believe it, and nobody could disprove it. So the Brahmins may say what they please on that subject, may build up dogmas and mysteries without end, and not be detected ; but their ingenious countryman cannot persuade the frequenters of the Olympic Theatre that he performs a number of astonishing feats without actually giving proofs of what he says.—There is then in this sort of manual dexterity, first a gradual aptitude acquired to a given exertion of muscular power, from constant repetition, and in the next place, an exact knowledge how much is still wanting and necessary to be supplied. The obvious test is to increase the effort or nicety of the operation, and still to find it come true. The muscles ply instinctively to the dictates of habit. Certain movements and impressions of the hand and eye, having been repeated together an infinite number of times, are unconsciously but unavoidably cemented into closer and closer union ; the limbs require little more than to be put in motion for them to follow a regular track with ease and certainty : so that the mere intention of the will acts mathematically like touching the spring of a machine, and you come with Locksley in *Ivanhoe*, in shooting at a mark, " to allow for the wind."

Farther, what is meant by perfection in mechanical exercises is the performing certain feats to a uniform nicety, that is, in fact, undertaking no more than you can perform. You task yourself, the limit you fix is optional, and no more than human industry and skill can attain to ; but you have no abstract, independent standard of difficulty or excellence (other than the extent of your own powers). Thus he who can keep up four brass balls does this *to perfection ;* but he cannot keep up five at the same instant, and would fail every time he attempted it. That is, the mechanical performer undertakes to emulate himself, not to equal another.* But the artist undertakes to imitate another or to do what nature has done, and this it appears is more difficult—viz., to copy what she has set before us in the face of nature or " human face divine," entire and without a blemish, than to keep up four brass balls at the same instant, for the one is done by the power of human skill and industry, and the other never was nor will be. Upon the whole, therefore, I have more respect for Reynolds than I have for Richer ; for, happen how it will, there have been more people in the world who could dance on a rope like the one than who could paint like Sir Joshua. The latter was but a bungler in his profession to the other, it is true ; but then he had a harder taskmaster to obey, whose will was more wayward and obscure, and whose instructions it was more difficult to practice. You can put a child apprentice to a tumbler or rope-dancer with a comfortable prospect of success, if they are but sound of wind and limb ; but you cannot do the same thing in painting. The odds are a million to one. You may make indeed as many Haydons and H——s as you put into that sort of machine, but not one Reynolds amongst them all, with his grace, his grandeur, his blandness

* If two persons play against each other at any game, one of them necessarily fails.

of *gusto*, "in tones and gestures hit," unless you could make the man over again. To snatch this grace beyond the reach of art is then the height of art—where fine art begins, and where mechanical skill ends. The soft suffusion of the soul, the speechless breathing eloquence, the looks "commercing with the skies," the ever-shifting forms of an eternal principle, that which is seen but for a moment, but dwells in the heart always, and is only seized as it passes by strong and secret sympathy, must be taught by nature and genius, not by rules or study. It is suggested by feeling, not by laborious microscopic inspection; in seeking for it without, we lose the harmonious clue to it within; and in aiming to grasp the substance, we let the very spirit of art evaporate. In a word, the objects of fine art are not the objects of sight but as these last are the objects of taste and imagination, that is, as they appeal to the sense of beauty, of pleasure, and of power in the human breast, and are explained by that finer sense, and revealed in their inner structure to the eye in return. Nature is also a language. Objects, like words, have a meaning; and the true artist is the interpreter of this language, which he can only do by knowing its application to a thousand other objects in a thousand other situations. Thus the eye is too blind a guide of itself to distinguish between the warm or cold tone of a deep-blue sky, but another sense acts as a monitor to it, and does not err. The colour of the leaves in autumn would be nothing without the feeling that accompanies it; but it is that feeling that stamps them on the canvas, faded, seared, blighted, shrinking from the winter's flaw, and makes the sight as true as touch—

> " And visions, as poetic eyes avow,
> Cling to each leaf and hang on every bough."

The more ethereal, evanescent, more refined and sublime part of art is the seeing nature through the medium of sentiment and passion, as each object is a symbol of the affections and a link in the chain of our endless being. But the unravelling this mysterious web of thought and feeling is alone in the Muse's gift—namely, in the power of that trembling sensibility which is awake to every change and every modification of its ever-varying impressions, that

" Thrills in each nerve, and lives along the line."

This power is indifferently called genius, imagination, feeling, taste ; but the manner in which it acts upon the mind can neither be defined by abstract rules, as is the case in science, nor verified by continual unvarying experiments, as is the case in mechanical performances. The mechanical excellence of the Dutch painters in colouring and handling is that which comes the nearest in fine art to the perfection of certain manual exhibitions of skill. The truth of the effect and the facility with which it is produced are equally admirable. Up to a certain point, everything is faultless. The hand and eye have done their part. There is only a want of taste and genius. It is after we enter upon that enchanted ground that the human mind begins to droop and flag as in a strange road, or in a thick mist, benighted and making little way with many attempts and many failures, and that the best of us only escape with half a triumph. The undefined and the imaginary are the regions that we must pass like Satan, difficult and doubtful, "half flying, half on foot." The object in sense is a positive thing, and execution comes with practice.

Cleverness is a certain *knack* or aptitude at doing certain things, which depend more on a particular adroitness and off-hand readiness than on force or perseverance, such as making puns, making epigrams, making extempore verses, mimicking the company, mimicking a style, etc. Cleverness is either liveliness and smartness, or something answering to *sleight of hand*, like letting a glass fall sideways off a table, or else a trick, like knowing the secret spring of a watch. Accomplishments are certain external graces, which are to be learned from others, and which are easily displayed to the admiration of the beholder—namely, dancing, riding, fencing, music, and so on. These ornamental acquirements are only proper to those who are at ease in mind and fortune. I know an individual who, if he had been born to an estate of five thousand a-year, would have been the most accomplished gentleman of the age. He would have been the delight and envy of the circle in which he moved—would have graced by his manners the liberality flowing from the openness of his heart, would have laughed with the women, have argued with the men, have said good things and written agreeable ones, have taken a hand at piquet or the lead at the harpsichord, and have set and sung his own verses —*nugæ canoræ*—with tenderness and spirit ; a Rochester without the vice, a modern Surrey ! As it is, all these capabilities of excellence stand in his way. He is too versatile for a professional man, not dull enough for a political drudge, too gay to be happy, too thoughtless to be rich. He wants the enthusiasm of the poet, the severity of the prose-writer, and the application of the man of business.—Talent is the capacity of doing anything that depends on application and industry, such as writing a criticism, making a speech, studying the law. Talent differs from genius, as voluntary differs from involuntary power. Ingenuity is genius in trifles, greatness is genius in undertakings of much pith and moment. A clever or ingenious man is one who can do anything well, whether it is worth doing or not ; a great man is one who can do that which when done is of the highest importance. Themistocles said he could not play on the flute, but that he could make of a small city a great one. This gives one a pretty good idea of the distinction in question.

Greatness is great power, producing great effects. It is not enough that a man has great power in himself, he must show it to all the world in a way that cannot be hid or gainsaid. He must fill up a certain idea in the public mind. I have no other notion of greatness than this two-fold definition, great results springing from great inherent energy. The great in visible objects has relation to that which extends over space : the great in mental ones has to do with space and time. No man is truly great who is great only in his life-time. The test of greatness is the page of history. Nothing can be said to be great that has a distinct limit, or that borders on something evidently greater than itself. Besides, what is short-lived and pampered into mere notoriety, is of a gross and vulgar quality in itself. A Lord Mayor is hardly a great man. A city orator or patriot of the day only show, by reaching the height of their wishes, the distance they are at from any true ambition. Popularity is neither fame nor greatness. A king (as such) is not a great man. He has great power, but it is not his own. He merely wields the lever of the state, which a child, an idiot, or a mad-man can do. It is the office, not the man we gaze at. Any one else in the same situation would be just as much an object of abject curiosity. We laugh at the country girl who having seen a king expressed her disappointment by saying, "Why, he is only a man!" Yet, knowing this, we run to see a king as if he was something more than a man.—To display the greatest powers, unless they are applied to great purposes, makes nothing for the character of greatness. To throw a barley-corn through the eye of a needle, to multiply nine figures by nine in the memory, argues definite dexterity of body and capacity of mind, but nothing comes of either. There is a surprising power at work, but the effects are not proportionate, or such as take hold of the imagination. To impress the idea of power on others, they must be made in some way to feel it. It must be communicated to their understandings in the shape of an increase of knowledge, or it must subdue and overawe them by subjecting their wills. Admiration to be solid and lasting must be founded on proofs from which we have no means of escaping; it is neither a slight nor a voluntary gift. A mathematician who solves a profound problem, a poet who creates an image of beauty in the mind that was not there before, imparts knowledge and power to others, in which his greatness and his fame consists, and on which it reposes. Jedediah Buxton will be forgotten; but Napier's bones will live. Lawgivers, philosophers, founders of religion, conquerors and heroes, inventors and great geniuses in arts and sciences, are great men, for they are great public benefactors, or formid-able scourges to mankind. Among ourselves, Shakespeare, Newton, Bacon, Milton, Cromwell, were great men, for they showed great power by acts and thoughts, which have not yet been consigned to oblivion. They must needs be men of lofty stature, whose shadows lengthen out to remote posterity. A great farce-writer may be a great man; for Molière was but a great farce-writer. In my mind, the author of *Don Quixote* was a great man. So have there been many others. A great chess-player is not a great man, for he leaves the world as he found it. No act terminating in itself constitutes greatness. This will apply to all displays of power or trials of skill, which are confined to the momentary, individual effort, and construct no permanent image or trophy of themselves without them. Is not an actor, then, a great man, because "he dies and leaves the world no copy?" I must make an exception for Mrs. Siddons, or else give up my definition of greatness for her sake. A man at the top of his profession is not therefore a great man. He is great in his way, but that is all, unless he shows the marks of a great moving intellect, so that we trace the master-mind, and can sympathise with the springs that urge him on. The rest is but a craft or *mystery*. John Hunter was a great man—*that* any one might see without the smallest skill in surgery. His style and manner showed the man. He would set about cutting up the carcase of a whale with the same greatness of *gusto* that Michael Angelo would have hewn a block of marble. Lord Nelson was a great naval commander; but for myself, I have not much opinion of a seafaring life. Sir Humphry Davy is a great chemist, but I am not sure that he is a great man. I am not a bit the wiser for any of his discoveries; I never met with any one that was. But it is in the nature of greatness to propagate an idea of itself, as wave impels wave, circle without circle. It is a contradiction in terms for a coxcomb to be a great man. A really great man has always an idea of something greater than himself. I have observed that certain sectaries and polemical writers have no higher compliment to pay their most shining lights than to say that "such a one was a considerable man in his day." Some new elucidation of a text sets aside the authority of the old interpretation, and a "great scholar's memory outlives him half a century," at the utmost. A rich man is not a great man.

except to his dependants and his steward. A lord is a great man in the idea we have of his ancestry, and probably of himself, if we know nothing of him but his title. I have heard a story of two bishops, one of whom said (speaking of St. Peter's at Rome) that when he first entered it, he was rather awestruck, but that as he walked up it, his mind seemed to swell and dilate with it, and at last to fill the whole building : the other said that as he saw more of it, he appeared to himself to grow less and less every step he took, and in the end to dwindle into nothing. This was in some respects a striking picture of a great and little mind—for greatness sympathises with greatness, and littleness shrinks into itself. The one might have become a Wolsey ; the other was only fit to become a Mendicant Friar—or there might have been court-reasons for making him a bishop. The French have to me a character of littleness in all about them; but they have produced three great men that belong to every country, Moliére, Rabelais, and Montaigne.

To return from this digression, and conclude the Essay. A singular instance of manual dexterity was shown in the person of the late John Cavanagh, whom I have several times seen. His death was celebrated at the time in an article in the *Examiner* newspaper (Feb. 7, 1819), written apparently between jest and earnest : but as it is *pat* to our purpose, and falls in with my own way of considering such subjects, I shall here take leave to quote it.

· "Died at his house in Burbage Street, St. Giles's, John Cavanagh, the famous hand fives-player. When a person dies, who does any one thing better than any one else in the world, which so many others are trying to do well, it leaves a gap in society. It is not likely that any one will now see the game of fives played in its perfection for many years to come—for Cavanagh is dead, and has not left his peer behind him. It may be said that there are things of more importance than striking a ball against a wall—there are things indeed that make more noise and do as little good, such as making war and peace, making speeches and answering them, making verses and blotting them ; making money and throwing it away. But the game of fives is what no one despises who has ever played at it. It is the finest exercise for the body, and the best relaxation for the mind. The Roman poet said that 'Care mounted behind the horseman and stuck to his skirts.' But this remark would not have applied to the fives-player. He who takes to playing at fives is twice young. He feels neither the past nor future ' in the instant.' Debts, taxes, 'domestic treason, foreign levy, nothing can touch him further.' He has no other wish, no other thought, from the moment the game begins, but that of striking the ball, of placing it, of *making* it ! This Cavanagh was sure to do. Whenever he touched the ball, there was an end of the chase. His eye was certain, his hand fatal, his presence of mind complete. He could do what he pleased, and he always knew exactly what to do. He saw the whole game, and played it ; took instant advantage of his adversary's weakness, and recovered balls, as if by a miracle and from sudden thought, that every one gave for lost. He had equal power and skill, quickness and judgment. He could either outwit his antagonist by finesse, or beat him by main strength. Sometimes, when he seemed preparing to send the ball with the full swing of his arm, he would by a slight turn of his wrist drop it within an inch of the line. In general, the ball came from his hand, as if from a racket, in a straight horizontal line ; so that it was in vain to attempt to overtake or stop it. As it was said of a great orator that he never was at a loss for a word, and for the properest word, so Cavanagh always could tell the degree of force necessary to be given to a ball, and the precise direction in which it should be sent. He did his work with the greatest ease ; never took more pains than was necessary ; and while others were fagging themselves to death, was as cool and collected as if he had just entered the court. His style of play was as remarkable as his power of execution. He had no affectation, no trifling. He did not throw away the game to show off an attitude, or try an experiment. He was a fine, sensible, manly player, who did what he could, but that was more than any one else could even affect to do. His blows were not undecided and ineffectual—lumbering like Mr. Wordsworth's epic poetry, nor wavering like Mr. Coleridge's lyric prose, nor short of the mark like Mr. Brougham's speeches, nor wide of it like Mr. Canning's wit, nor foul like the *Quarterly*, not *let* balls like the *Edinburgh Review*. Cobbet and Junius together would have made a Cavanagh. He was the best *up-hill* player in the world ; even when his adversary was fourteen, he would play on the same or better, and as he never flung away the game through carelessness and conceit, he never gave it up through laziness or want of heart. The only peculiarity of his play was that he never *volleyed*, but let the balls hop ; but if they rose an inch from the ground, he never missed having them. There was not only nobody equal, but nobody second to him. It is supposed that he could give any other player half the game, or beat them with his left hand. His service was tremendous. He once played Woodward and Meredith together (two of the best players in England) in the Fives-court, St. Martin's Street, and made seven-and-twenty aces following by services alone—a thing unheard of. He another time played Peru, who was considered a first-rate fives-player, a match of the best out of five games, and in the three first games, which of course decided the match, Peru got only one ace. Cavanagh was an Irishman by birth, and a house-painter by profession. He had once laid aside his working-dress, and walked up, in his smartest clothes, to the Rosemary Branch to have an afternoon's pleasure. A person accosted him, and asked him if he would have a game. So they agreed to play for half-a-crown a game, and a bottle of cider. The first game began—it was seven, eight, ten, thirteen, fourteen, all. Cavanagh won it. The next was the same. They played on, and each game was hardly contested. ' There,' said the unconscious fives-player, ' there was a stroke that Cavanagh could not take : I never played better in my life, and yet I can't win a game. I don't know how it is !' However, they played on, Cavanagh winning every game, and the bystanders drinking the cider and laughing all the time. In the twelfth game, when Cavanagh was only four, and the stranger thirteen, a person came in, and said, 'What! are you here, Cavanagh?' The words were no sooner pronounced than the astonished player let the ball drop from his hand, and saying, 'What! have I been breaking my heart all this time to beat Cavanagh?' refused to make another effort. 'And yet, I give you my word,' said Cavanagh, telling the story with some triumph, 'I played all the while with my clenched fist.'—He used frequently to play matches at Copenhagen House for wagers and dinners. The wall against which they play is the same that supports the kitchen chimney, and when the wall resounded louder than usual, the cooks exclaimed, 'Those are the Irishman's balls,' and the joints trembled on the spit!— Goldsmith consoled himself that there were places where he too was admired; and Cavanagh was the admiration of all the fives-courts where he ever played. Mr. Powell, when he played matches in the Court in St. Martin's Street, used to fill his gallery at half-a-crown a-head, with amateurs and admirers of talent in whatever department it is shown. He could not have shown himself in any ground in England but he would have been immediately surrounded with inquisitive gazers, trying to find out in what part of his frame his unrivalled skill lay, as politicians wonder to see the balance of Europe suspended in Lord Castlereagh's face, and admire the trophies of the British Navy lurking under Mr. Croker's hanging brow. Now, Cavanagh was as good-looking a man as the Noble Lord, and much better looking than the Right Hon. Secretary. He had a clear, open countenance, and did not look sideways or down, like Mr. Murray, the bookseller. He was a young fellow of sense, humour, and courage. He once had a quarrel with a waterman at Hungerford Stairs, and, they say, served him out in great style. In a word, there are hundreds at this day who cannot mention his name without admiration, as the best fives-player that perhaps ever lived (the greatest excellence of which they have any notion)—and the noisy shout of the ring happily stood him in stead of the unheard voice of posterity! —The only person who seems to have excelled as much in another way as Cavanagh did in his was the late John Davies, the racket-player. It was remarked of him that he did not seem to follow the ball, but the ball seemed to follow him. Give him a foot of wall, and he was sure to make the ball. The four best racket-players of that day were Jack Spines, Jem Harding, Armitage, and Church. Davies could give any one of these two hands a time—that is, half the game—and each of these, at their best, could give the best player now in London the same odds. Such are the gradations in all exertions of human skill and art. He once played four capital players together, and beat them. He was also a first-rate tennis-player, and an excellent fives-player. In the Fleet or King's Bench, he would have stood against Powell, who was reckoned the best open-ground player of his time. This last-mentioned player is at present the keeper of the Fives-court, and we might recommend to him for a motto over his door—'Who enters here, forgets himself, his country, and his friends.' And the best of it is, that by the calculation of the odds, none of the three are worth remembering I—Cavanagh died from the bursting of a blood-vessel, which prevented him from playing for the last two or three years. This, he was often heard to say, he thought hard upon him. He was fast recovering, however, when he was suddenly carried off, to the regret of all who knew him. As Mr. Peel made it a qualification of the present Speaker, Mr. Manners Sutton, that he was an excellent moral character, so Jack Cavanagh was a zealous Catholic, and could not be persuaded to eat meat on a Friday, the day on which he died. We have paid this willing tribute to his memory.

> " Let no rude hand deface it,
> And his forlorn ' *Hic Jacet.*' "

THE OPERA.

THE Opera is a fine thing: the only question is, whether it is not too fine. It is the most fascinating, and at the same time the most tantalising, of all places. It is not the *too little*, but the *too much*, that offends us. Every object is there collected, and displayed in ostentatious profusion, that can strike the senses or dazzle the imagination ; music, dancing, painting, poetry, architecture, the blaze of beauty, "the glass of fashion, and the mould of form ;" and yet one is not satisfied—for the multitude and variety of objects distract the attention, and, by flattering us with a vain show of the highest gratification of every faculty and wish, leave us at last in a state of listlessness, disappointment, and *ennui*. The powers of the mind are exhausted, without being invigorated ; our expectations are excited, not satisfied ; and we are at some loss to distinguish an excess of irritation from the height of enjoyment. To sit at the Opera for a whole evening is like undergoing the process of animal magnetism for the same length of time. It is an illusion and a mockery, where the mind is made "the fool of the senses," and cheated of itself ; where pleasure after pleasure courts us, as in a fairy palace ; where the Graces and the Muses, weaving in a gay, fantastic round with one another, still turn from our pursuit ; where art, like an enchantress with a thousand faces, still allures our giddy admiration, shifts her mask, and again eludes us. The Opera, in short, proceeds upon a false estimate of taste and morals ; it supposes that the capacity for enjoyment may be multiplied with the objects

calculated to afford it. It is a species of intellectual pros-
titution; for we can no more receive pleasure from all our
faculties at once than we can be in love with a number of
mistresses at the same time. Though we have different senses,
we have but one heart ; and, if we attempt to force it into the
service of them all at once, it must grow restive or torpid,
hardened or enervated. The spectator may say to the sister-
arts of Painting, Poetry, and Music, as they advance to him in
a *pas-de-trois* at the Opera, "How happy could I be with
either, were t'other dear charmers away;" but while "they all
tease him together," the heart gives a satisfactory answer to
none of them ;—is ashamed of its want of resources to supply
the repeated calls upon its sensibility, seeks relief from the
importunity of endless excitement in fastidious apathy or
affected levity; and in the midst of luxury, pomp, vanity,
indolence, and dissipation, feels only the hollow, aching void
within, the irksome craving of unsatisfied desire, because more
pleasures are placed within its reach than it is capable of
enjoying, and the interference of one object with another ends
in a double disappointment. Such is the best account I can
give of the nature of the Opera,—of the contradiction between
our expectations of pleasure and our uneasiness there,—of our
very jealousy of the flattering appeals which are made to our
senses, our passions, and our vanity, on all sides,—of the little
relish we acquire for it, and the distaste it gives us for other
things. Any one of the sources of amusement to be found there
would be enough to occupy and keep the attention alive ; the
tout ensemble fatigues and oppresses it. One may be stifled to
death with roses. A headache may be produced by a profusion of sweet smells or of sweet sounds ; but we do not
like the headache the more on that account. Nor are we
reconciled to it, even at the Opera.

What makes the difference between an opera of Mozart's
and the singing of a thrush confined in a wooden cage at the
corner of the street? The one is nature, and the other is art :
the one is paid for, and the other is not. Madame Foder sang
the air of *Vedrai Carino* in "Don Giovanni" so divinely,

because she was hired to sing it; she sang it to please the audience, not herself, and did not always like to be *encored* in it; but the thrush that awakes us at daybreak with its song, does not sing because it is paid to sing, or to please others, or to be admired or criticised. It sings because it is happy: it pours the thrilling· sounds from its throat, to relieve the overflowings of its own heart—the liquid notes come from, and go to the heart, dropping balm into it, as the gushing spring revives the traveller's parched and fainting lips. That stream of joy comes pure and fresh to the longing sense, free from art and affectation; the same that rises over vernal groves, mingled with the breath of morning, and the perfumes of the wild hyacinth; it waits for no audience, it wants no rehearsing, and still—

"Hymns its good God, and carols sweet of love."

This is the great difference between nature and art, that the one *is* what the other *seems* to be, and gives all the pleasure it expresses, because it feels it itself. Madame Fodor sang as a musical instrument may be made to play a tune, and perhaps with no more real delight; but it is not so with the linnet or the thrush, that sings because God pleases, and pours out its little soul in pleasure. This is the reason why its singing is (so far) so much better than melody or harmony, than bass or treble, than the Italian or the German school, than quavers or crotchets, or half-notes, or canzonets, or quartetts, or anything in the world but truth and nature!

The Opera is the most artificial of all things. It is not only art, but ostentatious, unambiguous, exclusive art. It does not subsist as an imitation of nature, but in contempt of it; and, instead of seconding, its object is to pervert and sophisticate all our natural impressions of things. When the Opera first made its appearance in this country, there were strong prejudices entertained against it, and it was ridiculed as a species of the *mock-heroic*. The prejudices have worn out with time, and the ridicule has ceased; but the grounds for both remain the same in the nature of the thing itself. At the theatre we see and hear what has been said, thought, and done by various people elsewhere ; at the Opera we see and hear what was never said, thought, or done any where but at the Opera. Not only is all communication with nature cut off, but every appeal to the imagination is sheathed and softened in the melting medium of Siren sounds. The ear is cloyed and glutted with warbled ecstasies or agonies ; while every avenue to terror and pity is carefully stopped up and guarded by song and recitative. Music is not made the vehicle of poetry, but poetry of music ; the very meaning of the words is lost or refined away in the effeminacy of a foreign language. A grand serious Opera is a tragedy wrapped up in soothing airs, to suit the tender feelings of the nurslings of fortune—where tortured victims swoon on beds of roses, and the pangs of despair sink in tremulous accents into downy repose. Just so much of human misery is given as is proper to lull those who are exempted from it into a deeper sense of their own security : just enough of the picture of human life is shewn to relieve their languor without disturb- ing their indifference ;—it is calculated not to excite their sympathy, but "with some sweet, oblivious antidote," to pamper their sleek and sordid apathy. In a word, the whole business of the Opera is to stifle emotion in its birth, and to intercept every feeling in its progress to the heart. Every impression that, left to itself, might sink deep into the mind, and wake it to real sympathy, is overtaken and baffled by means of some other impression, plays round the surface of the imagination, trembles into airy sound, or expires in an empty pageant. In the grand carnival of the senses the pulse of life is suspended, the link which binds us to humanity is broken ; the soul is fretted by the sense of excessive softness into a feverish hectic dream ; truth becomes a fable ; good and evil matters of perfect indifference, except as they can be made subservient to our selfish gratification ; and there is hardly a vice for which the mind is not thus gradually prepared, no virtue of which it is not rendered incapable !

OF PERSONS ONE WOULD WISH TO HAVE SEEN.

"Come like shadows—so depart."

LAMB it was, I think, who suggested this subject, as well as the defence of Guy Faux, which I urged him to execute. As, however, he would undertake neither, I suppose I must do both, a task for which he would have been much fitter, no less from the temerity than the felicity of his pen—

"Never so sure our rapture to create
As when it touch'd the brink of all we hate."

Compared with him, I shall, I fear, make but a commonplace piece of business of it; but I should be loth the idea was entirely lost, and, besides, I may avail myself of some hints of his in the progress of it. I am sometimes, I suspect, a better reporter of the ideas of other people than expounder of my own. I pursue the one too far into paradox or mysticism; the others I am not bound to follow farther than I like, or than seems fair and reasonable.

On the question being started, Ayrton said, "I suppose the two first persons you would choose to see would be the two greatest names in English literature, Sir Isaac Newton and Mr. Locke?" In this Ayrton, as usual, reckoned without his host. Every one burst out a-laughing at the expression on Lamb's face, in which impatience was restrained by courtesy. "Yes, the greatest names," he stammered out hastily; "but they were not persons—not persons." "Not persons," said Ayrton, looking wise and foolish at the same time, afraid his triumph might be premature. "That is," rejoined Lamb, "not characters, you know. By Mr. Locke and Sir Isaac Newton, you mean the

Essay on the Human Understanding, and the *Principia,* which we have to this day. Beyond their contents there is nothing personally interesting in the men. But what we want to see any one *bodily* for, is when there is something peculiar, striking in the individuals, more than we can learn from their writings, and yet are curious to know. I dare say Locke and Newton were very like Kneller's portraits of them. But who could paint Shakespeare?"—"Ay," retorted Ayrton, "there it is; then I suppose you would prefer seeing him and Milton instead?" —"No," said Lamb, "neither. I have seen so much of Shakespeare on the stage and on bookstalls, in frontispieces and on mantelpieces, that I am quite tired of the everlasting repetition : and as to Milton's race, the impressions that have come down to us of it I do not like ; it is too starched and puritanical ; and I should be afraid of losing some of the manna of his poetry in the leaven of his countenance and the precisian's band and gown."—"I shall guess no more," said Ayrton. "Who is it, then, you would like to see ' in his habit as he lived,' if you had your choice of the whole range of English literature?" Lamb then named Sir Thomas Browne and Fulke Greville, the friend of Sir Philip Sidney, as the two worthies whom he should feel the greatest pleasure to encounter on the floor of his apartment in their nightgown and slippers and to exchange friendly greeting with them. At this Ayrton laughed outright, and conceived Lamb was jesting with him ; but as no one followed his example, he thought there might be something in it, and waited for an explanation in a state of whimsical suspense. Lamb then (as well as I can remember a conversation that passed twenty years ago—how time slips !) went on as follows. "The reason why I pitch upon these two authors is, that their writings are riddles, and they themselves the most mysterious of personages. They resemble the sooth-sayers of old, who dealt in dark hints and doubtful oracles ; and I should like to ask them the meaning of what no mortal but themselves, I should suppose, can fathom. There is Dr. Johnson : I have no curiosity, no strange uncertainty about him ; he and Boswell together have pretty well let me into the secret of what passed through his mind. He and other writers like him are sufficiently explicit: my friends, whose repose I should be tempted to disturb (were it in my power), are implicit, inextricable, inscrutable.

"When I look at that obscure but gorgeous prose composition, the *Urn-burial*, I seem to myself to look into a deep abyss, at the bottom of which are hid pearls and rich treasure; or it is like a stately labyrinth of doubt and withering speculation, and I would invoke the spirit of the author to lead me through it. Besides, who would not be curious to see the lineaments of a man who, having himself been twice married, wished that mankind were propagated like trees! As to Fulke Greville, he is like nothing but one of his own 'Prologues spoken by the ghost of an old king of Ormus,' a truly formidable and inviting personage : his style is apocalyptical, cabalistical, a knot worthy of such an apparation to untie; and for the unravelling a passage or two, I would stand the brunt of an encounter with so portentous a commentator!"—"I am afraid, in that case," said Ayrton, "that if the mystery were once cleared up, the merit might be lost;" and turning to me, whispered a friendly apprehension, that while Lamb continued to admire these old crabbed authors, he would never become a popular writer. Dr. Donne was mentioned as a writer of the same period, with a very interesting countenance, whose history was singular, and whose meaning was often quite as *uncomeatable*, without a personal citation from the dead, as that of any of his contemporaries. The volume was produced; and while some one was expatiating on the exquisite simplicity and beauty of the portrait prefixed to the old edition, Ayrton got hold of the poetry, and exclaiming "What have we here?" read the following :

"Here lies a She-Sun and a He-Moon there—
She gives the best light to his sphear
Or each is both, and all, and so
They unto one another nothing owe."*

* Epithalamion on Frederick, Count Palatina of the Rhyne and the Lady Elizabeth.

There was no resisting this, till Lamb, seizing the volume, turned to the beautiful " Lines to his Mistress," dissuading her from accompanying him abroad, and read them with suffused features and a faltering tongue :

" By our first strange and fatal interview,
 By all desires which thereof did ensue,
 By our long starving hopes, by that remorse
 Which my words' masculine perswasive force
 Begot in thee, and by the memory
 Of hurts, which spies and rivals threatned me,
 I calmely beg. But by thy father's wrath,
 By all paines which want and divorcement hath,
 I conjure thee ; and all the oathes which I
 And thou have sworne to seale joynt constancy
 Here I unsweare, and overswear them thus—
 Thou shalt not love by wayes so dangerous.
 Temper, O fair love ! love's impetuous rage,
 Be my true mistris still, not my faign'd Page ;
 I'll goe, and, by thy kinde leave, leave behinde
 Thee I onely worthy to nurse it in my minde.
 Thirst to come backe ; O, if thou die before,
 My soule, from other lands to thee shall soare.
 Thy (else almighty) beautie cannot move
 Rage from the seas, nor thy love teach them love,
 Nor tame wild Boreas' harshnesse : thou hast reade
 How roughly hee in peeces shivered
 Fair Orithea, whom he swore he lov'd.
 Fall ill or good, 'tis madnesse to have prov'd
 Dangers unurg'd : Feed on this flattery,
 That absent lovers one in th' other be.
 Dissemble nothing, not a boy ; nor change
 Thy bodie's habite, not minde ; be not strange
 To thyselfe onely. All will spie in thy face
 A blushing, womanly, discovering grace.
 Richly-cloath'd apes are call'd apes, and as soon
 Eclips'd as bright, we call the moone the moon,
 Men of France, changeable camelions,
 Spittles of diseases, shops of fashions,
 Love's fuellers, and the rightest company

Of players, which upon the world's stage be,
Will quickly know thee . . .
O stay here ! for for thee
England is onely a worthy gallerie,
To walke in expectation ; till from thence
Our greatest King call thee to his presence.
When I am gone, dreame me some happinesse,
Nor let thy lookes our long-hid love confesse,
Nor praise, nor dispraise me ; nor blesse, nor curse
Openly love's force, nor in bed fright thy nurse
With midnight's startings, crying out, Ob, oh,
Nurse, oh, my love is slaine, I saw him goe
O'er the white Alpes alone ; I saw him, I,
Assail'd, fight, taken, stabb'd, bleed, fall, and die.
Augure me better chance, except dread Jove
Thinke it enough for me to have had thy love."

Someone then inquired of Lamb if we could not see from the window the Temple-walk in which Chaucer used to take his exercise ; and on his name being put to the vote, I was pleased to find that there was a general sensation in his favour in all but Ayrton, who said something about the ruggedness of the metre, and even objected to the quaintness of the orthography. I was vexed at this superficial gloss, pertinaciously reducing everything to its own trite level, and asked "if he did not think it would be worth while to scan the eye that had first greeted the Muse in that dim twilight and early dawn of English literature ; to see the head round which the visions of fancy must have played like gleams of inspiration or a sudden glory ; to watch those lips that 'lisped in numbers, for the numbers came'—as by a miracle, or as if the dumb should speak? Nor was it alone that he had been the first to tune his native tongue (however imperfectly to modern ears); but he was himself a noble, manly character, standing before his age and striving to advance it ; a pleasant humourist withal, who has not only handed down to us the living manners of his time, but had, no doubt, store of curious and quaint devices, and would make as hearty a companion as mine

host of the Tabard. His interview with Petrarch 'is fraught
with interest. Yet I would rather have seen Chaucer in
company with the author of the *Decameron*, and have heard
them exchange their best stories together—the *Squire's Tale*
against the story of the *Falcon*, the *Wife of Bath's Prologue*
against the *Adventures of Friar Albert.* How fine to see
the high mysterious brow which learning then wore, relieved
by the gay, familiar tone of men of the world, and by
the courtesies of genius I Surely, the thoughts and feelings
which passed through the minds of these great revivers
of learning, these Cadmuses who sowed the teeth of letters,
must have stamped an expression on their features as
different from the moderns as their books, and well worth
the perusal Dante," I continued, " is as interesting a person
as his own Ugolino, one whose lineaments curiosity would
as eagerly devour in order to penetrate his spirit, and the
only one of the Italian poets I should care much to see. There
is a fine portrait of Ariosto by no less a hand than Titian's ;
light, Moorish, spirited, but not answering our idea. The same
artist's large colossal profile of Peter Aretine is the only likeness
of the kind that has the effect of conversing with ' the mighty
dead ; ' and this is truly spectral, ghastly, necromantic."
Lamb put it to me if I should like to see Spenser as well
as Chaucer ; and I answered, without hesitation, " No ; for
that his beauties were ideal, visionary, not palpable or personal,
and therefore connected with less curiosity about the man.
His poetry was the essence of romance, a very halo round
the bright orb of fancy ; and the bringing in the individual
might dissolve the charm. No tones of voice could come
up to the mellifluous cadence of his verse ; no form but of
a winged angel could vie with the airy shapes he has described.
He was (to my apprehension) rather a 'creature of the
element, that lived in the rainbow and played in the plighted
clouds,' than an ordinary mortal Or if he did appear, I
should wish it to be as a mere vision, like one of his own
pageants, and that he should pass by unquestioned like a
dream or sound

'———*That* was Arion crown'd :
So went he playing on the wat'ry plain'"

Captain Burney muttered something about Columbus, and
Martin Burney hinted at the Wandering Jew; but the last
was set aside as spurious, and the first made over to the
New World.

"I should like," said Mrs. Reynolds, "to have seen Pope
talk with Patty Blount; and I *have* seen Goldsmith." Every
one turned round to look at Mrs. Reynolds, as if by so doing
they could get a sight at Goldsmith.

"Where," asked a harsh, croaking voice, "was Dr. Johnson
in the years 1745-46? He did not write anything that we
know of, nor is there any account of him in Boswell during
those two years. Was he in Scotland with the Pretender?
He seems to have passed through the scenes in the Highlands
in company with Boswell, many years after, 'with lack-lustre
eye,' yet as if they were familiar to him, or associated in his
mind with interests that he durst not explain. If so, it would
be an additional reason for my liking him; and I would give
something to have seen him seated in the tent with the youthful
Majesty of Britain, and penning the Proclamation to all true
subjects and adherents of the legitimate Government."

"I thought," said Ayrton, turning short round upon Lamb,
"that you of the Lake School did not like Pope?"—"Not like
Pope! My dear sir, you must be under a mistake—I can read
him over and over for ever!"—"Why, certainly, the *Essay on
Man* must be allowed to be a masterpiece."—"It may be so,
but I seldom look into it."—"Oh! then it's his Satires you
admire?"—"No, not his Satires, but his friendly Epistles and
his compliments."—"Compliments! I did not know he ever
made any."—"The finest," said Lamb "that were ever paid by
the wit of man. Each of them is worth an estate for life—
nay, is an immortality. There is that superb one to Lord
Cornbury:

'Despise low joys, low gains;
Disdain whatever Cornbury disdains;
Be virtuous, and be happy for your pains.'

Was there ever more artful insinuation of idolatrous praise?
And then that noble apotheosis of his friend Lord Mansfield
(however little deserved), when, speaking of the House of
Lords, he adds:

> ' Conspicuous scene ! another yet is nigh,
> (More silent far) where kings and poets lie ;
> Where Murray (long enough his country's pride)
> Shall be no more than Tully or than Hyde ! '

And with what a fine turn of indignant flattery he addresses
Lord Bolingbroke :

> ' Why rail they then, if but one wreath of mine,
> Oh ! all-accomplish'd St. John, deck thy shrine ? '

Or turn," continued Lamb, with a slight hectic on his cheek and
his eye glistening, " to his list of early friends :

> ' But why then publish ? Granville the polite,
> And knowing Walsh, would tell me I could write ;
> Well-natured Garth inflamed with early praise,
> And Congreve loved, and Swift endured my lays:
> The courtly Talbot, Somers, Sheffield read,
> Ev'n mitred Rochester would nod the head ;
> And St. John's self (great Dryden's friend before)
> Received with open arms one poet more.
> Happy my studies, if by these approved !
> Happier their author, if by these beloved !
> From these the world will judge of men and books,
> Not from the Burnets, Oldmixons, and Cooks.' "

Here his voice totally failed him, and throwing down the book,
he said, " Do you think I would not wish to have been friends
with such a man as this ? "

" What say you to Dryden ? "—" He rather made a show of
himself, and courted popularity in that lowest temple of fame, a
coffee-shop, so as in some measure to vulgarise one's idea of

him. Pope, on the contrary, reached the very *beau ideal* of
what a poet's life should be ; and his fame while living seemed
to be an emanation from that which was to circle his name after
death. He was so far enviable (and one would feel proud to
have witnessed the rare spectacle in him) that he was almost
the only poet and man of genius who met with his reward on
this side of the tomb, who realised in friends, fortune, the
esteem of the world, the most sanguine hopes of a youthful
ambition, and who found that sort of patronage from the great
during his lifetime which they would be thought anxious to
bestow upon him after his death. Read Gay's verses to him on
his supposed return from Greece, after his translation of Homer
was finished, and say if you would not gladly join the bright
procession that welcomed him home, or see it once more land
at Whitehall stairs."—" Still," said Mrs. Reynolds, " I would
rather have seen him talking with Patty Blount, or riding by in
a coronet-coach with Lady Mary Wortley Montagu !"

Erasmus Phillips, who was deep in a game of piquet at the
other end of the room, whispered to Martin Burney to ask if
Junius would not be a fit person to invoke from the dead.
" Yes," said Lamb, " provided he would agree to lay aside
his mask."

We were now at a stand for a short time, when Fielding was
mentioned as a candidate ; only one, however, seconded the
proposition. " Richardson ?"—" By all means, but only to look
at him through the glass door of his back shop, hard at work
upon one of his novels (the most extraordinary contrast that
ever was presented between an author and his works) ; not to
let him come behind his counter, lest he should want you to
turn customer, or to go upstairs with him, lest he should offer
to read the first manuscript of Sir Charles Grandison, which
was originally written in eight-and-twenty volumes octavo, or
get out the letters of his female correspondents, to prove that
Joseph Andrews was low."

There was but one statesman in the whole of English history
that any one expressed the least desire to see—Oliver Cromwell, with his fine, frank, rough, pimply face, and wily policy ;

and one enthusiast, John Bunyan, the immortal author of the *Pilgrim's Progress.* It seemed that if he came into the room, dreams would follow him, and that each person would nod under his golden cloud, "nigh-sphered in heaven," a canopy as strange and stately as any in Homer.

Of all persons near our own time, Garrick's name was received with the greatest enthusiasm, who was proposed by Baron Field. He presently superseded both Hogarth and Handel, who had been talked of, but then it was on condition that he should act in tragedy and comedy, in the play and the farce, *Lear* and *Wildair* and *Abel Drugger.* What a *sight for sore eyes* that would be! Who would not part with a year's income at least, almost with a year of his natural life, to be present at it? Besides, as he could not act alone, and recitations are unsatisfactory things, what a troop he must bring with him—the silver-tongued Barry, and Quin, and Shuter and Weston, and Mrs. Clive and Mrs. Pritchard, of whom I have heard my father speak as so great a favourite when he was young. This would indeed be a revival of the dead, the restoring of art ; and so much the more desirable, as such is the lurking scepticism mingled with our overstrained admiration of past excellence, that though we have the speeches of Burke, the portraits of Reynolds, the writings of Goldsmith, and the conversation of Johnson, to show what people could do at that period, and to confirm the universal testimony to the merits of Garrick ; yet, as it was before our time, we have our misgivings, as if he was probably, after all, little better than a Bartlemy-fair actor, dressed out to play *Macbeth* in a scarlet coat and laced cocked-hat. For one, I should like to have seen and heard with my own eyes and ears. Certainly, by all accounts, if any one was ever moved by the true histrionic *æstus,* it was Garrick. When he followed the Ghost in *Hamlet,* he did not drop the sword, as most actors do, behind the scenes, but kept the point raised the whole way round, so fully was he possessed with the idea, or so anxious not to lose sight of his part for a moment. Once at a splendid dinner-party at Lord ——'s, they suddenly missed Garrick, and could not

imagine what was become of him, till they were drawn to the
window by the convulsive screams and peals of laughter of a
young negro boy, who was rolling on the ground in an ecstasy
of delight to see Garrick mimicking a turkey-cock in the court-
yard, with his coat-tail stuck out behind, and in a seeming
flutter of feathered rage and pride. Of our party only two
persons present had seen the British Roscius ; and they seemed
as willing as the rest to renew their acquaintance with their old
favourite.

We were interrupted in the hey-day and mid-career of this
fanciful speculation, by a grumbler in a corner, who declared it
was a shame to make all this rout about a mere player and
farce-writer, to the neglect and exclusion of the fine old
dramatists, the contemporaries and rivals of Shakespeare.
Lamb said he had anticipated this objection when he had
named the author of *Mustapha* and *Alaham;* and, out of
caprice, insisted upon keeping him to represent the set, in
preference to the wild, hare-brained enthusiast, Kit Marlowe ;
to the sexton of St. Ann's, Webster, with his melancholy yew-
trees and death's-heads ; to Decker, who was but a garrulous
proser; to the voluminous Heywood; and even to Beaumont
and Fletcher, whom we might offend by complimenting the
wrong author on their joint productions. Lord Brooke, on the
contrary, stood quite by himself, or, in Cowley's words, was "a
vast species alone." Some one hinted at the circumstance of
his being a lord, which rather startled Lamb, but he said a
ghost would perhaps dispense with strict etiquette, on being
regularly addressed by his title. Ben Jonson divided our
suffrages pretty equally. Some were afraid he would begin to
traduce Shakespeare, who was not present to defend himself.
"If he grows disagreeable," it was whispered aloud, "there is
Godwin can match him." At length, his romantic visit to
Drummond of Hawthornden was mentioned, and turned the
scale in his favour.

Lamb inquired if there was any one that was hanged that I
would choose to mention? And I answered, Eugene Aram.
The name of the "Admirable Crichton" was suddenly started

as a splendid example of *waste* talents, so different from the generality of his countrymen. This choice was mightily approved by a North-Briton present, who declared himself descended from that prodigy of learning and accomplishment, and said he had family plate in his possession as vouchers for the fact, with the initials A. C.—*Admirable Crichton !* Hunt laughed, or rather roared, as heartily at this as I should think he has done for many years.

The last-named Mitre-courtier* then wished to know whether there were any metaphysicians to whom one might be tempted to apply the wizard spell? I replied, there were only six in modern times deserving the name—Hobbes, Berkeley, Butler, Hartley, Hume, Leibnitz ; and perhaps Jonathan Edwards, a Massachusetts man.† As to the French, who talked fluently of having *created* this science, there was not a tittle in any of their writings that was not to be found literally in the authors I had mentioned. [Horne Tooke, who might have a claim to come in under the head of Grammar, was still living.] None of these names seemed to excite much interest, and I did not plead for the reappearance of those who might be thought best fitted by the abstracted nature of their studies for the present spiritual and disembodied state, and who, even while on this living stage, were nearly divested of common flesh and blood. As Ayrton, with an uneasy, fidgety face, was about to put some question about Mr. Locke and Dugald Stewart, he was prevented by Martin Burney, who observed, " If J—— was here,

---

* Lamb at this time occupied chambers in Mitre Court, Temple.

† Bacon is not included in this list, nor do I know where he should come in. It is not easy to make room for him and his reputation together. This great and celebrated man in some of his works recommends it to pour a bottle of claret into the ground of a morning, and to stand over it, inhaling the perfumes. So he sometimes enriched the dry and barren soil of speculation with the fine aromatic spirit of his genius. His *Essays* and his *Advancement of Learning* are works of vast depth and scope of observation. The last, though it contains no positive discoveries, is a noble chart of the human intellect, and a guide to all future inquirers.

he would undoubtedly be for having up those profound and redoubted socialists, Thomas Aquinas and Duns Scotus." I said this might be fair enough in him who had read, or fancied he had read, the original works, but I did not see how we could have any right to call up these authors to give an account of themselves in person till we had looked into their writings.

By this time it should seem that some rumour of our whimsical deliberation had got wind, and had disturbed the *irritable genus* in their shadowy abodes, for we received messages from several candidates that we had just been thinking of. Gray declined our invitation, though he had not yet been asked ; Gay offered to come, and bring in his hand the Duchess of Bolton, the original Polly ; Steele and Addison left their cards as Captain Sentry and Sir Roger de Coverley ; Swift came in and sat down without speaking a word, and quitted the room as abruptly ; Otway and Chatterton were seen lingering on the opposite side of the Styx, but could not muster enough between them to pay Charon his fare ; Thomson fell asleep in the boat, and was rowed back again ; and Burns sent a low fellow, one John Barleycorn, an old companion of his, who had conducted him to the other world, to say that he had during his lifetime been drawn out of his retirement as a show, only to be made an exciseman of, and that he would rather remain where he was. He desired, however, to shake hands by his representative —the hand, thus held out, was in a burning fever, and shook prodigiously.

The room was hung round with several portraits of eminent painters. While we were debating whether we should demand speech with these masters of mute eloquence, whose features were so familiar to us, it seemed that all at once they glided from their frames, and seated themselves at some little distance from us. There was Leonardo, with his majestic beard and watchful eye, having a bust of Archimedes before him ; next him was Raphael's graceful head turned round to the Fornarina ; and on his other side was Lucretia Borgia, with calm, golden locks ; Michael Angelo had placed the model of St. Peter's on the table before him : Correggio had an angel at

his side ; Titian was seated with his mistress between himself
and Giorgione ; Guido was accompanied by his own Aurora,
who took a dice-box from him ; Claude held a mirror in his
hand ; Rubens patted a beautiful panther (led in by a satyr) on
the head ; Vandyke appeared as his own Paris, and Rembrandt
was hid under firs, gold chains, and jewels, which Sir Joshua
eyed closely, holding his hand so as to shade his forehead.
Not a word was spoken ; and as we rose to do them homage,
they still presented the same surface to the view. Not being
hond-fide representations of living people, we got rid of the
splendid apparitions by signs and dumb show. As soon as
they had melted into thin air, there was a loud noise at the
outer door, and we found it was Giotto, Cimabue, and Ghirlandaio, who had been raised from the dead by their earnest
desire to see their illustrious successors—

> " Whose names on earth
> In Fame's eternal records live for aye ! "

Finding them gone, they had no ambition to be seen after
them, and mournfully withdrew. "Egad !" said Lamb, "these
are the very fellows I should like to have had some talk with, to
know how they could see to paint when all was dark around
them."

"But shall we have nothing to say," interrogated G. J——,
"to the *Legend of Good Women ?*"—"Name, name, Mr. J——,"
cried Hunt in a boisterous tone of friendly exultation, "name as
many as you please, without reserve or fear of molestation !"
J—— was perplexed between so many amiable recollections,
that the name of the lady of his choice expired in a pensive
whiff of his pipe ; and Lamb impatiently declared for the
Duchess of Newcastle. Mrs. Hutchinson was no sooner
mentioned, than she carried the day from the Duchess. We
were the less solicitous on this subject of filling up the
posthumous lists of Good Women, as there was already one in
the room as good, as sensible, and in all respects as exemplary,
as the best of them could be for their lives ! "I should like
vastly to have seen Ninon de l'Enclos," said that incomparable

person ; and this immediately put us in mind that we had neglected to pay honour due to our friends on the other side of the Channel : Voltaire, the patriarch of levity, and Rousseau, the father of sentiment ; Montaigne and Rabelais (great in wisdom and in wit) ; Molière and that illustrious group that are collected round him (in the print of that subject) to hear him read his comedy of the *Tartuffe* at the house of Ninon ; Racine, La Fontaine, Rochefoucalt, St. Evremont, etc.

"There is one person," said a shrill, querulous voice, "I would rather see than all these—Don Quixote !"

"Come, come !" said Hunt ; "I thought we should have no heroes, real or fabulous. What say you, Mr. Lamb? Are you for ekeing out your shadowy list with such names as Alexander, Julius Cæsar, Tamerlane, or Ghengis Khan ?"—"Excuse me," said Lamb ; "on the subject of characters in active life, plotters and disturbers of the world, I have a crotchet of my own, which I beg leave to reserve."—"No, no! come out with your worthies !"—"What do you think of Guy Fawkes and Judas Iscariot ?" Hunt turned an eye upon him like a wild Indian, but cordial and full of smothered glee. "Your most exquisite reason !" was echoed on all sides ; and Ayrton thought that Lamb had now fairly entangled himself. "Why, I cannot but think," retorted he of the wistful countenance, "that Guy Fawkes, that poor, fluttering, annual scarecrow of straw and rags, is an ill-used gentleman. I would give something to see him sitting pale and emaciated, surrounded by his matches and his barrels of gunpowder, and expecting the moment that was to transport him to Paradise for his heroic self-devotion ; but if I say any more, there is that fellow Godwin will make something of it. And as to Judas Iscariot, my reason is different. I would fain see the face of him who, having dipped his hand in the same dish with the Son of Man, could afterwards betray him. I have no conception of such a thing ; nor have I ever seen any picture (not even Leonardo's very fine one) that gave me the least idea of it."—"You have said enough, Mr. Lamb, to justify your choice."

"Oh ! ever right, Menenius—ever right !"

"There is only one other person I can ever think of after this," continued Lamb ; but without mentioning a name that once put on a semblance of mortality. "If Shakespeare was to come into the room, we should all rise up to meet him ; but if that person was to come into it, we should all fall down and try to kiss the hem of his garment ! "

As a lady present seemed now to get uneasy at the turn the conversation had taken, we rose up to go. The morning broke with that dim, dubious light by which Giotto, Cimabue, and Ghirlandaio must have seen to paint their earliest works ; and we parted to meet again and·renew similar topics at night, the next night, and the night after that, till that night overspread Europe which saw no dawn. The same event, in truth, broke up our little Congress that broke up the great one. But that was to meet again : our deliberations have never been resumed.

A FAREWELL TO ESSAY-WRITING.

" This life is best, if quiet life is best."

FOOD, warmth, sleep, and a book ; these are all I at present ask—the *ultima Thule* of my wandering desires. Do you not then wish for

" A friend in your retreat,
Whom you may whisper, solitude is sweet ? "

Expected, well enough :—gone, still better. Such attractions are strengthened by distance. Nor a mistress ? " Beautiful mask ! I know thee ! " When I can judge of the heart from the face, of the thoughts from the lips, I may again trust myself. Instead of these give me the robin redbreast, pecking the crumbs at the door, or warbling on the leafless spray, the same glancing form that has followed me wherever I have been, and "done its spiriting gently ;" or the rich notes of the thrush that startle the ear of winter, and seem to have drunk up the full draught of joy from the very sense of contrast. To these I adhere, and am faithful, for they are true to me ; and, dear in themselves, are dearer for the sake of what is departed, leading me back (by the hand) to that dreaming world, in the innocence of which they sat and made sweet music, waking the promise of future years, and answered by the eager throbbings of my own breast. But now " the credulous hope of mutual minds is o'er," and I turn back from the world that has deceived me, to nature that lent it a false beauty, and that keeps up the illusion of the past. As I quaff my libations of tea in a morning, I love to watch the clouds sailing from the

west, and fancy that "the spring comes slowly up this way."
In this hope, while "fields are dank and ways are mire," I
follow the same direction to a neighbouring wood, where,
having gained the dry, level greensward, I can see my way for
a mile before me, closed in on each side by copse-wood, and
ending in a point of light more or less brilliant, as the day is
bright or cloudy.   What a walk is this to me!   I have
no need of book or companion—the days, the hours, the
thoughts of my youth are at my side, and blend with the
air that fans my cheek.   Here I. can saunter for hours,
bending my eye forward, stopping and turning to look back,
thinking to strike off into some less trodden path, yet
hesitating to quit the one I am in, afraid to snap the brittle
threads of memory.   I remark the shining trunks and slender
branches of the birch trees, waving in the idle breeze; or a
pheasant springs up on whirring wing; or I recall the spot
where I once found a wood-pigeon at the foot of a tree,
weltering in its gore, and think how many seasons have flown
since "it left its little life in air."   Dates, names, faces come
back—to what purpose?   Or why think of them now?   Or
rather why not think of them oftener?   We walk through life,
as through a narrow path, with a thin curtain drawn around it;
behind are ranged rich portraits, airy harps are strung—yet we
will not stretch forth our hands and lift aside the veil, to catch
glimpses of the one, or sweep the chords of the other.   As in a
theatre, when the old-fashioned green curtain drew up, groups
of figures, fantastic dresses, laughing faces, rich banquets,
stately columns, gleaming vistas appeared beyond; so we have
only at any time to "peep through the blanket of the past," to
possess ourselves at once of all that has regaled our senses, that
is stored up in our memory, that has struck our fancy, that
has pierced our hearts:—yet to all this we are indifferent,
insensible, and seem intent only on the present vexation, the
future disappointment.   If there is a Titian hanging up in the
room with me, I scarcely regard it: how then should I be
expected to strain the mental eye so far, or to throw down, by
the magic spells of the will, the stone-walls that enclose it in the

Louvre? There is one head there of which I have often thought, when looking at it, that nothing should ever disturb me again, and I would become the character it represents— such perfect calmness and self-possession reigns in it! Why do I not hang an image of this in some dusky corner of my brain, and turn an eye upon it ever and anon, as I have need of some such talisman to calm my troubled thoughts? The attempt is fruitless, if not natural; or, like that of the French, to hand garlands on the grave, and to conjure back the dead by miniature pictures of them while living! It is only some actual coincidence or 'local association that tends, without violence, to "open all the cells where memory slept." I can easily, by stooping over the long-sprent grass and clay cold clod, recall the tufts of primroses, or purple hyacinths, that formerly grew on the same spot, and cover the bushes with leaves and singing-birds, as they were eighteen summers ago; or prolonging my walk and hearing the sighing gale rustle through a tall, straight wood at the end of it, can fancy that I distinguish the cry of hounds, and the fatal group issuing from it, as in the tale of *Theodore and Honoria*. A moaning gust of wind aids the belief; I look once more to see whether the trees before me answer to the idea of the horror-stricken grove, and an air-built city towers over their grey tops.

> " Of all the cities in Romanian lands,
> The chief and most renown'd Ravenna stands."

I return home resolved to read the entire poem through, and, after dinner, drawing my chair to the fire, and holding a small print close to my eyes, launch into the full tide of Dryden's couplets (a stream of sound), comparing his didactic and descriptive pomp with the simple pathos and picturesque truth of Boccacio's story, and tasting with a pleasure, which none but an habitual reader can feel, some quaint examples of pronunciation in this accomplished versifier.

> " Which when Honoria view'd,
> The fresh *impulse* her former fright renew'd."

> " And made th' *insult*, which in his grief appears,
>   The means to mourn thee with my pious tears."

These trifling instances of the wavering and unsettled state of the language give double effect to the firm and stately march of the verse, and make me dwell with a sort of tender interest on the difficulties and doubts of an earlier period of literature. They pronounced words then in a manner which we should laugh at now ; and they wrote verse in a manner which we can do anything but laugh at. The pride of a new acquisition seems to give fresh confidence to it ; to impel the rolling syllables through the moulds provided for them, and to overflow the envious bounds of rhyme into time-honoured triplets.

What sometimes surprises me in looking back to the past is, with the exception already stated, to find myself so little changed in the time. The same images and trains of thought stick by me : I have the same tastes, likings, sentiments, and wishes that I had then. One great ground of confidence and support has, indeed, been struck from under my feet ; but I have made it up to myself by proportionable pertinacity of opinion. The success of the great cause, to which I had vowed myself, was to me more than all the world : I had a strength in its strength, a resource which I knew not of, till it failed me for the second time.

> " Fall'n was Glenartny's stately tree !
>   Oh ! ne'er to see Lord Ronald more ! "

It was not till I saw the axe laid to the root that I found the full extent of what I had to lose and suffer. But my conviction of the right was only established by the triumph of the wrong ; and my earliest hopes will be my last regrets. One source of this unbendingness (which some may call obstinacy) is that, though living much alone, I have never worshipped the Echo. I see plainly enough that black is not white, that the grass is green, that kings are not their subjects ; and, in such self-evident cases, do not think it necessary to collate my opinions with the received prejudices. In subtler questions, and matters that admit of doubt, as I do not impose my opinion on others without a reason, so I will not give up mine to them without a better reason ; and a person calling me names, or giving himself airs of authority, does not convince me of his having taken more pains to find out the truth than I have, but the contrary. Mr. Gifford once said, that "while I was sitting over my gin and tobacco-pipes, I fancied myself a Leibnitz." He did not so much as know that I had ever read a metaphysical book :— was I, therefore, out of complaisance or deference to him, to forget whether I had or not ? Leigh Hunt is puzzled to reconcile the shyness of my pretensions with the inveteracy and sturdiness of my principles. I should have thought they were nearly the same thing. Both from disposition and habit, I can *assume* nothing in word, look, or manner. I cannot steal a march upon public opinion in any way. My standing upright, speaking loud, entering a room gracefully, proves nothing ; therefore I neglect these ordinary means of recommending myself to the good graces and admiration of strangers (and, as it appears, even of philosophers and friends). Why ? Because I have other resources, or, at least, am absorbed in other studies and pursuits. Suppose this absorption to be extreme, and even morbid—that I have brooded over an idea till it has become a kind of substance in my brain, that I have reasons for a thing which I have found out with much labour and pains, and to which I can scarcely do justice without the utmost violence of exertion (and that only to a few persons)—is this a reason for my playing off my out-of-the-way notions in all companies, wearing a prim and self-complacent air, as if I were "the admired of all observers?" or is it not rather an argument (together with a want of animal spirits), why I should retire into myself, and perhaps acquire a nervous and uneasy look, from a consciousness of the disproportion between the interest and conviction I feel on certain subjects, and my ability to communicate what weighs upon my own mind to others? If my ideas, which I do not avouch, but suppose, lie below the surface, why am I to be always attempting to dazzle superficial people with them, or smiling, delighted, at my own want of success ?

In matters of taste and feeling, one proof that my conclusions have not been quite shallow or hasty, is the circumstance of their having been lasting. I have the same favourite books, pictures, passages that I ever had : I may, therefore, presume that they will last me my life—nay, I may indulge a hope that my thoughts will survive me. This continuity of impression is the only thing on which I pride myself. Even Lamb, whose relish of certain things is as keen and earnest as possible, takes a surfeit of admiration, and I should be afraid to ask about his select authors or particular friends, after a lapse of ten years. As to myself, anyone knows where to have me. What I have once made up my mind to, I abide by to the end of the chapter. One cause of my independence of opinion is, I believe, the liberty I give to others, or the very diffidence and distrust of making converts. I should be an excellent man on a jury. I might say little, but should starve "the other eleven obstinate fellows " out. I remember Mr. Godwin writing to Mr. Wordsworth, that "his tragedy of 'Antonio' could not fail of success." It was damned past all redemption. I said to Mr. Wordsworth that I thought this a natural consequence ; for how could anyone have a dramatic turn of mind who judged entirely of others from himself? Mr. Godwin might be convinced of the excellence of his work ; but how could he know that others would be convinced of it, unless by supposing that they were as wise as himself, and as infallible critics of dramatic poetry—so many Aristotles sitting in judgment on Euripides ! This shows why pride is connected with shyness and reserve ; for the really proud have not so high an opinion of the generality as to suppose that they can understand them, or that there is any common measure between them. So Dryden exclaims of his opponents with bitter disdain—

" Nor can I think what thoughts they can conceive."

I have not sought to make partisans, still less did I dream of making enemies ; and have therefore kept my opinions myself, whether they were currently adopted or not. To get others to come into our ways of thinking, we must go over to theirs ;

and it is necessary to follow, in order to lead. At the time I lived here formerly, I had no suspicion that I should ever become a voluminous writer, yet I had just the same confidence in my feelings before I had ventured to air them in public as I have now. Neither the outcry *for* or *against* moves me a jot : I do not say that the one is not more agreeable than the other.

Not far from the spot where I write, I first read Chaucer's *Flower and Leaf*, and was charmed with that young beauty, shrouded in her bower, and listening with ever-fresh delight to the repeated song of the nightingale close by her—the impression of the scene, the vernal landscape, the cool of the morning, the gushing notes of the songstress,

"And ayen methought she sung close by mine ear,"

is as vivid as if it had been of yesterday ; and nothing can persuade me that that is not a fine poem. I do not find this impression conveyed in Dryden's version, and therefore nothing can persuade me that that is as fine. I used to walk out at this time with Mr. and Miss Lamb of an evening, to look at the Claude Lorraine skies over our heads melting from azure into purple and gold, and to gather mushrooms, that sprung up at our feet, to throw into our hashed mutton at supper. I was at that time an enthusiastic admirer of Claude, and could dwell for ever on one or two of the finest prints from him hung round my little room ; the fleecy flocks, the bending trees, the winding streams, the groves, the nodding temples, the air-wove hills, and distant sunny vales ; and tried to translate them into their lovely living hues. People then told me that Wilson was much superior to Claude : I did not believe them. Their pictures have since been seen together at the British Institution, and all the world have come into my opinion. I have not, on that account, given it up. I will not compare our hashed mutton with Amelia's ; but it put us in mind of it, and led to a discussion, sharply seasoned and well sustained, till midnight, the result of which appeared some years after in the *Edinburgh Review*. Have I a better opinion of those criticisms on that account, or should I therefore maintain them with greater vehemence and tenaciousness? Oh no; both rather with less, now that they are before the public, and it is for them to make their election.

It is in looking back to such scenes that I draw my best consolation for the future. Later impressions come and go, and serve to fill up the intervals; but these are my standing resource, my true classics. If I have had few real pleasures or advantages, my ideas, from their sinewy texture, have been to ne in the nature of realities; and if I should not be able to add to the stock, I can live by husbanding the interest. As to my speculations, there is little to admire in them but my admiration of others; and whether they have an echo in time to come or not, I have learned to set a grateful value on the past, and am content to wind up the account of what is personal only to myself and the immediate circle of objects in which I have moved, with an act of easy oblivion,

"And curtain-close such scene from every future view."

THE SICK CHAMBER.

FROM the crowded theatre to the sick chamber, from the noise, the glare, the keen delight, to the loneliness, the darkness, the dulness, and the pain, there is but one step. A breath of air, an overhanging cloud, effects it; and though the transition is made in an instant, it seems as if it would last for ever. A sudden illness not only puts a stop to the career of our triumphs and agreeable sensations, but blots out all recollection of and desire for them. We lose the relish of enjoyment; we are effectually cured of our romance. Our bodies are confined to our beds; nor can our thoughts wantonly detach themselves and take the road to pleasure, but turn back with doubt and loathing at the faint evanescent phantom which has usurped its place. If the folding-doors of the imagination were thrown open or left ajar, so that from the disordered couch where we lay, we could still hail the vista of the past or future, and see the gay and gorgeous visions floating at a distance, however denied to our embrace, the contrast, though mortifying, might have something soothing in it, the mock-splendour might be the greater for the actual gloom, but the misery is that we cannot conceive anything beyond or better than the present evil: we are shut up and spell-bound in that, the curtains of the mind are drawn close, we cannot escape from "the body of this death," our souls are conquered, dismayed, "couped and cabined in," and thrown with the lumber of our corporeal frames in one corner of a neglected and solitary room.

We hate ourselves and everything else; nor does one ray of comfort "peep through the blanket of the dark" to give us hope. How should we entertain the image of grace and beauty when our bodies writhe with pain? To what purpose invoke the echo of some rich strain of music, when we ourselves can scarcely breathe? The very attempt is an impossibility. We give up the vain task of linking delight to agony, of urging torpor into ecstasy, which makes the very heart sick. We feel the present pain, and an impatient longing to get rid of it. This were indeed "a consummation devoutly to be wished:" on this we are intent, in earnest, inexorable, all else is impertinence and folly; and could we but obtain Ease (that Goddess of the infirm and suffering) at any price, we think we could forswear all other joy and all other sorrow. *Hoc erat in votis.* All other things but our disorder and its cure seem less than nothing and vanity. It assumes a palpable form; it becomes a demon, a spectre, an incubus hovering over and oppressing us: we grapple with it; it strikes its fangs into us, spreads its arms round us, infects us with its breath, glares upon us with its hideous aspect; we feel it take possession of every fibre and of every faculty; and we are at length so absorbed and fascinated by it, that we cannot divert our reflections from it for an instant, for all other things but pain (and that which we suffer most acutely) appear to have lost their pith and power to interest. They are turned to dust and stubble. This is the reason of the fine resolutions we sometimes form in such cases, and of the vast superiority of the sick-bed to the pomps and thrones of the world. We easily renounce wine when we have nothing but the taste of physic in our mouths; the rich banquet tempts us not, when "our very gorge rises" within us. Love and Beauty fly from a bed twisted into a thousand folds by restless lassitude and tormenting cares, the nerve of pleasure is killed by the pains that shoot through the head or rack the limbs; and indigestion seizes you with its leaden grasp and giant force (down Ambition!)—you shiver and tremble like a leaf in a fit of the ague. (Avarice, let go your palsied hold!) We then are in mood,

without ghostly advice, to betake ourselves to the life of the
"hermit poor,"

"In pensive place obscure,"

and should be glad to prevent the return of a fever raging in
the blood by feeding on pulse, and slaking our thirst at the
limpid brook.   The sudden resolutions, however, or "vows
made in pain as violent and void," are generally of short
duration : the excess and the sorrow for it are alike selfish ; and
those repentances which are the most loud and passionate are
the surest to end speedily in a relapse ; for both originate in
the same cause, the being engrossed by the prevailing feeling
(whatever it may be), and an utter incapacity to look beyond it

"The Devil was sick, the Devil a monk would be :
The Devil grew well, the Devil a monk was he !"

It is amazing how little effect physical suffering or local
circumstances have upon the mind, except while we are subject
to their immediate influence.   While the impression lasts they
are everything ; when it is gone they are nothing.   We toss
and tumble about in a sick-bed ; we lie on our right side, we
then change to the left ; we stretch ourselves on our backs, we
turn on our faces ; we wrap ourselves under the clothes to
exclude the cold, we throw them off to escape the heat and
suffocation ; we grasp the pillow in agony, we fling ourselves
out of bed, we walk up and down the room with hasty or feeble
steps ; we return to bed ; we are worn out with fatigue and
pain, yet can get no repose for the one, nor intermission for the
other ; we summon all our patience, or give vent to passion and
petty rage ; nothing avails ; we seem wedded to our disease,
"like life and death in disproportion met ;" we make new
efforts, try new expedients, but nothing appears to shake it off,
or promise relief from our grim foe : it infixes its sharp sting
into us, or overpowers us by its sickly and stunning-weight ;
every moment is as much as we can bear, and yet there
seems no end of our lengthening tortures ; we are ready to
faint with exhaustion or work ourselves up to a frenzy : we

"trouble deaf Heaven with our bootless prayers;" we think our last hour has come, or peevishly wish it were, to put an end to the scene; we ask questions as to the origin of evil, and the necessity of pain; we "moralise our complaints into a thousand similes;" we deny the use of medicine *in toto*, we have a full persuasion that all doctors are mad or knaves, that our object is to gain relief, and theirs (out of the perversity of human nature, or to seem wiser than we) to prevent it; we catechise the apothecary, rail at the nurse, and cannot so much as conceive the possibility that this state of things should not last for ever; we are even angry at those who would give us encouragement as if they would make dupes or children of us; we might seek a release by poison, a halter, or the sword, but we have not strength of mind enough—our nerves are too shaken to attempt even this poor revenge—when lo! a change comes, the spell falls off, and the next moment we forget all that has happened to us. No sooner does our disorder turn its back upon us than we laugh at it. The state we have been in sounds like a dream—a fable; health is the order of the day, strength is ours *de jure* and *de facto;* and we discard all uncalled-for evidence to the contrary with a smile of contemptuous incredulity, just as we throw our physic-bottles out of the window! I see (as I awake from a short uneasy doze) a golden light shine through the white window-curtains on the opposite wall;—is it the dawn of a new day, or the departing light of evening? I do not well know, for the opium "they have drugged my posset with" has made strong havoc with my brain, and I am uncertain whether time has stood still, or advanced, or gone backward. By "puzzling o'er the doubt," my attention is drawn a little out of myself to external objects; and I consider whether it would not administer some relief to my monotonous langour if I call up a vivid picture of an evening sky I witnessed a short time before—the white, fleecy clouds, the azure vault, the verdant fields, and balmy air! In vain! The wings of fancy refuse to mount from my bedside. The air without has nothing in common with the closeness within; the clouds disappear, the sky is instantly overcast and black. I walk out in this scene soon after I recover ; and with those favourite and well-known objects interposed, can no longer recall the tumbled pillow, the juleps, or the labels, or the wholesome dungeon in which I was before immured. What is contrary to our present sensations or settled habits amalgamates indifferently with our belief ; the imagination rules over imaginary themes ; the senses and customs have a narrower sway, and admit but one guest at a time. It is hardly to be wondered at that we dread physical calamities so little before-hand ; we think no more of them after they have happened. Out of sight, out of mind. This will perhaps explain why all actual punishment has so little effect ; it is a state contrary to Nature, alien to the will. If it does not touch honour and conscience (and where these are not how can it touch them?) it goes for nothing ; and where these are, it rather sears and hardens them. The gyves, the cell, the meagre fare, the hard labour, are abhorrent to the mind of the culprit on whom they are imposed, who carries the love of liberty or indulgence to licentiousness ; and who throws the thought of them behind him (the moment he can evade the penalty) with scorn and laughter,

" Like Samson his green wythes."

So, in travelling, we often meet with great fatigue and inconvenience from heat or cold, or other accident, and resolve never to go a journey again ; but we are ready to set off on a new excursion to-morrow. We remember the landscape, the change of scene, the romantic expectation, and think no more of the heat, the noise, and the dust. The body forgets its grievances till they recur ; but imagination, passion, pride, have a longer memory and quicker apprehensions. To the first, the pleasure or pain is nothing when once over ; to the last, it is only then that they begin to exist. The line in Metastasio,

" The worst of every evil is the fear,"

is true only when applied to this latter sort. It is curious that, on coming out of a sick room, where one has been pent up some time, and grown weak and nervous, and looking at Nature for the first time, the objects that present themselves have a very questionable and spectral appearance ; the people in the street resemble flies crawling about, and seem scarce half alive. It is we who are just risen from a torpid and unwholesome state, and who impart our imperfect feelings of existence, health, and motion to others. Or it may be that the violence and exertion of the pain we have gone through make common everyday objects seem unreal and unsubstantial. It is not till we have established ourselves in form in the sitting-room, wheeled round the arm-chair to the fire (for this makes part of our re-intro-duction to the ordinary modes of being in all seasons), felt our appetite return, and taken up a book, that we can be con-sidered as at all returned to ourselves. And even then our sensations are rather empirical than positive, as after sleep we stretch out our hands to know whether we are awake. This is the time for reading. Books are then indeed "a world both pure and good," into which we enter with all our hearts, after our revival from illness and respite from the tomb, as with the freshness and novelty of youth. They are not merely accept-able as without too much exertion they pass the time and relieve *ennui ;* but from a certain suspension and deadening of the passions, and abstraction of worldly pursuits, they may be said to bring back and be friendly to the guileless and enthusi-astic tone of feeling with which we formerly read them. Sickness has weaned us *pro tempore* from contest and cabal ; and we are fain to be docile and children again. All strong changes in our present pursuits throw us back upon the past. This is the shortest and most complete emancipation from our late discomfiture. We wonder that anyone who has read the *History of a Foundling* should labour under an indigestion, nor do we comprehend how a perusal of the *Fairy Queen* should not ensure the true believer an uninterrupted succession of halcyon days. Present objects bear a retrospective meaning, and point to "a foregone conclusion." Returning back to life with half-strung nerves and shattered strength, we seem as when we first entered it with uncertain purposes and faltering aims. The machine has received a shock, and it moves on more tremulously than before, and not all at once in the beaten track. Startled at the approach of death, we are willing to get as far from it as we can by making a proxy of our former selves; and finding the precarious tenure by which we hold existence, and its last sands running out, we gather up and make the most of the fragments that memory has stored up for us. Everything is seen through a medium of reflection and contrast. We hear the sound of merry voices in the street, and this carries us back to the recollections of some country town or village group—

> " We see the children sporting on the shore,
> And hear the mighty waters roaring evermore."

A cricket chirps on the hearth, and we are reminded of Christmas gambols long ago. The very cries in the street seem to be of a former date, and the dry toast eats very much as it did—twenty years ago. A rose smells doubly sweet after being stifled with tinctures and essences, and we enjoy the idea of a journey and an inn the more for having been bed-rid. But a book is the secret and sure charm to bring all these implied associations to a focus. I should prefer an old one, Mr. Lamb's favourite, the *Journey to Lisbon*, or the *Decameron*, if I could get it; but, if a new one, let it be *Paul Clifford*. That book has the singular advantage of being written by a gentleman, and not about his own class. The characters he commemorates are every moment at fault between life and death, hunger and forced loan on the public; and therefore the interest they take in themselves, and which we take in them, has no cant or affectation in it, but is "lively, audible, and full of vent." A set of well-dressed gentlemen, picking their teeth with a graceful air after dinner, and endeavouring to keep their cravats from the slightest discomposure, and saying the most insipid things in the most insipid manner, do not make a scene. Well, then, I have got the new paraphrase on the *Beggar's Opera*, am fairly embarked in it; and at the end of the first volume, where I am galloping across the heath with the three highwaymen, while the moon is shining full upon them, feel my nerves so braced, and my spirits so exhilarated, that, to say truth, I am scarce sorry for the occasion that has thrown me upon the work and the author—have quite forgot my SICK ROOM, and am more than ready to recant the doctrine that *Free-Admission* to the theatre is

> "The true pathos, and sublime
> Of human life,"

for I feel as I read that if the stage shows us the masks of men and the pageant of the world, books let us into their souls and lay open to us the secrets of our own.   They are the first and last, the most home-felt, the most heart-felt of all our enjoyments !

ON WIT AND HUMOUR.

MAN is the only animal that laughs and weeps ; for he is the only animal that is struck with the difference between what things are and what they ought to be. We weep at what thwarts or exceeds our desires in serious matters : we laugh at what only disappoints our expectations in trifles. We shed tears from sympathy with real and necessary distress, as we burst into laughter from want of sympathy with that which is unreasonable and unnecessary, the absurdity of which pro- vokes our spleen or mirth, rather than any serious reflections on it.

To explain the nature of laughter and tears is to account for the condition of human life, for it is in a manner compounded of these two ! It is a tragedy or a comedy—sad or merry, as it happens. The crimes and misfortunes that are inseparable from it shock and wound the mind when they once seize upon it, and when the pressure can no longer be borne, seek relief in tears ; the follies and absurdities that men commit, or the odd accidents that befall them, afford us amusement from the very rejection of these false claims upon our sympathy, and end in laughter. If everything that went wrong, if every vanity or weakness in another, gave us a sensible pang, it would be hard indeed ; but as long as the disagreeableness of the consequences of a sudden disaster is kept out of sight by the immediate oddity of the circumstances, and the absurdity or unaccount- ableness of a foolish action is the most striking thing in it, the ludicrous prevails over the pathetic, and we receive pleasure instead of pain from the farce of life which is played before us, and which discomposes our gravity as often as it fails to move our anger or our pity !

Tears may be considered as the natural and involuntary resource of the mind overcome by some sudden and violent emotion before it has had time to reconcile its feelings to the change of circumstances, while laughter may be defined to be the same sort of convulsive and involuntary movement, occasioned by mere surprise or contrast (in the absence of any more serious emotion), before it has time to reconcile its belief to contradictory appearances. If we hold a mask before our face, and approach a child with this disguise on, it will at first, from the oddity and incongruity of the appearance, be inclined to laugh ; if we go nearer to it, steadily, and without saying a word, it will begin to be alarmed, and be half inclined to cry ; if we suddenly take off the mask, it will recover from its fears, and burst out a-laughing ; but if, instead of presenting the old well-known countenance, we have concealed a satyr's head or some frightful caricature behind the first mask, the suddenness of the change will not in this case be a source of merriment to it, but will convert its surprise into an agony of consternation, and will make it scream out for help, even though it may be convinced that the whole is a trick at bottom.

The alternation of tears and laughter, in this little episode in common life, depends almost entirely on the greater or less degree of interest attached to the different changes of appearance. The mere suddenness of the transition, the mere baulking our expectations, and turning them abruptly into another channel, seems to give additional liveliness and gaiety to the animal spirits ; but the instant the change is not only sudden, but threatens serious consequences, or calls up the shape of danger, terror supersedes our disposition to mirth, and laughter gives place to tears. It is usual to play with infants, and make them laugh by clapping your hands suddenly before them ; but if you clap your hands too loud, or too near their sight, their countenances immediately change, and they hide them in the nurse's arms. Or suppose the same child, grown up a little older, comes to a place, expecting to meet a person it is particularly fond of, and does not find that person there, its countenance suddenly falls, its lips begin to quiver, its cheek turns pale, its eye glistens, and it vents its little sorrow (grown too big to be concealed) in a flood of tears. Again, if the child meets the same person unexpectedly after long absence, the same effect will be produced by an excess of joy, with different accompaniments; that is, the surprise and the emotion excited will make the blood come into his face, his eyes sparkle, his tongue falter or be mute; but in either case the tears will gush to his relief, and lighten the pressure about his heart. On the other hand, if a child is playing at hide-and-seek, or blindman's buff, with persons it is ever so fond of, and either misses them where it had made sure of finding them, or suddenly runs up against them where it had least expected it, the shock or additional impetus given to the imagination by the disappointment or the discovery, in a matter of this indifference, will only vent itself in a fit of laughter.* The transition here is not from one thing of importance to another, or from a state of indifference to a state of strong excitement; but merely from one impression to another that we did not at all expect, and when we had expected just the contrary. The mind having been led to form a certain conclusion, and the result producing an immediate solution of continuity in the chain of our ideas, this alternate excitement and relaxation of the imagination; the object also striking upon the mind more vividly in its loose, unsettled state, and before it has had time to recover and collect itself, causes that alternate excitement and relaxation, or irregular convulsive movement of the muscular and nervous system, which constitutes physical laughter. The *discontinuous* in our sensations produces a correspondent jar and discord in the frame. The steadiness of our faith and of our features begins to give way at the same time. We turn with an

---

* A child that has hid itself out of the way in sport is under a great temptation to laugh at the unconsciousness of others as to its situation. A person concealed from assassins is in no danger of betraying his situation by laughing

incredulous smile from a story that staggers our belief ; and we are ready to split our sides with laughing at an extravagance that sets all common sense and serious concern at defiance.

To understand or define the ludicrous, we must first know what the serious is. Now, the serious is the habitual stress which the mind lays upon the expectation of a given order of events, following one another with a certain regularity and weight of interest attached to them. When this stress is increased beyond its usual pitch of intensity, so as to overstrain the feelings by the violent opposition of good to bad, or of objects to our desires, it becomes the pathetic or tragical. The ludicrous, or comic, is the unexpected loosening or relaxing this stress below its usual pitch of intensity, by such an abrupt transposition of the order of our ideas, as taking the mind unawares, throws it off its guard, startles it into a lively sense of pleasure, and leaves no time nor inclination for painful reflections.

The essence of the laughable, then, is the incongruous, the disconnecting one idea from another, or the jostling of one feeling against another. The first and most obvious cause of laughter is to be found in the simple succession of events, as in the sudden shifting of a disguise, or some unlooked-for accident, without any absurdity of character or situation. The accidental contradiction between our expectations and the event can hardly be said, however, to amount to the ludicrous : it is merely laughable. The ludicrous is where there is the same contradiction between the object and our expectations, heightened by some deformity or inconvenience, that is, by its being contrary to what is customary or desirable ; as the ridiculous, which is the highest degree of the laughable, is that which is contrary not only to custom, but to sense and reason, or is a voluntary departure from what we have a right to expect from those who are conscious of absurdity and propriety in words, looks, and actions.

Of these different kinds or degrees of the laughable, the first is the most shallow and short-lived ; for the instant the immediate surprise of a thing's merely happening one way or another is over, there is nothing to throw us back upon our former expectation, and renew our wonder at the event a second time. The second sort, that is, the ludicrous arising out of the improbable or distressing, is more deep and lasting, either because the painful catastrophe excites a greater curiosity, or because the old impression, from its habitual hold on the imagination, still recurs mechanically, so that it is longer before we can seriously make up our minds to the unaccountable deviation from it. The third sort, or the ridiculous arising out of absurdity as well as improbability, that is, where the defect or weakness is of a man's own seeking, is the most refined of all, but not always so pleasant as the last, because the same contempt and disapprobation which sharpens and subtilises our sense of the impropriety, adds a severity to it inconsistent with perfect ease and enjoyment. This last species is properly the province of satire. The principle of contrast is, however, the same in all the stages, in the simply laughable, the ludicrous, the ridiculous; and the effect is only the more complete, the more durably and pointedly this principle operates.

To give some examples in these different kinds. We laugh, when children, at the sudden removing of a pasteboard mask; we laugh, when grown-up, more gravely at the tearing off the mask of deceit. We laugh at absurdity; we laugh at deformity. We laugh at a bottle-nose in a caricature; at a stuffed figure of an alderman in a pantomime; and at the tale of Slaukenbergius. A giant standing by a dwarf makes a contemptible figure enough. Rosinante and Dapple are laughable from contrast, as their masters from the same principle make two for a pair. We laugh at the dress of foreigners, and they at ours. Three chimney-sweepers meeting three Chinese in Lincoln's Inn Fields, they laughed at one another till they were ready to drop down. Country people laugh at a person because they never saw him before. Anyone dressed in the height of the fashion, or quite out of it, is equally an object of ridicule. One rich source of the ludicrous is distress with which we cannot sympathise from its absurdity or insignificance. Women laugh at their lovers. We laugh at a damned author, in spite of our teeth, and though he may be our friend. "There is something in the misfortunes of our best friends that pleases us." We laugh at people on the top of a stage-coach, or in it, if they seem in great extremity. It is hard to hinder children from laughing at a stammerer, at a negro, at a drunken man, or even at a madman. We laugh at mischief. We laugh at what we do not believe. We say that an argument or an assertion that is very absurd, is quite ludicrous. We laugh to show our satisfaction with ourselves, or our contempt for those about us, or to conceal our envy or our ignorance. We laugh at fools, and at those who pretend to be wise—at extreme simplicity, awkwardness, hypocrisy, and affectation. "They were talking of me," says Scrub, "for they laughed *consumedly*." Lord Foppington's insensibility to ridicule, and airs of ineffable self-conceit, are no less admirable ; and Joseph Surface's cant maxims of morality, when once disarmed of their power to do hurt, become sufficiently ludicrous. We laugh at that in others which is a serious matter to ourselves ; because our self-love is stronger than our sympathy, sooner takes the alarm, and instantly turns our heedless mirth into gravity, which only enhances the jest to others. Someone is generally sure to be the sufferer by a joke. What is sport to one is death to another. It is only very sensible or very honest people who laugh as freely at their own absurdities as at those of their neighbours. In general the contrary rule holds, and we only laugh at those misfortunes in which we are spectators, not sharers. The injury, the disappointment, shame, and vexation that we feel put a stop to our mirth ; while the disasters that come home to us, and excite our repugnance and dismay, are an amusing spectacle to others. The greater resistance we make, and the greater the perplexity into which we are thrown, the more lively and *piquant* is the intellectual display of cross-purposes to the bystanders. Our humiliation is their triumph. We are occupied with the disagreeableness of the result instead of its oddity or unexpectedness. Others see only the conflict of motives, and the sudden alternation of events ; we feel the pain as well, which more than counterbalances the speculative entertainment we might receive from the contemplation of our abstract situation.

You cannot force people to laugh : you cannot give a reason why they should laugh : they must laugh of themselves, or not at all. As we laugh from a spontaneous impulse, we laugh the more at any restraint upon this impulse. We laugh at a thing merely because we ought not. If we think we must not laugh, this perverse impediment makes our temptation to laugh the greater ; for by endeavouring to keep the obnoxious image out of sight, it comes upon us more irresistibly and repeatedly ; and the inclination to indulge our mirth, the longer it is held back, collects its force, and breaks out the more violently in peals of laughter. In like manner, anything we must not think of makes us laugh, by its coming upon us by stealth and unawares, and from the very efforts we make to exclude it. A secret, a loose word, a wanton jest, make people laugh. Aretine laughed himself to death at hearing a lascivious story. Wickedness is often made a substitute for wit ; and in most of our good old comedies, the intrigue of the plot and the double meaning of the dialogue go hand-in-hand, and keep up the ball with wonderful spirit between them. The consciousness, however it may arise, that there is something that we ought to look grave at, is almost always a signal for laughing outright : we can hardly keep our countenance at a sermon, a funeral, or a wedding. What an excellent old custom was that of throwing the stocking ! What a deal of innocent mirth has been spoiled by the disuse of it ! It is not an easy matter to preserve decorum in courts of justice. The smallest circumstance that interferes with the solemnity of the proceedings throws the whole place into an uproar of laughter. People at the point of death often say smart things. Sir Thomas More jested with his executioner. Rabelais and Wycherley both died with a *bon-mot* in their mouths.

Misunderstandings (*mal-entendus*), where one person means one thing, and another is aiming at something else, are another great source of comic humour, on the same principle of ambiguity and contrast. There is a high-wrought instance

of this in the dialogue between Aimwell and Gibbet, in the
"Beaux' Stratagem," where Aimwell mistakes his companion
for an officer in a marching regiment, and Gibbet takes it for
granted that the gentleman is a highwayman. The alarm and
consternation occasioned by someone saying to him, in the
course of common conversation, "I apprehend you," is the most
ludicrous thing in that admirably natural and powerful performance, Mr. Emery's "Robert Tyke." Again, unconsciousness in
the person himself of what he is about, or of what others think
of him, is also a great heightener of the sense of absurdity.
It makes it come the fuller home upon us from his insensibility
to it. His simplicity sets off the satire, and gives it a finer
edge. It is a more extreme case still where the person is
aware of being the object of ridicule, and yet seems perfectly
reconciled to it as a matter of course. So wit is often the more
forcible and pointed for being dry and serious, for it then seems
as if the speaker himself had no intention in it, and we were
the first to find it out. Irony, as a species of wit, owes its force
to the same principle. In such cases it is the contrast between
the appearance and the reality, the suspense of belief and the
seeming incongruity, that gives point to the ridicule, and makes
it enter the deeper when the first impression is overcome.
Excessive impudence, as in the "Liar;" or excessive modesty,
as in the hero of "She stoops to Conquer;" or a mixture of the
two, as in the "Busy Body," are equally amusing. Lying is a
species of wit and humour. To lay anything to a person's
charge from which he is perfectly free, shows spirit and
invention; and the more incredible the effrontery, the greater
is the joke.

There is nothing more powerfully humorous than what is
called *keeping* in comic character, as we see it very finely
exemplified in Sancho Panza and Don Quixote. The pro-
verbial phlegm and the romantic gravity of these two celebrated
persons may be regarded as the height of this kind of excellence. The deep feeling of character strengthens the sense of
the ludicrous. Keeping in comic character is consistency in
absurdity; a determined and laudable attachment to the

incongruous and singular. The regularity completes the contradiction ; for the number of instances of deviation from the right line, branching out in all directions, shows the inveteracy of the original bias to any extravagance or folly, the natural improbability, as it were, increasing every time with the multiplication of chances for a return to common sense, and in the end mounting up to an incredible and unaccountably ridiculous height, when we find our expectations as invariably baffled. The most curious problem of all is this truth of absurdity to itself. That reason and good sense should be consistent is not wonderful : but that caprice, and whim, and fantastical prejudice should be uniform and infallible in their results, is the surprising thing. But while this characteristic clue to absurdity helps on the ridicule, it also softens and harmonises its excesses ; and the ludicrous is here blended with a certain beauty and decorum, from this very truth of habit and sentiment, or from the principle of similitude in dissimilitude. The devotion to nonsense, and enthusiasm about trifles, is highly affecting as a moral lesson : it is one of the striking weaknesses and greatest happinesses of our nature. That which excites so lively and lasting an interest in itself, even though it should not be wisdom, is not despicable in the sight of reason and humanity. We cannot suppress the smile on the lip ; but the tear should also stand ready to start from the eye. The history of hobby-horses is equally instructive and delightful ; and after the pair I have just alluded to, My Uncle Toby's is one of the best and gentlest that "ever lifted leg !" The inconveniences, odd accidents, falls, and bruises, to which they expose their riders, contribute their share to the amusement of the spectators ; and the blows and wounds that the Knight of the Sorrowful Countenance received in his many perilous adventures have applied their healing influence to many a hurt mind. In what relates to the laughable, as it arises from unforeseen accidents or self-willed scrapes, the pain, the shame, the mortification, and utter helplessness of situation, add to the joke, provided they are momentary, or overwhelming only to the imagination of the sufferer. Malvolio's punishment and apprehensions are as comic, from our knowing that they are not real, as Christopher Sly's drunken transformation and short-lived dream of happiness are for the like reason. Parson Adams's fall into the tub at the 'Squire's, or his being discovered in bed with Mrs. Slipslop, though pitiable, are laughable accidents nor do we read with much gravity of the loss of his " Æschylus," serious as it was to him at the time. A Scotch clergyman, as he was going to church, seeing a spruce, conceited mechanic who was walking before him, suddenly covered all over with dirt, either by falling into the kennel, or by some other calamity befalling him, smiled and passed on : but afterwards seeing the same person, who had stopped to refit, seated directly facing him in the gallery, with a look of perfect satisfaction and composure, as if nothing of the sort had happened to him, the idea of his late disaster and present self-complacency struck him so powerfully that, unable to resist the impulse, he flung himself back in the pulpit, and laughed till he could laugh no longer. I remember reading a story in an odd number of the *European Magazine*, of an old gentleman who used to walk out every afternoon, with a gold-headed cane, in the fields opposite Baltimore House, which were then open, only with footpaths crossing them. He was frequently accosted by a beggar with a wooden leg, to whom he gave money, which only made him more importunate. One day, when he was more troublesome than usual, a well-dressed person happening to come up, and observing how saucy the fellow was, said to the gentleman, "Sir, if you will lend me your cane for a moment, I'll give him a good thrashing for his impertinence." The old gentleman, smiling at the proposal, handed him his cane, which the other no sooner was going to apply to the shoulders of the culprit, than he immediately whipped off his wooden leg, and scampered off with great alacrity, and his chastiser after him as hard as he could go. The faster the one ran, the faster the other followed him, brandishing the cane, to the great astonishment of the gentleman who owned it, till having fairly crossed the fields, they suddenly turned a corner, and nothing more was seen of either of them.

In the way of mischievous adventure, and a wanton exhibition of ludicrous weakness in character, nothing is superior to the comic parts of the *Arabian Nights' Entertainments.* To take only the set of stories of the Little Hunchback, who was choked with a bone, and the Barber of Bagdad and his seven brothers—there is that of the tailor who was persecuted by the miller's wife, and who, after toiling all night in the mill, got nothing for his pains ;—of another who fell in love with a fine lady who pretended to return his passion, and inviting him to her house, as the preliminary condition of her favour, had his eyebrows shaved, his clothes stripped off, and being turned loose into a winding gallery, he was to follow her, and by overtaking obtain all his wishes ; but, after a turn or two, stumbled on a trap-door, and fell plump into the street, to the great astonishment of the spectators and his own, shorn of his eyebrows, naked, and without a ray of hope left ;—that of the castle-building pedlar who, in kicking his wife, the supposed daughter of an emperor, kicks down his basket of glass, the brittle foundation of his ideal wealth, his good fortune, and his arrogance ;—that, again, of the beggar who dined with the Barmecide, and feasted with him on the names of wines and dishes ;—and, last and best of all, the inimitable story of the Impertinent Barber himself, one of the seven, and worthy to be so ; his pertinacious, incredible, teasing, deliberate, yet unmeaning folly, his wearing out the patience of the young gentleman whom he is sent for to shave, his preparations and his professions of speed, his taking out an astrolabe to measure the height of the sun while his razors are getting ready, his dancing the dance of Zimri and singing the song of Zamtout, his disappointing the young man of an assignation, following him to the place of rendezvous, and alarming the master of the house in his anxiety for his safety, by which his unfortunate patron loses his hand in the affray ; and this is felt as an awkward accident. The danger which the same loquacious person is afterwards in of losing his head for want of saving who he was, because he would not forfeit his character of being "justly called the Silent," is a consummation of the jest, though, if it had really taken place, it would have been carrying the joke too far. There are a thousand instances of the same sort in the *Thousand and One Nights*, which are an inexhaustible mine of comic humour and invention, and which, from the manners of the East which they describe, carry the principle of callous indifference in a jest as far as it can go. The serious and marvellous stories in that work, which have been so much admired and so greedily read, appear to me monstrous and abortive fictions, like disjointed dreams, dictated by a preternatural dread of arbitrary and despotic power, as the comic and familiar stories are rendered proportionately amusing and interesting from the same principle operating in a different direction, and producing endless uncertainty and vicissitude, and an heroic contempt for the untoward accidents and petty vexations of human life. It is the gaiety of despair, the mirth and laughter of a respite during pleasure from death. The strongest instances of effectual and harrowing imagination are in the story of Amine and her three sisters, whom she led by her side as a leash of hounds, and of the *goul* who nibbled grains of rice for her dinner, and preyed on human carcasses. In this condemnation of the serious parts of the *Arabian Nights*, I have nearly all the world, and in particular the author of the "Ancient Mariner," against me, who must be allowed to be a judge of such matters, and who said, with a subtlety of philosophical conjecture which he alone possesses, "That if I did not like them, it was because I did not dream." On the other hand, I have Bishop Atterbury on my side, who, in a letter to Pope, fairly confesses that "he could not read them in his old age."

There is another source of comic humour which has been but little touched on or attended to by the critics—not the infliction of casual pain, but the pursuit of uncertain pleasure and idle gallantry. Half the business and gaiety of comedy turns upon this. Most of the adventures, difficulties, demurs, hair-breadth 'scapes, disguises, deceptions, blunders, disappointments, successes, excuses, all the dexterous manœuvres, artful inuendoes, assignations, billets-doux, *double entendres*, sly allusions, and elegant flattery, have an eye to this—to the obtaining of those "favours secret, sweet, and precious," in which love and pleasure consist, and which when attained, and the *equivoque* is at an end, the curtain drops, and the play is over. All the attractions of a subject that can only be glanced at indirectly, that is a sort of forbidden ground to the imagination, except under severe restrictions, which are constantly broken through; all the resources it supplies for intrigue and invention; the bashfulness of the clownish lover, his looks of alarm and petrified astonishment; the foppish affectation and easy confidence of the happy man; the dress, the airs, the languor, the scorn, and indifference of the fine lady; the bustle, pertness, loquaciousness, and tricks of the chambermaid; the impudence, lies, and roguery of the valet; the match-making and unmaking; the wisdom of the wise; the sayings of the witty, the folly of the fool; "the soldier's, scholar's, courtier's eye, tongue, sword, the glass of fashion and the mould of form," have all a view to this. It is the closest in "Blue-Beard." It is the life and soul of Wycherley, Congreve, Vanbrugh, and Farquhar's plays. It is the salt of comedy, without which it would be worthless and insipid. It makes Horner decent, and Millamant divine. It is the jest between Tattle and Miss Prue. It is the bait with which Olivia, in the "Plain Dealer," plays with honest Manly. It lurks at the bottom of the catechism which Archer teaches Cherry, and which she learns by heart. It gives the finishing grace to Mrs. Amlet's confession—"Though I'm old, I'm chaste." Valentine and his Angelica would be nothing without it; Miss Peggy would not be worth a gallant; and Slender's "sweet Anne Page" would be no more! "The age of comedy would be gone, and the glory of our playhouses extinguished for ever." Our old comedies would be invaluable, were it only for this, that they keep alive this sentiment, which still survives in all its fluttering grace and breathless palpitations on the stage.

Humour is the describing the ludicrous as it is in itself; wit is the exposing it, by comparing or contrasting it with something else.　Humour is, as it were, the growth of nature and accident ; wit is the product of art and fancy.　Humour, as it is shown in books, is an imitation of the natural or acquired absurdities of mankind, or of the ludicrous in accident, situation, and character : wit is the illustrating and heightening the sense of that absurdity by some sudden and unexpected likeness or opposition of one thing to another, which sets off the quality we laugh at or despise in a still more contemptible or striking point of view.　Wit, as distinguished from poetry, is the imagination or fancy inverted, and so applied to given objects, as to make the little look less, the mean more light and worthless ; or to divert our admiration or wean our affections from that which is lofty and impressive, instead of producing a more intense admiration and exalted passion, as poetry does.　Wit may sometimes, indeed, be shown in compliments as well as satire ; as in the common epigram—

> " Accept a miracle, instead of wit :
> See two dull lines with Stanhope's pencil writ."

But then the mode of paying it is playful and ironical, and contradicts itself in the very act of making its own performance an humble foil to another's.　Wit hovers round the borders of the light and trifling, whether in matters of pleasure or pain ; for as soon as it describes the serious seriously, it ceases to be wit, and passes into a different form.　Wit is, in fact, the eloquence of indifference, or an ingenious and striking exposition of those evanescent and glancing impressions of objects which affect us more from surprise or contrast to the train of our ordinary and literal preconceptions, than from anything in the objects themselves exciting our necessary sympathy or lasting hatred.　The favourite employment of wit is to add littleness to littleness, and heap contempt on insignificance by all the arts of petty and incessant warfare ; or if it ever affects to aggrandise, and use the language of hyperbole, it is only to betray into derision by a fatal comparison, as in the mock-heroic ; or if it treats of serious passion, it must do it so as to lower the tone of intense and high-wrought sentiment, by the

introduction of burlesque and familiar circumstances. To give
an instance or two. Butler, in his *Hudibras*, compares the
change of night into day, to the change of colour in a boiled
lobster—

> " The sun had long since, in the lap
> Of Thetis, taken out his nap ;
> And like a lobster boil'd, the morn
> From black to red, began to turn :
> When Hudibras, whom thoughts and aching
> 'Twixt sleeping kept all night, and waking,
> Began to rub his drowsy eyes,
> And from his couch prepared to rise,
> Resolving to dispatch the deed
> He vow'd to do with trusty speed."

Compare this with the following stanzas in Spenser, treating of
the same subject :—

> " By this the Northern Waggoner had set
> His seven-fold team behind the stedfast star,
> That was in Ocean waves yet never wet,
> But firm is fix'd and sendeth light from far
> To all that in the wide deep wand'ring are :
> And cheerful chanticleer with his note shrill,
> Had warned once that Phoebus' fiery car
> In haste was climbing up the eastern hill,
> Full envious that the night so long his room did fill.
>
> At last the golden oriental gate
> Of greatest heaven 'gan to open fair,
> And Phoebus, fresh as bridegroom to his mate,
> Came dancing forth, shaking his dewy hair,
> And hurl'd his glist'ring beams through gloomy air :
> Which when the wakeful elf perceiv'd, straightway
> He started up and did himself prepare
> In sun-bright arms and battailous array,
> For with that pagan proud he combat will that day."

In this last passage, every image is brought forward that can
give effect to our natural impression of the beauty, the

splendour, and solemn grandeur of the rising sun ; pleasure
and power wait on every line and word ; whereas, in the other,
the only memorable thing is a grotesque and ludicrous
illustration of the alteration which takes place from darkness to
gorgeous light, and that brought from the lowest instance, and
with associations that can only disturb and perplex the
imagination in its conception of the real object it describes.
There cannot be a more witty, and at the same time degrading
comparison, than that in the same author, of the Bear turning
round the pole-star to a bear tied to a stake :—

> " But now a sport more formidable
> Had raked together village rabble;
> 'Twas an old way of recreating
> Which learned butchers call bear-baiting.
> A bold adventrous exercise
> With ancient heroes in high prize,
> For authors do affirm it came
> From Isthmian or Nemæan game;
> Others derive it from the Bear
> That's fixed in northern hemisphere,
> And round about his pole does make
> A circle like a bear at stake,
> That at the chain's end wheels about
> And overturns the rabble rout."

I need not multiply examples of this sort. Wit or ludicrous
invention produces its effect oftenest by comparison, but not
always. It frequently effects its purposes by unexpected and
subtle distinctions. For instance, in the first kind, Mr.
Sheridan's description of Mr. Addington's administration as
the fag end of Mr. Pitt's, who had remained so long on the
treasury bench that, like Nicias in the fable, "he left the
sitting part of the man behind him," is as fine an example
of metaphorical wit as any on record. •The same idea
seems, however, to have been included in the old well-known
nickname of the *Rump* Parliament. Almost as happy an
instance of the other kind of wit, which consists in sudden

retorts, in turns upon an idea, and diverting the train of your adversary's argument abruptly and adroitly into another channel, may be seen in the sarcastic reply of Porson, who hearing some one observe, that "certain modern poets would be read and admired when Homer and Virgil were forgotten," made answer—"And not till then!" Sir Robert Walpole's definition of the gratitude of place-expectants, "That it is a lively sense of *future* favours," is no doubt wit, but it does not consist in the finding out any coincidence or likeness, but in suddenly transposing the order of time in the common account of this feeling, so as to make the professions of those who pretend to it correspond more with their practice. It is filling up a blank in the human heart with a word that explains its hollowness at once. Voltaire's saying, in answer to a stranger who was observing how tall his trees grew— "That they had nothing else to do"—was a quaint mixture of wit and humour, making it out as if they really led a lazy, laborious life ; but there was here neither allusion or metaphor. Again, that master-stroke in Hudibras is sterling wit and profound satire, where speaking of certain religious hypocrites he says that they

> " Compound for sins they are inclin'd to,
> By damning those they have no mind to ; "

but the wit consists in the truth of the character, and in the happy exposure of the ludicrous contradiction between the pretext and the practice ; between their lenity towards their own vices, and their severity to those of others. The same principle of nice distinction must be allowed to prevail in those lines of the same author, where he is professing to expound the dreams of judicial astrology.

> " There's but the twinkling of a star
> Betwixt a man of peace and war ;
> A thief and justice, fool and knave,
> A huffing officer and a slave ;
> A crafty lawyer and pickpocket,
> A great philosopher and a blockhead ;

> A formal preacher and a player,
> A learn'd physician and man slayer."

The finest piece of wit I know of is in the lines of Pope on the Lord Mayor's show—

> "Now night descending, the proud scene is o'er,
> But lives in Settle's numbers one day more."

This is certainly as mortifying an inversion of the idea of poetical immortality as could be thought of; it fixes the *maximum* of littleness and insignificance : but it is not by likeness to anything else that it does this, but by literally taking the lowest possible duration of ephemeral reputation, marking it (as with a slider) on the scale of endless renown, and giving a rival credit for it as his loftiest praise. In a word, the shrewd separation or disentangling of ideas that seem the same, or where the secret contradiction is not sufficiently suspected, and is of a ludicrous and whimsical nature, is wit just as much as the bringing together those that appear at first sight totally different. There is then no sufficient ground for admitting Mr. Locke's celebrated definition of wit, which he makes to consist in the finding out striking and unexpected resemblances in things as so to make pleasant pictures in the fancy, while judgment and reason, according to him, lie the clean contrary way, in separating and nicely distinguishing those wherein the smallest difference is to be found.*

His words are—" If in having our ideas in the memory ready at hand consists quickness of parts, in this of having them unconfused, and being able nicely to distinguish one thing from another, where there is but the least difference, consists in a great measure the exactness of judgment and clearness of reason, which is to be observed in one man above another. And hence, perhaps, may be given some reason of that common observation, that men who have a great deal of wit and prompt memories, have not always the clearest judgment or deepest reason. For wit lying mostly in the assemblage of ideas, and putting them together with quickness and variety, wherein can be found any resemblance or congruity, thereby

On this definition Harris, the author of *Hermes*, has very well observed that the demonstrating the equality of the three angles of a right-angled triangle to two right ones, would, upon the principle here stated, be a piece of wit instead of an act of the judgment or understanding, and *Euclid's Elements* a collection of epigrams. On the contrary, it has appeared that the detection and exposure of difference, particularly where this implies nice and subtle observation, as in discriminating between pretence and practice, between appearance and reality, is common to wit and satire with judgment and reasoning, and certainly the comparing and connecting our ideas together is an essential part of reason and judgment, as well as of wit and fancy. Mere wit, as opposed to reason or argument, consists in

---

to make up pleasant pictures and agreeable visions in the fancy; judgment, on the contrary, lies quite on the other side, in separating carefully one from another, ideas wherein can be found the least difference, thereby to avoid being misled by similitude, and by affinity to take one thing for another." This definition, such as it is, Mr. Locke took without acknowledgment from Hobbes, who says in his *Leviathan*, "This difference of quickness is caused by the difference of men's passions that love and dislike some one thing, some another, and therefore some men's thoughts run one way, some another, and are held to, and observe differently the things that pass through their imagination. And whereas in this succession of men's thoughts there is nothing to observe in the things they think on, but either in what they be like one another, or in what they be unlike, . . . those that observe their similitudes, in case they be such as are but rarely observed by others, are said to have a good wit, by which on this occasion is meant a good fancy. But they that observe their differences and dissimilitudes, which is called distinguishing and discerning, and judging between thing and thing, in case such discerning be not easy, are said to have a good judgment; and particularly in matter of conversation and business; wherein times, places, and persons are to be discerned, this virtue is called discretion. The former, that is, fancy, without the help of judgment, is not commended for a virtue; but the latter, which is judgment or discretion, is commended for itself, without the help of fancy.'

striking out some casual and partial coincidence which has
nothing to do, or at least implies no necessary connection with
the nature of the things which are forced into a seeming
analogy by a play upon words, or some irrelevant conceit,
as in puns, riddles, alliteration, etc. The jest, in all such cases,
lies in the sort of mock-identity, or nominal resemblance,
established by the intervention of the same words expressing
different ideas, and countenancing as it were, by a fatality of
language, the mischievous insinuation which the person who
has the wit to take advantage of it wishes to convey. So
when the disaffected French wits applied to the new order
of the *Fleur du lys* the *double entendre* of *Compagnons d'Ulysse*,
or companions of Ulysses, meaning the animal into which the
fellow-travellers of the hero of the *Odyssey* were transformed,
this was a shrewd and biting intimation of a galling truth (if
truth it were) by a fortuitous concourse of letters of the alphabet,
jumping in "a foregone conclusion," but there was no proof of
the thing, unless it was self-evident. And, indeed, this may be
considered as the best defence of the contested maxim—That
ridicule is the test of truth; viz., that it does not contain or
tempt a formal proof of it, but owes its power of conviction
to the bare suggestion of it, so that if the thing when once
hinted is not clear in itself, the satire fails of its effect and
falls to the ground. The sarcasm here glanced at the character
of the new or old French noblesse may not be well founded ;
but it is so like truth, and "comes in such a questionable
shape," backed with the appearance of an identical proposition,
that it would require a long train of facts and laboured argu-
ments to do away the impression, even if we were sure of the
honesty and wisdom of the person who undertook to refute it.
A flippant jest is as good a test of truth as a solid bribe ;
and there are serious sophistries,

"Soul-killing lies, and truths that work small good,"

as well as idle pleasantries. Of this we may be sure, that
ridicule fastens on the vulnerable points of a cause, and
finds out the weak sides of an argument : if those who resort

to it sometimes rely too much on its success, those who are chiefly annoyed by it almost always are so with reason, and cannot be too much on their guard against deserving it. Before we can laugh at a thing, its absurdity must at least be open and palpable to common apprehension. Ridicule is necessarily built on certain supposed facts, whether true or false, and on their inconsistency with certain acknowledged maxims, whether right or wrong. It is, therefore, a fair test, if not of philosophical or abstract truth, at least of what is truth according to public opinion and common sense; for it can only expose to instantaneous contempt that which is condemned by public opinion, and is hostile to the common sense of mankind. Or to put it differently, it is the test of the quantity of truth that there is in our favourite prejudices. To show how nearly allied wit is thought to be to truth, it is not unusual to say of any person—" Such a one is a man of sense, for though he said nothing, he laughed in the right place." Alliteration comes in here under the head of a certain sort of verbal wit; or, by pointing the expression, sometimes points the sense. Mr. Grattan's wit or eloquence (I don't know by what name to call it) would be nothing without this accompaniment. Speaking of some ministers whom he did not like, he said, " Their only means of government are the guinea and the gallows." There can scarcely, it must be confessed, be a more effectual mode of political conversion than one of these applied to a man's friends, and the other to himself. The fine sarcasm of Junius on the effect of the supposed ingratitude of the Duke of Grafton at court—" The instance might be painful, but the principle would please "—notwithstanding the profound insight into human nature it implies, would hardly pass for wit without the alliteration, as some poetry would hardly be acknowledged as such without the rhyme to clench it. A quotation or a hackneyed phrase dexterously turned or wrested to another purpose, has often the effect of the liveliest wit. An idle fellow who had only fourpence left in the world, which had been put by to pay for the baking some meat for his dinner, went and laid it out to buy a new string for a guitar. An old acquaintance, on hearing this story, repeated those lines out of the L' Allegro "—

> " And ever against *eating* cares
> Lap me in soft Lydian airs."

The reply of the author of the periodical paper called the *World* to a lady at church, who seeing him look thoughtful, asked what he was thinking of—" The next World "—is a perversion of an established formula of language, something of the same kind. Rhymes are sometimes a species of wit, where there is an alternate combination and resolution or decomposition of the elements of sound, contrary to our usual division and classification of them in ordinary speech, not unlike the sudden separation and reunion of the component parts of the machinery in a pantomime. The author who excels infinitely the most in this way is the writer of *Hudibras.* He also excels in the invention of single words and names which have the effect of wit by sounding big, and meaning nothing :—" full of sound and fury, signifying nothing." But of the artifices of this author's burlesque style I shall have occasion to speak hereafter. It is not always easy to distinguish between the wit of words and that of things ; " For thin partitions do their bounds divide." Some of the late Mr. Curran's *bon-mots* or *jeux d'esprit* might be said to owe their birth to this sort of equivocal generation ; or were a happy mixture of verbal wit and a lively and picturesque fancy, of legal acuteness in detecting the variable applications of words, and of a mind apt at perceiving the ludicrous in external objects. " Do you see anything ridiculous in this wig ?" said one of his brother judges to him. " Nothing but the head," was the answer. Now here instantaneous advantage was taken of the slight technical ambiguity in the construction of language, and the matter-of-fact is flung into the scale as a thumping makeweight. After all, verbal and accidental strokes of wit, though the most surprising and laughable, are not the best and most lasting. That wit is the most refined and effectual which is founded on the detection of unexpected likeness or distinction in things, rather than in words. It is more severe and galling—that is, it is more unpardonable though less surprising, in proportion as the thought suggested is more complete and satisfactory from its being inherent in the nature of the things themselves. *Hæret lateri lethalis arundo.* Truth makes the greatest libel ; and it is that which barbs the darts of wit. The Duke of Buckingham's saying, " Laws are not like women, the worse for being old," is an instance of a harmless truism and the utmost malice of wit united. This is, perhaps, what has been meant by the distinction between true and false wit. Mr. Addison, indeed, goes so far as to make it the exclusive test of true wit that it will bear translation into another language—that is to say, that it does not depend at all on the form of expression. But this is by no means the case. Swift would hardly have allowed of such a strait-laced theory to make havoc with his darling conundrums, though there is no one whose serious wit is more that of things, as opposed to a mere play either of words or fancy. I ought, I believe, to have noticed before, in speaking of the difference between wit and humour, that wit is often pretended absurdity, where the person overacts or exaggerates a certain part with a conscious design to expose it as if it were another person, as when Mandrake in the *Twin Rivals* says, " This glass is too big, carry it away. I'll drink out of the bottle." On the contrary, when Sir Hugh Evans says, very innocently, " 'Od's plessed will, I will not be absence at the grace," though there is here a great deal of humour, there is no wit. This kind of wit of the humorist, where the person makes a butt of himself, and exhibits his own absurdities or foibles purposely in the most pointed and glaring lights, runs through the whole of the character of Falstaff, and is, in truth, the principle on which it is founded. It is an irony directed against one's self. Wit is, in fact, a voluntary act of the mind, or exercise of the invention, showing the absurd and ludicrous consciously, whether in ourselves or another. Cross-readings, where the

" The deadly arrow still sticks in his side.'

blunders are designed, are wit; but if any one were to light upon them through ignorance or accident, they would be merely ludicrous.

It might be made an argument of the intrinsic superiority of poetry or imagination to wit, that the former does not admit of mere verbal combinations. Whenever they do occur, they are uniformly blemishes. It requires something more solid and substantial to raise admiration or passion. The general forms and aggregate masses of our ideas must be brought more into play to give weight and magnitude. Imagination may be said to be the finding out something similar in things generally alike, or with like feelings attached to them; while wit principally aims at finding out something that seems the same, or amounts to a momentary deception where you least expected it—namely, in things totally opposite. The reason why more slight and partial, or merely accidental and nominal resemblances serve the purposes of wit, and indeed characterise its essence as a distinct operation and faculty of the mind, is, that the object of ludicrous poetry is naturally to let down and lessen; and it is easier to let down than to raise up; to weaken than to strengthen; to disconnect our sympathy from passion and power, than to attach and rivet it to any object of grandeur or interest; to startle and shock our preconceptions by incongruous and equivocal combinations, than to confirm, enforce, and expand them by powerful and lasting associations of ideas, or striking and true analogies. A slight cause is sufficient to produce a slight effect. To be indifferent or sceptical, requires no effort; to be enthusiastic and in earnest, requires a strong impulse and collective power. Wit and humour (comparatively speaking, or taking the extremes to judge of the gradations by) appeal to our indolence, our vanity, our weakness, and insensibility; serious and impassioned poetry appeals to our strength, our magnanimity, our virtue, and humanity. Anything is sufficient to heap contempt upon an object; even the bare suggestion of a mischievous allusion to what is improper dissolves the whole charm, and puts an end to our admiration of the sublime or beautiful. Reading the finest passage in Milton's *Paradise Lost* in a false tone, will make it seem insipid and absurd. The cavilling at, or invidiously pointing out, a few slips of the pen, will embitter the pleasure, or alter our opinion of a whole work, and make us throw it down in disgust. The critics are aware of this vice and infirmity in our nature, and play upon it with periodical success. The meanest weapons are strong enough for this kind of warfare, and the meanest hands can wield them. Spleen can subsist on any kind of food. The shadow of a doubt, the hint of an inconsistency, a word, a look, a syllable, will destroy our best-formed convictions. What puts this argument in as striking a point of view as anything, is the nature of parody or burlesque, the secret of which lies merely in transposing or applying at a venture to anything, or to the lowest objects, that which is applicable only to certain given things, or to the highest matters. "From the sublime to the ridiculous there is but one step." The slightest want of unity of impression destroys the sublime; the detection of the smallest incongruity is an infallible ground to rest the ludicrous upon. But in serious poetry, which aims at riveting our affections, every blow must tell home. The missing a single time is fatal, and undoes the spell. We see how difficult it is to sustain a continued flight of impressive sentiment : how easy it must be then to travestie or burlesque it, to flounder into nonsense, and be witty by playing the fool. It is a common mistake, however, to suppose that parodies degrade, or imply a stigma on the subject ; on the contrary, they in general imply something serious or sacred in the originals. Without this, they would be good for nothing, for the immediate contrast would be wanting, and with this they are sure to tell. The best parodies are, accordingly, the best and most striking things reversed. Witness the common travesties of Homer and Virgil. Mr. Canning's court parodies on Mr. Southey's popular odes, are also an instance in point (I do not know which were the cleverest) ; and the best of the *Rejected Addresses* is the parody on Crabbe, though I do not certainly think that Crabb·· is the most ridiculous poet now living.

Lear and the Fool are the sublimest instance I know of passion and wit united, or of imagination unfolding the most tremendous sufferings, and of burlesque on passion playing with it, aiding and relieving its intensity by the most pointed, but familiar and indifferent illustrations of the same thing in different objects, and on a meaner scale. The Fool's reproaching Lear with "making his daughters his mothers," his snatches of proverbs and old ballads, "The hedge-sparrow fed the cuckoo so long, that it had its head bit off by its young," and "Whoop jug, I know when the horse follows the cart," are a running commentary of trite truisms, pointing out the extreme folly of the infatuated old monarch, and in a manner reconciling us to its inevitable consequences.

Lastly, there is a wit of sense and observation, which consists in the acute illustration of good sense and practical wisdom, by means of some far-fetched conceit or quaint imagery. The matter is sense, but the form is wit. Thus the lines in Pope—

> " 'Tis with our judgments as our watches, none
> Go just alike ; yet each believes his own "—

are witty, rather than poetical ; because the truth they convey is a mere dry observation on human life, without elevation or enthusiasm, and the illustration of it is of that quaint and familiar kind that is merely curious and fanciful. Cowley is an instance of the same kind in almost all his writings. Many of the jests and witticisms in the best comedies are moral aphorisms and rules for the conduct of life, sparkling with wit and fancy in the mode of expression. The ancient philosophers also abounded in the same kind of wit, in telling home truths in the most unexpected manner. In this sense Æsop was the greatest wit and moralist that ever lived. Ape and slave, he looked askance at human nature, and beheld its weaknesses and errors transferred to another species. Vice and virtue were to him as plain as any objects of sense. He saw in man a talking, absurd, obstinate, proud, angry animal ; and clothed these abstractions with wings, or a beak, or tail, or claws, or long ears, as they appeared embodied in these hieroglyphics in the brute creation. His moral philosophy is natural history. He makes an ass bray wisdom, and a frog croak humanity. The store of moral truth, and the fund of invention in exhibiting it in eternal forms, palpable and intelligible, and delightful to children and grown persons, and to all ages and nations, are almost miraculous. The invention of a fable is to me the most enviable exertion of human genius : it is the discovering a truth to which there is no clue, and which, when once found out, can never be forgotten. I would rather have been the author of *Æsop's Fables*, than of *Euclid's Elements!* That popular entertainment, Punch and the Puppet-show, owes part of its irresistible and universal attraction to nearly the same principle of inspiring inanimate and mechanical agents with sense and consciousness. The drollery and wit of a piece of wood is doubly droll and farcical. Punch is not merry in himself, but "he is the cause of heartfelt mirth in other men." The wires and pulleys that govern his motions are conductors to carry off the spleen, and all "that perilous stuff that weighs upon the heart." If we see a number of people turning the corner of a street, ready to burst with secret satisfaction, and with their faces bathed in laughter, we know what is the matter —that they are just come from a puppet-show. Who can see three little painted, patched-up figures, no bigger than one's thumb, strut, squeak and gibber, sing, dance, chatter, scold, knock one another about the head, give themselves airs of importance, and "imitate humanity most abominably," without laughing immoderately? We overlook the farce and mummery of human life in little, and for nothing ; and what is still better, it costs them who have to play in it nothing. We place the mirth, and glee, and triumph, to our own account ; and we know that the bangs and blows they have received go for nothing, as soon as the showman puts them up in his box and marches off quietly with them, as jugglers of a less amusing description sometimes march off with the wrongs and rights of mankind in their pockets !—I have heard no bad judge of such matters say, that "he liked a comedy better than a tragedy, a farce better than comedy, a pantomime better than a farce, but a puppet-show best of all." I look upon it, that he who invented puppet-shows was a greater benefactor to his species than he who invented operas !

I shall conclude this imperfect and desultory sketch of wit and humour with Barrow's celebrated description of the same subject. He says,—"But first it may be demanded, what the thing we speak of is, or what this facetiousness doth import ; to which question I might reply, as Democritus did to him that asked the definition of a man—*'tis that which we all see and know* ; and one better apprehends what it is by acquaintance, than I can inform him by description. It is, indeed, a thing so versatile and multiform, appearing in so many shapes, so many postures, so many garbs, so variously apprehended by several eyes and judgments, that it seemeth no less hard to settle a clear and certain notice thereof, than to make a portrait of Proteus, or to define the figure of fleeting air. Sometimes it lieth in pat allusion to a known story, or in seasonable application of a trivial saying, or in forging an apposite tale : sometimes it playeth in words and phrases, taking advantage from the ambiguity of their sense, or the affinity of their sound : sometimes it is wrapped in a dress of luminous expression ; sometimes it lurketh under an odd similitude. Sometimes it is lodged in a sly question, in a smart answer ; in a quirkish reason ; in a shrewd intimation ; in cunningly diverting or cleverly restoring an objection : sometimes it is couched in a bold scheme of speech ; in a tart irony ; in a lusty hyperbole ; in a startling metaphor ; in a plausible reconciling of contradictions, or in acute nonsense : sometimes a scenical representation of persons or things, a counterfeit speech, a mimical look or gesture passeth for it ; sometimes an affected simplicity, sometimes a presumptuous bluntness giveth it being ; sometimes it riseth only from a lucky hitting upon what is strange : sometimes from a crafty wresting obvious matter to the purpose : often it consisteth in one knows not what, and springeth up one can hardly tell how. Its ways are unaccountable and inexplicable, being answerable to the numberless rovings of fancy and windings of language. It is, in short, a manner of speaking out of the simple and plain way (such as reason teacheth and knoweth things by), which by a pretty surprising uncouthness in conceit or expression doth affect and amuse the fancy, showing in it some wonder, and breathing some delight thereto. It raiseth admiration, as signifying a nimble sagacity of apprehension, a special felicity of invention, a vivacity of spirit, and reach of wit more than vulgar : it seeming to argue a rare quickness of parts, that one can fetch in remote conceits applicable ; a notable skill that he can dexterously accommodate them to a purpose before him, together with a lively briskness of humour, not apt to damp those sportful flashes of imagination. (Whence in Aristotle such persons are termed επιδεξιοι, dexterous men, and ευτροποι, men of facile or versatile manners, who can easily turn themselves to all things, or turn all things to themselves.) It also procureth delight by gratifying curiosity with its rareness or semblance of difficulty (as monsters, not for their beauty but their rarity ; as juggling tricks, not for their use but their abstruseness, are beheld with pleasure) ; by diverting the mind from its road of serious thoughts ;. by instilling gaiety and airiness of spirit ; by provoking to such dispositions of spirit, in way of emulation or complaisance, and by seasoning matter, otherwise distasteful or insipid, with an unusual and thence grateful tang."

I will only add by way of general caution, that there is nothing more ridiculous than laughter without a cause, nor anything more troublesome than what are called laughing people. A professed laugher is as contemptible and tiresome a character as a professed wit : the one is always contriving something to laugh at, the other is always laughing at nothing. An excess of levity is as impertinent as an excess of gravity. A character of this sort is well personified by Spenser, in the " Damsel of the Idle Lake "—

> " ————Who did assay
> To laugh at shaking of the leaves light."

Anyone must be mainly ignorant or thoughtless who is surprised at everything he sees ; or wonderfully conceited, who expects everything to conform to his standard of propriety. Clowns and idiots laugh on all occasions ; and the common failing of wishing to be thought satirical often runs through whole families in country places, to the great annoyance of their neighbours. To be struck with incongruity in whatever comes before us, does not argue great comprehension or refinement of perception, but rather a looseness and flippancy of mind and temper, which prevents the individual from connecting any two ideas steadily or consistently together. It is owing to a natural crudity and precipitateness of the imagination, which assimilates nothing properly to itself. People who are always laughing, at length laugh on the wrong side of their faces, for they cannot get others to laugh with them. In like manner, an affectation of wit by degrees hardens the heart, and spoils good company and good manners. A perpetual succession of good things puts an end to common conversation. There is no answer to a jest, but another ; and even where the ball can be kept up in this way without ceasing, it tires the patience of the bystanders, and runs the speakers out of breath. Wit is the salt of conversation, not the food.

The four chief names for comic humour out of our own language are Aristophanes and Lucian among the ancients, Molière and Rabelais among the moderns. Of the two first I shall say, for I know, but little. I should have liked Aristophanes better if he had treated Socrates less scurvily, for he has treated him most scurvily both as to wit and argument. His Plutus and his Birds are striking instances, the one of dry humour, the other of airy fancy. Lucian is a writer who appears to deserve his full fame : he has the licentious and extravagant wit of Rabelais, but directed more uniformly to a purpose ; and his comic productions are interspersed with beautiful and eloquent descriptions, full of sentiment, such as the exquisite account of the fable of the halcyon put into the mouth of Socrates, and the heroic eulogy on Bacchus, which is conceived in the highest strain of glowing panegyric.

The two other authors I proposed to mention are modern,

and French. Molière, however, in the spirit of his writings, is almost as much an English as a French author—quite a *barbare* in all in which he really excelled. He was unquestionably one of the greatest comic geniuses that ever lived ; a man of infinite wit, gaiety, and invention—full of life, laughter, and whim. But it cannot be denied that his plays are in general mere farces, without scrupulous adherence to nature, refinement of character, or common probability. The plots of several of them could not be carried on for a moment without a perfect collusion between the parties to wink at contradictions, and act in defiance of the evidence of their senses. For instance, take the *Medecin malgrè lui* (the "Mock Doctor"), in which a common wood-cutter takes upon himself, and is made success-fully to support through a whole play, the character of a learned physician, without exciting the least suspicion ; and yet, not-withstanding the absurdity of the plot, it is one of the most laughable and truly comic productions that can well be imagined. The rest of his lighter pieces, the "Bourgeois Gentilhomme," "Monsieur Pourceaugnac," "George Dandin" (or "Barnaby Brittle"), etc., are of the same description—gratuitous assumptions of character, and fanciful and outrageous caricatures of nature. He indulges at his peril in the utmost license of burlesque exaggeration, and gives a loose to the intoxication of his animal spirits. With respect to his two most laboured comedies, the "Tartuffe" and "Misanthrope," I confess that I find them rather hard to get through : they have much of the improbability and extravagance of the others, united with the endless commonplace prosing of French decla-mation. What can exceed, for example, the absurdity of the Misanthrope, who leaves his mistress, after every proof of her attachment and constancy, for no other reason than that she will not submit to the *technical formality* of going to live with him in a wilderness ? The characters, again, which Celimene gives of her female friends near the opening of the play, are admirable satires (as good as Pope's characters of women), but not exactly in the spirit of comic dialogue. The strictures of Rousseau on this play, in his Letter to D'Alembert, are a fine specimen of the best philosophical criticism. The same remarks apply in a greater degree to the "Tartuffe." The long speeches and reasonings in this play tire one almost to death : they may be very good logic, or rhetoric, or philosophy, or anything but comedy. If each of the parties had retained a special pleader to speak his sentiments, they could not have appeared more verbose or intricate. The improbability of the character of Orgon is wonderful. This play is in one point of view invaluable, as a lasting monument of the credulity of the French to all verbal professions of wisdom or virtue ; and its existence can only be accounted for from that astonishing and tyrannical predominance which words exercise over things in the mind of every Frenchman. The *Ecole des Femmes,* from which Wycherley has borrowed his "Country Wife," with the true spirit of original genius, is, in my judgment, the masterpiece of Molière. The set speeches in the original play, it is true, would not be borne on the English stage, nor indeed on the French, but that they are carried off by the verse. The *Critique de l'Ecole des Femmes,* the dialogue of which is prose, is written in a very different style. Among other things, this little piece contains an exquisite and almost unanswerable defence of the superiority of comedy over tragedy. Molière was to be excused for taking this side of the question.

A writer of some pretensions among ourselves has reproached the French with "an equal want of books and men." There is a common French print, in which Molière is represented reading one of his plays in the presence of the celebrated Ninon de l'Enclos, to a circle of the wits and first men of his own time. Among these are the great Corneille ; the tender, faultless Racine ; Fontaine, the artless old man, unconscious of immortality ; the accomplished St. Evremond ; the Duke de la Rochefoucault, the severe anatomiser of the human breast ; Boileau, the flatterer of courts and judge of men ! Were these men nothing ? They have passed for men (and great ones) hitherto, and though the prejudice is an old one, I should hope it may still last our time.

Rabelais is another name that might have saved this unjust censure. The wise sayings and heroic deeds of Gargantua and Pantagruel ought not to be set down as nothing. I have already spoken my mind at large of this author; but I cannot help thinking of him here, sitting in his easy chair, with an eye languid with excess of mirth, his lip quivering with a new-born conceit, and wiping his beard after a well-seasoned jest, with his pen held carelessly in his hand, his wine-flagons, and his books of law, of school divinity, and physic, before him, which were his jest-books, whence he drew endless stores of absurdity; laughing at the world and enjoying it by turns, and making the world laugh with him again, for the last three hundred years, at his teeming wit and its own prolific follies. Even to those who have never read his works, the name of Rabelais is a cordial to the spirits, and the mention of it cannot consist with gravity or spleen!

NOTES.

——◆◆——

The Periodical Essayists.

This Essay is taken from the Lectures on the *English Comic Writers*. It is claimed for these pages, because the whole matter referring to the *Tatler* appeared in the *Examiner* as No. 10 of the *Round Table* Essays, March 5th, 1815: in the index, entitled "Characters of Sir R. Steele and Addison as Essayists." It was republished in the *Round Table Essays*, 2 vols., 1817, as "On the Tatler."

Hazlitt here states clearly what, to his mind, is the nature and purpose of the Essay. "It plays the whole game of life over before us. . . . It inquires what human life is and has been, to show what it ought to be. We put faith in the testimony of the essayist, for we know that it is true."

In the *Round Table* we have the first fruits of Hazlitt's essay-writing. He had yet to approve himself, according to the picture he has here drawn. This he certainly did. The *London Magazine* had to be born. The *New Monthly* had to find in him a new contributor. Hence came the series of Essays, republished in four volumes as *Table Talk* and *The Plain Speaker*.

Hazlitt loved old books as old books. An original edition of the *Tatler* is of rare interest to him, even in its list of subscribers.

The felicitous comparison of Burke and Johnson prepares us for Hazlitt's great admiration of Burke as a writer. Indeed, his pen was always as ready thus to praise Burke's style as to depreciate him as a politician.

It will be noted that it is in this paper Hazlitt makes his famous compensation to Johnson. It has been said that Hazlitt had not a sympathetic audience; nevertheless, he did not fail to make some fine

points, and this one should be held in generous remembrance.
Sergeant Talfourd (introduced by Lamb to Wordsworth, as his
(Lamb's) "only admirer") was present at these lectures, and he
records that when Hazlitt mentioned Johnson's "carrying the unfortunate victim of disease on his back up through Fleet Street," a
titter arose from some of the audience, who were struck by the picture
as ludicrous, "and a murmur from others, who deemed the allusion
unfit for ears polite." He paused for an instant, and then added in his
sturdiest and most impressive manner, "An act which realises the
parable of the good Samaritan," at which his moral and delicate hearers
"shrunk rebuked into deep silence."

In leaving the lectures, we may mark two other points made by
Hazlitt. At the outset, says Talfourd, he startled many of his audience
by the observation that, since Jacob's dream, "the heavens have gone
further off, and became astronomical." The other point speaks for itself,
in the lecture on the "Living Poets." He prefaced his reading Wordsworth's poem, "Hart-Leap Well," with these words :—"Those who do
not feel the beauty and the force of it may save themselves the trouble of
inquiring further." What an air of bounty and disdain is there in this
short sentence. "Here is a poem for your admiration; you who know
not Wordsworth shall now learn with what he delights our ears and
imaginations; if you cannot appreciate it, lose no time—go back to
your bathos." De Quincey distinguished three periods in Wordsworth's
reputation—persecuted, militant, triumphant. During the poet's
persecuted and militant periods Hazlitt's voice in public was of great
effect, although he denounced Wordsworth the politician as much as he
praised Wordsworth the poet.

MY FIRST ACQUAINTANCE WITH POETS.

In the *Examiner* of 8th September 1816 Hazlitt severely criticised
Coleridge's *Lay Sermon*, before it had appeared in print. On the 29th
December he noticed it when it had appeared; and on the 12th
January 1817, in the same periodical, he wrote a letter on the subject
signed *Semper ego Auditor.* This letter complained of Coleridge's
change of opinion. A whimpering letter :—If, twenty years ago,
Coleridge preached such a sermon (which Hazlitt described), why,
in the name of the dread political furies, dare he publish this *Lay
Sermon?* That epistle, brief and ill-tempered, contained the beautiful

passage in this essay, an amaranth in a desert, beginning, "It was January 1798 that I," etc., to, "Like to that sanguine flower inscribed with woe."

In *Political Tracts* the letter was reprinted. In 1822 the ill-fated *Liberal* was founded, as already explained. The contributions worthiest of the venture were Byron's " Vision of Judgment," and the amplification by Hazlitt of the *Examiner*-letter into the above essay. Hunt would have added Shelley's translations of Goethe's "Mayday Night."

Hazlitt makes beautiful use of quotations. He is free in the use of them without inverted commas. " Like a worm by the wayside." He had lectured on Chaucer, and marked that heart-breaking utterance of Griselda—

> " Wherefore, I you pray,
> Let me not like a worm go by the way !"

"*Longings infinite*" he adopts from Wordsworth without quotation marks.

> " Then I should have sight
> Of him I wait for day and night
> With love and longings infinite."

So ends a verse in the " Affliction of Margaret."

The offer of T. Wedgewood of a hundred and fifty pounds a-year was the turning-point in Coleridge's life. He gave up preaching. The artless Cottle puts it thus—" Up to this day, 18th February 1798 Coleridge held laxly the doctrines of Socinus."

"*Ever after, when I saw the sunset stream upon the objects facing it, I conceived I had made a discovery, or thanked Wordsworth for having made one for me.*"—This is as fine as Gray's sunrise—" It is very odd it makes no figure on paper ; yet I shall remember it as long as the sun—or, at least, as long as I endure. I wonder whether anybody ever saw it before : I hardly believe it." . . .

Here, in the room of an inn at Linton, we have Coleridge uttering the memorable saying, on finding a little worn-out copy of Thomson's *Seasons* lying on a window-seat—" That is true fame ! "

" *The next day Wordsworth arrived.*"—This was a meeting of young men, each of whom set his mark upon the present century. Wordsworth was twenty-eight years of age, Coleridge twenty-six, and Hazlitt twenty. Lamb and his sister had been visiting

Coleridge a little before, on which occasion Coleridge wrote the poem, " A lime-tree bower my prison is." Lamb's age was twenty three.

This Chester is a good picture of worthy, sincere, silent admirer. His happiness was consummated when his knees were beneath the same mahogany as Coleridge's. How delightfully this is put. They were to eat and drink together : there was a temporary equality between Chester and Coleridge—" John's felicity was complete."

" *My heart . . . has never found, nor will it ever find, a heart to speak to it.*"—Here we have the open secret—a sigh from the deeps— the tale of *Liber Amoris*.

" *Vision of Judgment which Mr. Murray.*"—This is a reference to Byron's satire, which had appeared in the first number of the *Liberal*.

On the Pleasure of Painting.

This Essay appeared in the *London Magazine* for December 1820, as No. 5 of *Table Talk*. This was the first year of the *London*. Its brilliant set of contributors included Thomas Carlyle, Allan Cunningham, De Quincey (his *Confessions of an Opium-Eater*), Cary (the translator of Dante), Thomas Hood, Landor, Keats. "Elia's" fame, too, lies in the pages of the *London ;* Hazlitt, therein, displayed his mature powers as Essayist. " The Pleasure of Painting " reappeared in the earliest pages of the first volume of *Table Talk*, and divided into two parts. For the sake of space, the first portion only is taken, being a good instance of his style when inspired by his passion for painting. His first picture was that of an old woman. He said, " I had seen an old head by Rembrandt at Burleigh House, and if I could produce a head at all like Rembrandt's in a year, in my life-time, it would be glory and felicity, and wealth and fame enough for me." Mrs. Charles Cowden Clarke, on reading this quotation, used in my *Hesperides*, wrote me from Genoa in May last, that " Hazlitt's aspiration was fulfilled by the incident of the portrait of his old nurse." This incident is thus given in Mr. and Mrs. Clarke's *Recollections* :—" The very first portrait that Hazlitt took was a mere head of his old nurse ; and so remarkable are the indications in it of early excellence in style and manner, that a member of the profession inquired of the person to whom Hazlitt lent it for his gratification, ' Why, where did you get that

Rembrandt ?' The upper part of the face was in strong shadow, from an overpending black silk bonnet, edged with black lace, that threw the forehead and eyes into darkened effect ; while this, as well as the wrinkled cheeks, the lines about the mouth, and the touches of actual and reflected light, were all given with a truth and vigour that might well recall the hand of the renowned Flemish master."—But of his visionary Burleigh, and that old woman's head, we shall hear from himself in an Essay further on.

The little pleasure Hazlitt finds in writing these Essays is given in the style of Montaigne, who said :—" I have neither fancy nor expression worth anything, and am ignorant beyond a child, of the phrases, and even the very words, proper to express the most common things." Luxurious self-dispraise, by the father of the Essay.

" *A picture of my father.*"—His father had died a few months before (16th July 1820). He loved that father ; his language respecting him is always gentle and reverential. The passage in the foregoing Essay gives evidence of this. So, also, does his reference to him in an Essay on the " Clerical Character." Out of the recollection of his attempting a picture of his father arose another Essay, which is to be found in the first volume of the *Plain Speaker*—" On Sitting for One's Picture."

Note that flash of the news of the battle of Austerlitz. A stormy soul in politics has Hazlitt proved long ere this. When Wordsworth, Coleridge, and he, twenty years ago, strolled in the green lanes round Nether-Stowey, the poet-charmed youth would have taken little interest in the nearness of a political spy ; but the time came when the fierce partisan spirit was roused in him, nevermore to be subdued.

On Actors and Acting.

This *Round Table* Essay appeared in the *Examiner* for the 5th of January 1817 ; and the same year it was published in the second volume of the *Round Table*. It is selected as a general Essay, best suited to introduce Hazlitt as the theatre-goer and critic. The stage is much lauded to-day by a select class which formerly eschewed it. They may further sharpen their judgments by the dogma of one whose defence is praise : " Wherever there is a playhouse, the world will go on not amiss." Perhaps actors, too, would take hints from the moralising of their loving friend, some of whose last thoughts were on a playhouse. The hand of death was on him when, in 1830, he wrote his Essay, "The Free Admission."

ON MR. KEAN'S "IAGO."

This paper appeared in the *Examiner* for 24th July, and was continued on 7th August 1814. The greater portion of it forms the eighth Essay in the first volume of *Round Table.* It was afterwards inserted complete in *View of the English Stage.* Kean first appeared in London at Drury Lane, 26th January of that year, as Shylock. On mention of that, two singular pictures arise, of the actor and the critic. After provincial training, Kean has come to London. Driven to despair by poverty and the ill-treatment of the Drury Lane directors, nearly bankrupted at that time, he is saved (22nd January) on his way from Cecil Street, half-intent on suicide, by the news that he is advertised to play Shylock on the twenty-sixth. The day arrived ; a drizzly, heart-depressing day. One rehearsal is given at noon. His interpretation of the Jew causes the manager to protest. The rehearsal is flat; failure is foretold by those whose business it is to know what acting ought to be, and what the public is. Kean goes to his lodgings, and shares with his wife "the unusual luxury of a dinner." Six o'clock is struck by St. Clement Danes's clock, sullenly answered through the dark rain from the neighbouring steeples. Kean takes a little bundle of such necessaries as an actor provides, and hurries off. " I wish I was going to be shot ! " spoken as he leaves, tells his sickness at heart. Into the foul night he goes—(but as Venus once in ambrosial cloud, so, now, the Muse of Tragedy is near her favourite son). On, through the slush of the street to a common dressing-room, amongst second-rate actors. There he prepares himself, and puts on—a black wig. Burbadge played "the red-haired Jew ; " Macklin revived the red-haired Jew. Can a great actor win upon the colour—black or red ? Insolence and scorn and disspiritment surround him, except an encouraging word from Bannister, a glass of brandy and water from Oxberry, a pleasant phrase from Dr. Drury. He is now at the wings. The stage, the house, all the world are before him. He goes across the stage, peeps through the eyelet hole, beholds the house—empty boxes and fifty people in the pit. But great actors always received their laurels from the pit. These fifty represent not five hundred, five thousand—but the world of London—fame, or dishonour. These fifty in the pit, and a critic unseen—William Hazlitt—have Cæsar and his fortunes in keeping. Nothing can he said here of the charm of intonation, the power, the grace. The night is won. The Muse of Tragedy has claimed her son at the voice of fifty and one. Through the rain and darkness Kean rushed to his lodgings. Husband and wife embrace each other. Tears are brighter than the rain; and in the sun of fortune they now flash brighter than jewels. "Mary, you shall ride in your carriage, and——;" he took their child from the cradle, "Charley!". . . The actor has a double life. But enough. The critic—William Hazlitt—saw Kean—and the fifty in the pit. The night was memorable through all his days. He had been wearied by the exigent trials and failures of Drury Lane; he could not have a good heart as to the man now to try the house—advertised as, "Mr. Kean, from the Theatre Royal, Exeter." His report in the *Morning Chronicle*, next day, told of the new star risen on the stage—"For voice, eye, action, and expression, no actor has come out for many years equal to him."

"Iago" was first played by Kean at Drury Lane in May; the second time in July 1814.

It soon appeared that Hazlitt's views in the Essay, or critique, were in opposition to those of the Theatrical Critic of the *Examiner*, who replied to Hazlitt's on the 4th of September 1814. Hazlitt gave the retort courteous in the following number. On September 18th the hostile critic made his final response, and the home-thrust proved a cruel one. In his letter Hazlitt spoke of Iago as the busy, meddling fiend "who rides in the whirlwind and directs the storm, triumphing over the scattered wrecks, and listening to the shrieks of death." The critic's reference to this shows how well Hazlitt's vehement idolatry of Napoleon was known amongst his fellow-labourers in the field of literature. "Perhaps he (Hazlitt) had some existing character before him; at any rate the picture bears a stronger resemblance to Buonaparte than to Shakspere's 'Ancient.'" The critic had a more severe revenge than this biting repartee. In three-quarters of a year Waterloo was fought. As an antidote to that passionate fencing, we have given some of Hazlitt's remarks on Mrs. Siddons—the first portion from "Whether Actors ought to sit in the Boxes:" the second from "Novelty and Familiarity."

ON A LANDSCAPE OF NICHOLAS POUSSIN

Appeared in the *London Magazine*, August 1821; republished in the second volume of *Table Talk*. This essay affords a good example of Hazlitt's art-criticism, which caused Hunt to say that his writings on that subject "cast a light like a painted window." Hunt's expression occurs in his short, sudden notice of Hazlitt's death, in the fourteenth number of Hunt's *Tatler*. The TATLER! Hunt took the opportunity of saying that Hazlitt "would not have thought it beneath his sympathy with greater things, to express his satisfaction at the *name* and the hopes of the paper." Of that, Hunt and the admirers of Hazlitt might be certain. He spake handsome praise of his friends, by the way: he made sure they should live if his own name lived.

In this Essay, as in others at opportune moments, Hazlitt never tires of mentioning certain names for which he has admiration any more than the world tires of mentioning Shakspere. Rembrandt, Rubens, Titian, Claude, Guido, Poussin, Caracci, Raphael, here in one cluster, are music upon the tongue and a scene of varying shades and splendours.

"*Et ego in Arcadia vixi!*"—I, too, lived in Arcadia. This is a reference to a picture by Poussin in the Louvre, where shepherds in the Vale of Tempe survey a tombstone bearing this inscription. This picture haunted Hazlitt with its colours and language through life.

I have spoken of Hazlitt's influence on other minds. The Louvre brings us to an instance. When Talfourd, with his wife, his eldest son, and niece, in 1841, made that happy tour which embraced Switzerland and its Alps, of course, when at Paris, he visited the Louvre. And these are his words following his slight description:—

"I regarded the Louvre with more interest as a great chapter in Hazlitt's intellectual history, than as the richest gallery of pictures in the world. The intensity of his first admiration; the association of the scene with the triumphs of his favourite hero; and the softened spirit in which he received it, when spoiled of its noblest trophies, and when that hero had been finally vanquished by what he regarded as the commonplace virtues and tyrannies of the world—gave to the place, in my mind, a personal interest, nearer, if lower, than its matchless treasures could inspire. Hazlitt's true history was all within—of the struggles and the winnings of thought ; and as thought will sympathise with thought itself, more perfectly than with thought's grandest objects, so here the tenderest associations this mighty collection rendered back were those which a mind, now snatched from human view, once imparted to its glories and its losses."

On Hogarth's Marriage-a-la-Mode.

This was published in the two volumes of the *Round Table,* essays eleven and twelve, and was taken into *Sketches of the Principal Picture Galleries in England.*

"*Boccaccio, the most refined.*"—This is one of Hazlitt's references to the great writer of the *Decameron,* which caused Leigh Hunt, in his *Bacchus in Tuscany,* to say that "Hazlitt was the first to point out to our own times the nobler character of Boccaccio."

The Reflector (1810-12) was a quarterly magazine, projected by Leigh Hunt's brother : edited by Leigh Hunt himself. In his Autobiography he says, "Some of the liveliest effusions of Lamb appeared in this magazine."

"*Lamb's Essay on the Genius of Hogarth.*"—The note here given is at the end of the essay as it appeared in the *Round Table.* When incorporated with *Sketches of Picture Galleries* (1824), the words following "C. Lamb" were left out. A glance at the advertisements at the end of the volume acquaints us with the reason. *Elia : Essays which have appeared under that signature in the London Magazine.* My copy of that original edition is now before me—"Elia," as Mr. P. Fitzgerald thought it pertinent to remark, "Elia," not the *Essays of Elia* as they became afterwards—in dark green cloth, clear in its type as its humour after sixty-five years. Looking again at the Taylor and Hessey advertisements, it is singular to note amongst those books then "just published" how many have become famous. The first in the list is Landor's *Imaginary Conversations*—there are Cary's Dante and Aristophanes ; Bowring's *Poetry and Romance of Spain ;* Coleridge's *Aids to Reflection ; Flora Domestica* (fragrant with anonymous contributions by Leigh Hunt) ; *Songs and Tales,* by Allan Cunningham ; the "Endymion," "Lamia," "Isabella," and "Eve of St. Agnes" of Keats; Clare's poems ; and *Elia.* It should be noted that the many-sided Coleridge did much to unseal the eyes as to discrimination of Hogarth's powers. This we learn through a quotation by Lamb from *The Friend.*

My copy of the original *Friend* shows me that Lamb quoted from the second of *Satyrane's Letters—The Friend*, No. 16, *Thursday, December 7th*, 1809—so that Coleridge's thought must have been germinating for years, too, in Lamb's mind. Lamb's best sentence in his Hogarth Essay refers to "the quantity of thought which Hogarth crowds into every picture." Lamb's limitation as art-critic is soon reached. Not so with Hazlitt. Enthusiasm in dallying with a favourite subject tricks it out with fruits and foliage not its own, and elevates it into one of the most supreme of human efforts, crying "Here is the Phœnix!" Lamb, indeed, did say—Shakspere and Hogarth! Hazlitt having Hogarth solely in his mind's regard, and angered with the world in its neglect of the painter, spoke, perhaps, in hardly less ardent terms. But Hazlitt had travelled through the lengths and breadths of the golden realms of this art, and in the higher hours of contemplation he had some other thing to say. Hogarth was not the artist for all nations and all time. To speak of the man is one thing; his relations to the great masters is another. This Hazlitt made manifest in his *Characteristics.* "Raphael's figures are sustained by ideas; Hogarth's are dictated by mechanical habits and instincts. It is elevation of thought that gives grandeur and delicacy of expression to passion. The expansion and refinement of the soul are seen in the face as in a mirror. . . . Now, if mental expression has this superior grandeur and grace, we can account at once for the superiority of Raphael. For there is no doubt that it is more difficult to give a whole, continuously and proportionably, than to give the parts separate and disjointed, or to diffuse the same subtle but powerful expression over a large mass than to caricature it in a single part or feature. The actions in Raphael are like a branch of a tree swept by the surging blast; those in Hogarth like straws whirled and twitched about in the gusts and eddies of passion. I do not mean to say that goodness alone constitutes greatness, but mental power does. Hogarth's Good Apprentice is insipid. Raphael has clothed Elymas the Sorcerer with all the dignity and grandeur of vice."

ON GOING A JOURNEY.

This Essay is of the first of the series of *Table Talk* which appeared in the *New Monthly*, 1822. A note at the commencement informs the reader that these essays "are by the well-known author of *Table Talk*, in one vol., 8vo, published during the last year." It is the third essay in the second volume of the republication of *Table Talk.*

"*Repeating the lines which I have just quoted from Mr. Coleridge's poem!*"—They are from Coleridge's "Ode to the Departing Year," referred to in the second essay. The lines he quotes appear in the following extract :—

> " O, my mother Isle !
> Thy valleys, fair as Eden's bowers,
> Glitter green with sunny showers ;
> Thy grassy upland's gentle swells
> Echo to the bleat of flocks ;
> (Those grassy hills, those glittering dells,
> Proudly ramparted with rocks,)
> And ocean mid his uproar wild
> Speaks safety to his island child."

"*I once took a party to Oxford.*"—Of course, this is the visit referred to in the Introduction, and memorialised by Lamb in *Vacation at Oxford*, and spoken upon, again, in *Conversation of Authors.*

On the Prose Style of Poets.

The reason for giving this extract is to afford a specimen of his loyalty to the Muses, even when his political passion is engaged. He never wearied, in or out of season, in praising and denouncing Burke. It is Hazlitt himself, and no other, to opine that Hunt required something of the heat and earnestness of the political partisan. Yet what would have destroyed the Ariel of essayists is the making of Hazlitt.

Whether Genius is Conscious of its Powers?

This essay is the twelfth in the first volume of the *Plain Speaker.*

"*I am not in the humour to pursue this argument any further at present, but to write a digression.*"—A transition as cheerful as it is abrupt, which transports us at once to Winterslow. He is happy in his seclusion there, as is told in other places. That sketch of Millimant was something he was proud of: also, that of Friscobaldo. Then another break, fresh as mountain spring: "I look out of my window and see that a shower has just fallen."

"*The circle of critics that beset a throne.*"—Of course, he has the arch-critic Gifford in his mind, as thus written in his letter to him afterwards:—"It is your business to keep a strict eye over all writers who differ in opinion with his Majesty's Ministers, and to measure their talents and attainments by the standard of their servility and meanness." To say that Leigh Hunt, Editor of the *Examiner*, was driven from country and friends because, ten years before, he had called a prince "an Adonis of fifty," is fevered exaggeration. Hunt was imprisoned for that offence, as is well known, but in the migration he simply suffered from the chances of political warfare. His own representation was that politics "different from ours, were triumphing all over Europe;" consequently, the *Examiner*, on which the fortunes of Hunt and his brother depended, declined. Byron proposed that he should go to Italy, and, in conjunction with himself and Shelley, "set up a Liberal publication." That was the origin of the *Liberal* of which Hazlitt was home editor. Twice Hazlitt's temper broke out in this essay.

ON THE CONVERSATION OF AUTHORS.

This Essay is dated "Winterslow Hut," appearing as number three of *Table Talk* in the *London* for September 1820; republished as Essays three and four in the first volume of the *Plain Speaker*.

These are the opening rays to the immortality which awaited Lamb's *Wednesdays*. Of these I have spoken of elsewhere, and abstain from other remarks, now that Hazlitt's descriptions are before the reader. Other reference will be found in Barry Cornwall's *Memoir of Lamb*, and Talfourd's *Letters of Lamb*.

The Indicator, as giving a good idea of Hunt's conversation; a kindly hint, again, for readers to make acquaintance of his friend's writings.

"*Mr. Northcote the painter.*"—An infatuation with Hazlitt. *Boswell-Redivivus* was Hazlitt's conversations with Northcote idealised. Mr. Carew Hazlitt illuminates the hero and the book in his *Memoirs of William Hazlitt*, vol. i., page 198. Enough here of his words, that Northcote was "a person of average conversational powers . . . an ill-conditioned, malevolent, mean-spirited person, for whom nobody probably ever entertained any real regard." "An old cynic," says Mr.

Leslie Stephen, "out of whom it does not seem that anybody else could strike many sparks." And thus reported a friend of a conversation with Hazlitt :—"What fine things Northcote says." "Yes, and what ill-natured things : they are all malicious to the last word. Lamb called him a little bottle of aqua-fortis, which, you know, corrodes everything it touches." "Except gold," interrupted Hazlitt ; "he never drops upon Sir Joshua or the great masters." "Well, but is he not flowing over with envy, hatred, and all uncharitableness? I am told that he is as spiteful as a woman. Then his niggardness ! Did he ever give anything away?" "Yes," retorted Hazlitt, "his advice, and very unpleasant it is."

"*Lamb once came down . . . we crossed the country to Oxford.*"—It was in the second year after Hazlitt's marriage—October 1809—that Lamb, with his sister and Martin Burney, made this visit. ("Martin says, if you can borrow a blanket or two, he can sleep on the floor without either bed or mattress, which would save his expenses at the *Hut. . . .* You may think it as well to make him up a bed in the best kitchen."—Mary Lamb to Mrs. Hazlitt, June 1809.) In Hazlitt's *Farewell to Essay-Writing,* written 1828, he pathetically refers to this visit :—"I used to walk out at this time with Mr. and Miss Lamb of an evening, to look at the Claude Lorraine skies over our heads, melting from azure into purple and gold ; and to gather mushrooms, that sprung up at our feet, to throw into our hashed mutton at supper." Hazlitt has already referred to the Oxford visit in *Going a Journey.*

On New Books.

Written in Florence, when on his wedding tour. Dated May 1825. *Lord Byron is dead.*—Yes, in the previous year—April 19, 1824. *Waverley romances.* Although it became an open secret, through the bankruptcy of Constable in January 1826, it was not till the dinner of the Theatrical Fund in Edinburgh, February 23, 1827, that Scott avowed his authorship of the romances. Sir Walter himself was in the chair. He wrote out for the occasion the three cardinal rules for the maintenance of this dignity, as became his boonful nature, and a fourth—"always speak short, and *skeoch doch na skiel*—cut a tale with a drink.

> This is the purpose and intent
> Of gude Schir Walter's testament.

Lord Meadowbank proposed Scott's health, and revealed the Great Unknown. The company rose to their feet, thence upon the chairs and tables, to vent their rapturous applause. Scott replied, and "dedicated a bumper to the health . . . of my friend Bailie Nicol Jarvie"—that was Mackay, the actor—who responded briefly—"My conscience! My worthy father the deacon could never have believed that his son would hae sic a compliment paid him by the Great Unknown."

"*If we read Irving's Orations, it is merely that we may go as a lounge to see the man.*"—Irving has entered the Scotch Church : has been a lesser light beside Chalmers in Glasgow : has arrived in London and become the hero of the Pulpit. He holds forth in the Caledonian Church, Cross Street, Covent Garden, and all fashionable London is now around him, to treasure every word of his Orations. He has "put new wine into old bottles," says Hazlitt, " or new cloth on old garments. He has taken the thorns and briars of scholastic divinity, and garlanded them with the flowers of modern literature."

"*Everyone in a crowd has power to throw dirt : nine out of ten have the inclination.*"—These words are only a figurative paraphrase of the Greek.

On Reading Old Books.

This appeared as seventh *Table Talk* in the *London*, February 1821, and is the third Essay in the second volume of the *Plain Speaker*.

Marcian Colonna.—A poetic tale of the passions, of sorrows, and death. It would suit Hazlitt's mood. Of it was written by the sweet Grecian hand of the time—W. B. Procter's (Barry Cornwall's), "heroine coming to the ball is delicious. He should always write of beauty and gentleness, and all beautiful and gentle things, whether in tears or smiles. If Titian could come to life again, to paint his portrait for him in gratitude for his love to Italy, he would put by the side of it a rose, bending with dew, from out a sunny glass."

"*Keats's Eve of St. Agnes.*"—This was timely spoken. All praise of Keats was now good, and it was a good thing for Hazlitt to measure Keats against Gifford in the *Spirit of the Age.* "Adonais" was written by Shelley in 1821, but not reprinted in England until 1829, and then with fear and trembling by some young admirers.

"*Like (these sentences) from the great preacher in the Caledonian Chapel.*"—This is praise indeed for Irving.

" *To understand an adversary is some praise: to admire him is more; I thought I did both: I knew I did one.*"—He puts his whole of loving, and liking, and hating into these words. Praise of Burke for his style to the last, and a disclaimer as to his politics.

THE FIGHT

Appeared in *New Monthly* 1822, republished as the eighteenth essay in Hazlitt's *Literary Remains.*

ON THE LOOK OF A GENTLEMAN

Appeared in the *London,* January 1821, as sixth essay of its *Table Talk,* and is the second essay in the second volume of the *Plain Speaker.* Take him at his word, that of manners he borrows of no one; take this as a mere society-essay, he the Observer and Plain Speaker. But then, what colour and life there is in it. "*Sir Charles Bunbury*" presents nothing startling. Ah, but then there is romance in him; "he is a gentleman of the first water" (the same that sixty years ago married the beautiful Lady Sarah Lennox, with whom the king was in love). Walking with Lamb in London, Crabb Robinson met Sir Charles, who shook hands with him. Lamb was all astonishment. "I had no idea that you knew Sheridan." "Nor do I. That is Sir Charles Bunbury." "That's impossible. I have known him to be Sheridan all my life. That *shall* be Sheridan. You thief! You have stolen my Sheridan."

"*Lord C——*" (Castlereagh), a well-hated man, cursed in his grave by poets. Leigh Hunt, late in life, wrote kindly of him and said, "How pleasant it is thus to find oneself reconciled to men whom we have ignorantly undervalued, and how fortunate to have lived long enough to say so." But these were political opponents.—The approach of the Marquis Wellesley, after the description of Castlereagh, is a masterly contrast.

"*Wycherley. . . . looking like a lord.*"—Any grace added to a writer of good English comedy would, with Hazlitt, add double lustre to him. Wycherley's marriage with the Countess of Drogheda would commend his memory further to Hazlitt; the persecution of jealousy he endured would win his sympathy. "Does not the reader wonder that he did not beat her, although she was a Countess?" says a biographer.

"It is not recorded, but we will hope that he did." He married a second time, "just at the eve of death"—that is eleven days before he died—to pay his debts with his wife's fortune.

" *The late George Dyer.*"—George Dyer did not remove from earth until 1841. He is here, nineteen years before, the victim of a joke-artifice which lies in the word "late." He was a respected, book-delving, slovenly, kindly, down-at-the-heel, forgetful man. This will be seen to some extent in Hazlitt's note on " New Books " and in Leigh Hunt's "Jack Abbot's Breakfast," where Goodall, the author of all the comic misery, is George Dyer. In 1800 Lamb spoke of him as " of burlesque memory;" another time he wrote—" George writes Odes, where the rhymes, like fashionable man and wife, keep a comfortable distance of six or eight lines apart, and calls that ' observing the laws of verse.' " Lamb also said, " All poems are *good* to George; all men *fine geniuses*; " Lamb, also, made George the good genius in his *Oxford in the Vacation,* and concluded by saying of him—" On the Muses' hill he is as happy, and good, as one of the Shepherds on the Delectable Mountains; and when he goes about with you to show you the halls and colleges, you think you have with you the Interpreter at the House Beautiful."

ON THE CONDUCT OF LIFE

Is the eleventh essay in *Literary Remains.* I read it as a paper addressed to "My dear old fellow," with a smack of childhood in it. I read it with Heine's baby-house poem in my mind, or with Coleridge's—

> "Life is but thought; so think I will
> That youth and I are house-mates still."

Nearly all the subjects in Emerson's *Conduct of Life* are touched upon by Hazlitt, from fate, power, culture, behaviour, and beauty, to illusions, although in a different key. We are in the school of the world, and reading " fellow " instead of " school-fellow," every one can obtain benefit from the serious and judicious directions and warnings. Hazlitt writes himself plainly in the essay. It is better than his *Characteristics,* ten times told. The worldly wisdom in it is condensed, pure, and powerful, as in the best of essays. Here comes in his favourite maxim, as a heritage of wisdom for his son. " *Desire to please, and you will infallibly please.*" When he speaks of marriage,

the wound of heart opens and bleeds afresh.   There, again, is the
wail from *Don Quixote,* " We hunt the wind, we worship a statue
—and cry aloud to the desert."   Out of that enough, in fitter place.   A
sigh from the *Liber Amoris* closes the penultimate paragraph.
Faithful to his admiration and art-affection, a cluster of painters concludes his great argument.   Of all the world of men they are to him
the finest spirits, and Northcote reappears, clothed with exhalations like
the dawn.

THE INDIAN JUGGLERS.

This Essay is the ninth in the first volume of *Table Talk.*

OF PERSONS ONE WOULD WISH TO HAVE SEEN

Appeared in *New Monthly,* 1826 ; republished as the eighteenth
essay in *Literary Remains.*   This is one of Lamb's *Wednesdays.*
   " *As, however, he would do neither, I suppose I must do both."*—There
is the joke of hide-and-seek in this.   Nay, Mr. Carew Hazlitt observes
on his grandfather's papers, which appeared in the   *Examiner*—
"Curiously enough, a few months afterwards (November 1823) Lamb
capped the *Examiner* 'Guy Faux' with a *London Magazine* 'Guy
Faux.'   The subject had been allowed to sleep thus far, and now in
the same year two of the principal authors of the day emptied out
their thoughts, etc."   Thus, in 1826, Hazlitt writes that Lamb had
suggested the subject, but as Lamb would not undertake it, he must.
Mr. Carew Hazlitt says that in "the same year"—1823—both
essays appeared ; but, in fact, Lamb's was in the November
London of that year, Hazlitt's in the November *Examiner* for 1821.
The loathness to reproduce both of these essays may have something
to do with the mystification.   Elia's Essay is made up of a long
extract from Hazlitt's "Guy Faux," a passage from one of Jeremy
Taylor's sermons, and some general remarks of his own, amidst
which, to the dirge-like sound of Elia's prose, the Houses of Parliament ascend to the stars, and became fixed there—a constellation
large, and bright, and wonderful.   Hazlitt did not aspire to such a
height.   He is more human.   He moves amongst principalities and
powers of the earth with explosive fury : praising martyrs and making
Guy Faux triumphant.   He regales his wrath by dwelling on Guy
Faux's sincere fanaticism.   " What lighted up the dungeon-gloom in

which Guy Faux buried himself alive?—The face of heaven open to receive him." He is not content with Guy Faux; he has tasted blood; he is on the track of carnage. He thrills at the heroism of Margaret Lambrun; he dwells, with unexpected praise, long and admiringly, on Southey's *Cid;* and at length sees Kean as a man of promptitude and valour, and worthy of being mentioned in the heroic mood.

We must now leave names to speak for themselves. If the reader is curious to inquire further, be will be as sure of his reward as though he were transported to the *Mermaid.*—Only, of Martin Burney by the way. He it was who went to Winterslow with the Lambs—five pounds in his pocket—prepared to "sleep on the floor without either bed or mattress." Martin's name is attached to two of Lamb's jokes. Earnestly explaining the three kinds of acids, he was stopped by Lamb, "The best of all kinds of acid, however, as you know, Martin, is *assid-uity.*" A person, speaking to Lamb, insisted on Martin's obstinacy. Lamb parried, but at last—" Well, I *like* a good solid, obstinacy—something may come of it. Besides, there's something to quarrel with. One's blows don't tell upon a fellow who goes whisking about like a ball of worsted, and won't stand up for his opinion. Martin's a freeholder, and insists upon having his vote."

A Farewell to Essay-Writing.

Written at Winterslow, February 20, 1828, but not printed until it appeared in the Winterslow volume, 1850.

Probably this Essay was intended to be sent to a magazine some day. Hazlitt's return to the past has a melancholy sweetness in it. When he first read the "Flower and the Leaf" of Chaucer!—Ah, and that time! We have already glanced at it more than once—when Charles and Mary Lamb visited Winterslow. He verifies his own words:— "I have learned to set a grateful value on the past."

The Sick Chamber.

"*A Free Admission.*"—We have reached the final year, 1830. Hazlitt contributed the *Free Admission* to the *New Monthly* this year, and in August the *Sick Chamber* to the same magazine. His earliest love speaks from the sick couch. Books—" they are the first and last, the most home-felt, the most heart-felt, of all our enjoyments." Then there is his latest wish—" I should like to leave some sterling work behind me." Earliest love! Yes, he was enamoured of Books before Pictures.

On Wit and Humour.

It is at "special request" that I insert this paper, which is introductory to Hazlitt's *Lectures on the English Comic Writers.* But a lecture is frequently nothing more than an essay delivered in public—there may be no inconsistency.

The Essay is all that the well-wisher could desire, and probably displays Hazlitt a little more at large as the literary critic. Then, it fails not to be Hazlittean : if this be not seen in the beginning, it will be felt at the end. Perhaps, also, in this : " *The essence of the laughable is the incongruous* " (page 272). There was no necessity, in dealing with Wit and Humour, to lay down such a doctrine. Of course, then, he needs must give us what men laugh at, and trips himself up in his catalogue. We laugh royally at things which are not incongruous—such are even specified by Hazlitt. He protests too much. Indeed, he can go to any extreme. He says, "You cannot give people a reason why they should laugh "—(page 275)—yet he would endeavour to give a reason why they should not laugh. Thus on Marvel, in this volume, he gives as an instance of the "fixed, far-fetched" method of treatment, the poet's line, where he says of the Hollanders, when their dykes overflowed—

> " The fish ofttimes the burgher dispossessed,
> And sat, not as a meat, but as a guest."

Now, Hunt has this remark—" Hazlitt made the same observation to Charles Lamb and myself, and was entering into a very acute discourse to prove that we ought *not to laugh* at such exaggerations, when we were forced to interrupt him by a fit of laughter uncontrollable."—Hazlitt's Essay should be read along with Leigh Hunt's on Wit and Humour. Hunt begins where Hazlitt ends, and he is a master-hand, having the animal spirits which he affirms Hazlitt wanted. This you feel with every quotation that Hunt makes. As for the definition of Wit and Humour, after having written as much as would serve for ten notes, we put it aside. Although we cannot agree with Hazlitt's theorising, it is well to acquiesce, and pass on : not worry with reasonings—especially

as he brings food for mirth.   For there are good specimens here of Wit
and Humour ; and to read such, like reading fine poetry, is better than
all the definitions in the world.   How a lecturer, apparently without
explanation or apology, could give, as a lecture on Comic Writers, one
upon "The Works of Hogarth," which Hazlitt does, would be inexplicable in any other person than William Hazlitt.   That lecture is
nothing else than the essay of this volume, *plus* remarks on Raphael
and Wilkie.   Then, again, *Reproached the French* "*with an equal
want of books and men.*"   This is not a worthy diversion ; but it is
an instance of Hazlitt's temper.   It is real saturnine humour, and
we can laugh at it.   See, after he raises the shadow, how he is beaten.
"The writer of some pretensions" is Wordsworth.   But neither
poet nor reader could be satisfied with Hazlitt's production of " Ninon
de Lenclos and her friends in a common French print."   Moreover,
Wordsworth would have refused to accept as names of greatness those
mentioned by Hazlitt, from Corneille to Boileau, who was not praised
by Byron, for his facile touch of

> " His country's creaking lyre,
> That whetstone of the teeth, monotony in wire."

As for Rabelais, great as he is, he is of a different order from the genius
of Milton, who is mentioned by Wordsworth.   Besides, Hazlitt is not
to the point.   Wordsworth spoke of great minds we have amongst us,
and remarks how strange it is that in her exigencies of revolution,
France had not produced such souls.

> " No single volume paramount, no code,
> No master-spirit, no determined road,
> But equally a want of books and men !"

New Illustrated Edition.

IN ONE VOLUME.

PRICE 3s. 6d.

COUNT TOLSTOÏ'S

MASTERPIECE,

ANNA KARENINA.

WITH TEN ILLUSTRATIONS

BY PAUL FRENZÉNY.

"As you read on you say, not, 'This is like life,' but, 'This is life.' It has not only the complexion, the very hue, of life, but its movement, its advances, its strange pauses, its seeming reversions to former conditions, and its perpetual change, its apparent isolations, its essential solidarity. It is a world, and you live in it while you read, and long afterward."—*W. D. Howells.*

AUTHORISED VERSION.

Crown 8vo, Cloth, Price 6s.

PEER GYNT: A Dramatic Poem.
BY HENRIK IBSEN.

TRANSLATED BY

WILLIAM AND CHARLES ARCHER.

This Translation, though unrhymed, preserves throughout the various rhythms of the original.

"In _Brand_ the hero is an embodied protest against the poverty of spirit and half-heartedness that Ibsen rebelled against in his country-men. In _Peer Gynt_ the hero is himself the embodiment of that spirit. In _Brand_ the fundamental antithesis, upon which, as its central theme, the drama is constructed, is the contrast between the spirit of compromise on the one hand, and the motto 'everything or nothing' on the other. And _Peer Gynt_ is the very incarnation of a compromising dread of decisive committal to any one course. In _Brand_ the problem of self-realisation and the relation of the individual to his surroundings is obscurely struggling for recognition, and in _Peer Gynt_ it becomes the formal theme upon which all the fantastic variations of the drama are built up. In both plays alike the problems of heredity and the influence of early surroundings are more than touched upon; and both alike culminate in the doctrine that the only redeeming power on earth or in heaven is the power of love."—Mr. P. H. WICKSTEED.

London : WALTER SCOTT, LIMITED, 24 Warwick Lane.

THE SCOTT LIBRARY.

Cloth, Uncut Edges, Gilt Top.　Price 1s. 6d. per Volume.

VOLUMES ALREADY ISSUED—

London : WALTER SCOTT, LIMITED, Paternoster Square.

THE SCOTT LIBRARY—continued.

14 GREAT ENGLISH PAINTERS. SELECTED FROM Cunningham's *Lives*. Edited by William Sharp.

15 BYRON'S LETTERS AND JOURNALS. SELECTED. with Introduction, by Mathilde Blind.

16 LEIGH HUNT'S ESSAYS. WITH INTRODUCTION AND Notes by Arthur Symons.

17 LONGFELLOW'S "HYPERION," "KAVANAH," AND "The Trouveres." With Introduction by W. Tirebuck.

18 GREAT MUSICAL COMPOSERS. BY G. F. FERRIS. Edited, with Introduction, by Mrs. William Sharp.

19 THE MEDITATIONS OF MARCUS AURELIUS. EDITED by Alice Zimmern.

20 THE TEACHING OF EPICTETUS. TRANSLATED FROM the Greek, with Introduction and Notes, by T. W. Rolleston.

21 SELECTIONS FROM SENECA. WITH INTRODUCTION by Walter Clode.

22 SPECIMEN DAYS IN AMERICA. BY WALT WHITMAN. Revised by the Author, with fresh Preface.

23 DEMOCRATIC VISTAS, AND OTHER PAPERS. BY Walt Whitman. (Published by arrangement with the Author.)

24 WHITE'S NATURAL HISTORY OF SELBORNE. WITH a Preface by Richard Jefferies.

25 DEFOE'S CAPTAIN SINGLETON. EDITED, WITH Introduction, by H. Halliday Sparling.

26 MAZZINI'S ESSAYS: LITERARY, POLITICAL, AND Religious. With Introduction by William Clarke.

27 PROSE WRITINGS OF HEINE. WITH INTRODUCTION by Havelock Ellis.

28 REYNOLDS'S DISCOURSES. WITH INTRODUCTION by Helen Zimmern.

29 PAPERS OF STEELE AND ADDISON. EDITED BY Walter Lewin.

30 BURNS'S LETTERS. SELECTED AND ARRANGED, with Introduction, by J. Logie Robertson, M.A.

London: Walter Scott, Limited, Paternoster Square.

THE SCOTT LIBRARY—continued.

. London : WALTER SCOTT, LIMITED, Paternoster Square.

THE SCOTT LIBRARY—continued.

London: WALTER SCOTT, LIMITED, Paternoster Square.

THE SCOTT LIBRARY—continued.

London: WALTER SCOTT, LIMITED, Paternoster Square.

THE SCOTT LIBRARY—continued.

London: WALTER SCOTT, LIMITED, Paternoster Square.

Great Writers.

A NEW SERIES OF CRITICAL BIOGRAPHIES.
Edited by E. ROBERTSON and F. T. MARZIALS.
Cloth, Uncut Edges, Gilt Top.   Price 1/6.

Longfellow	By Professor Eric S. Robertson
Coleridge	By Hall Caine
Dickens	By Frank T. Marzials
Dante Gabriel Rossetti	By J. Knight
Samuel Johnson	By Colonel F. Grant
Darwin	By G. T. Bettany
Charlotte Brontë	By A. Birrell
Carlyle	By R. Garnett, LL.D.
Adam Smith	By R. B. Haldane, M.P.
Keats	By W. M. Rossetti
Shelley	By William Sharp
Smollett	By David Hannay
Goldsmith	By Austin Dobson
Scott	By Professor Yonge
Burns	By Professor Blackie
Victor Hugo	By Frank T. Marzials
Emerson	By R. Garnett, LL.D.
Goethe	By James Sime
Congreve	By Edmund Gosse
Bunyan	By Canon Venables
Crabbe	By T. E. Kebbel
Heine	By William Sharp
Mill	By W. L. Courtney
Schiller	By Henry W. Nevinson
Marryat	By David Hannay
Lessing	By T. W. Rolleston
Milton	By R. Garnett, LL.D.
Balzac	By Frederick Wedmore
George Eliot	By Oscar Browning
Jane Austen	By Goldwin Smith
Browning	By William Sharp
Byron	By Hon. Roden Noel
Hawthorne	By Moncure D. Conway
Schopenbauer	By Professor Wallace
Sheridan	By Lloyd Sanders
Thackeray	By H. Merivale and F. T. Marzials
Cervantes	By H. E. Watts
Voltaire	By Francis Espinasse
Leigh Hunt	By Cosmo Monkhouse
Whittier	By W. J. Linton
Renan	By Francis Espinasse

A Complete Bibliography to each Volume, by
J. P. ANDERSON, British Museum, London.
Library Edition of "Great Writers," Demy 8vo, 2/6.

London : WALTER SCOTT, LIMITED.

IBSEN'S PROSE DRAMAS.

Edited by WILLIAM ARCHER.

Complete in Five Vols. Crown 8vo, Cloth, Price 3/6 each.
Set of Five Vols., in Case, 17/6; in Half Morocco, in Case, 32/6.

> "*We seem at last to be shown men and women as they are; and at first it is more than we can endure. . . . All Ibsen's characters speak and act as if they were hypnotised, and under their creator's imperious demand to reveal themselves. There never was such a mirror held up to nature before: it is too terrible. . . . Yet we must return to Ibsen, with his remorseless surgery, his remorseless electric-light, until we, too, have grown strong and learned to face the naked—if necessary, the flayed and bleeding—reality.*"—SPEAKER (London).

VOL. I. "A DOLL'S HOUSE," "THE LEAGUE OF YOUTH," and "THE PILLARS OF SOCIETY." With Portrait of the Author, and Biographical Introduction by WILLIAM ARCHER.

VOL. II. "GHOSTS," "AN ENEMY OF THE PEOPLE," and "THE WILD DUCK." With an Introductory Note.

VOL. III. "LADY INGER OF ÖSTRÅT," "THE VIKINGS AT HELGELAND," "THE PRETENDERS." With an Introductory Note and Portrait of Ibsen.

VOL. IV. "EMPEROR AND GALILEAN." With an Introductory Note by WILLIAM ARCHER.

VOL. V. "ROSMERSHOLM," "THE LADY FROM THE SEA," "HEDDA GABLER." Translated by WILLIAM ARCHER. With an Introductory Note.

The sequence of the plays *in each volume* is chronological; the complete set of volumes comprising the dramas thus presents them in chronological order.

"The art of prose translation does not perhaps enjoy a very high literary status in England, but we have no hesitation in numbering the present version of Ibsen, so far as it has gone (Vols. I. and II.), among the very best achievements, in that kind, of our generation."—*Academy*.

"We have seldom, if ever, met with a translation so absolutely idiomatic."—*Glasgow Herald*.

London: WALTER SCOTT, LIMITED, Paternoster Square.

COMPACT AND PRACTICAL.

In Limp Cloth; for the Pocket.   Price One Shilling.

THE EUROPEAN
CONVERSATION BOOKS.

FRENCH   ITALIAN

SPANISH   GERMAN

NORWEGIAN

CONTENTS.

Hints to Travellers—Everyday Expressions—Arriving at and Leaving a Railway Station—Custom House Enquiries—In a Train—At a Buffet and Restaurant—At an Hotel—Paying an Hotel Bill—Enquiries in a Town—On Board Ship—Embarking and Disembarking—Excursion by Carriage—Enquiries as to Diligences—Enquiries as to Boats—Engaging Apartments—Washing List and Days of Week—Restaurant Vocabulary—Telegrams and Letters, etc., etc.

The contents of these little handbooks are so arranged as to permit direct and immediate reference. All dialogues or enquiries not considered absolutely essential have been purposely excluded, nothing being introduced which might confuse the traveller rather than assist him. A few hints are given in the introduction which will be found valuable to those unaccustomed to foreign travel.

COUNT TOLSTOÏ'S WORKS.

The following Volumes are already issued—

A RUSSIAN PROPRIETOR
THE COSSACKS
IVAN ILYITCH, AND OTHER
   STORIES
MY RELIGION
LIFE
MY CONFESSION
CHILDHOOD, BOYHOOD,
   YOUTH
THE PHYSIOLOGY OF WAR
ANNA KARÉNINA. 3/6

WHAT TO DO?
WAR AND PEACE. (4 vols.)
THE LONG EXILE, AND
   OTHER STORIES FOR CHILD-
   REN
SEVASTOPOL
THE KREUTZER SONATA,
   AND FAMILY HAPPI-
   NESS
THE KINGDOM OF GOD IS
   WITHIN YOU.

Uniform with the above—

IMPRESSIONS OF RUSSIA. By DR. GEORG BRANDES.

NEW 'BOOKLETS' BY COUNT TOLSTOÏ.

Bound in White Grained Boards, with Gilt Lettering.
Price One Shilling each.

WHERE LOVE IS, THERE GOD
   IS ALSO
THE TWO PILGRIMS
WHAT MEN LIVE BY
THE GODSON

IF YOU NEGLECT THE FIRE,
   YOU DON'T PUT IT
   OUT
WHAT SHALL IT PROFIT
   MAN?

These little stories, issued in Russia as tracts for the people, possess all the grace, naïveté, and power which characterise the writings of Count Tolstoï; and while inculcating in the most penetrating way the fundamental Christian principles of love, humility, and charity, are perfect in their art-form as stories pure and simple.

London : WALTER SCOTT, LIMITED, Paternoster Square.

NEW ENGLAND LIBRARY.

GRAVURE EDITION.

PRINTED ON ANTIQUE PAPER. 2s. 6d. PER VOL.

Each Volume with a Frontispiece in Photogravure.

By NATHANIEL HAWTHORNE.

THE SCARLET LETTER.

THE HOUSE OF THE SEVEN GABLES.

THE BLITHEDALE ROMANCE.

TANGLEWOOD TALES.

TWICE-TOLD TALES.

A WONDER-BOOK FOR GIRLS AND BOYS.

OUR OLD HOME.

MOSSES FROM AN OLD MANSE.

THE SNOW IMAGE.

TRUE STORIES FROM HISTORY AND BIOGRAPHY.

THE NEW ADAM AND EVE.

LEGENDS OF THE PROVINCE HOUSE.

By OLIVER WENDELL HOLMES.

THE AUTOCRAT OF THE BREAKFAST-TABLE.

THE PROFESSOR AT THE BREAKFAST-TABLE.

THE POET AT THE BREAKFAST-TABLE.

ELSIE VENNER.

London: WALTER SCOTT, LIMITED, Paternoster Square.

SPECIAL EDITION OF THE
CANTERBURY POETS.
Square 8vo, Cloth, Gilt Top Elegant, Price 2s.

Each Volume with a Frontispiece in Photogravure.

1036756R0

Printed in Great Britain by
Amazon.co.uk, Ltd.,
Marston Gate.